STONE COUNTRY

An UNAUTHORIZED *History of Canada*

GEORGE BOWERING

PENGUIN
CANADA

PENGUIN CANADA

Published by the Penguin Group

Penguin Books, a division of Pearson Canada, 10 Alcorn Avenue, Toronto, Ontario,
Canada M4V 3B2

Penguin Books Ltd, 80 Strand, London WC2R ORL, England

Penguin Putnam Inc., 375 Hudson Street, New York, New York 10014, U.S.A.

Penguin Books Australia Ltd, 250 Camberwell Road, Camberwell, Victoria 3124, Australia

Penguin Books India (P) Ltd, 11, Community Centre, Panchsheel Park,
New Delhi – 110 017, India

Penguin Books (NZ) Ltd, cnr Rosedale and Airborne Roads, Albany, Auckland 1310,
New Zealand

Penguin Books (South Africa) (Pty) Ltd, 24 Sturdee Avenue, Rosebank 2196, South Africa

Penguin Books Ltd, Registered Offices: 80 Strand, London WC2R ORL, England

First published 2003

3 5 7 9 10 8 6 4 2

Copyright © George Bowering, 2003

Excerpt from "Lament for the Dorsets," by Al Purdy, reprinted with permission from
Beyond Remembering: The Collected Poems of Al Purdy, Harbour Publishing, 2000.

Excerpt from "Griffon" reprinted with permission from the author, Frank Davey.

Excerpt from "Comrade," by Dorothy Livesay, reprinted with
permission from the estate of Dorothy Livesay.

Printed and bound in Canada

NATIONAL LIBRARY OF CANADA CATALOGUING IN PUBLICATION

Bowering, George, 1935–
Stone country : an unauthorized history of Canada / George Bowering.

Includes bibliographical references and index.
ISBN 0-14-301397-1

1. Canada—History. I. Title.

FC164.B754 2003   971   C2003-900416-3
FI026.B754 2003

Visit Penguin Books' website at **www.penguin.ca**

This book is for Cynthia Good, with admiration and obedience

ALSO BY GEORGE BOWERING

Contents

Map of Canada   vi

1 BEFORE EUROPE   1
2 THERE GOES THE NEIGHBOURHOOD   18
3 MAKE WAR, NOT COLONIES   32
4 BRAVE NEW FRANCE   50
5 THE ENGLISH ARE COMING,
   THE ENGLISH ARE COMING!   65
6 THE YANKS ARE COMING,
   THE YANKS ARE COMING!   81
7 A LOYALIST NATION   97
8 WHERE IS LUNDY'S LANE?   113
9 REBELLIONS   130
10 GETTING TOGETHER   147
11 GET RIEL   164
12 GUNS ON THE PRAIRIES   180
13 A CENTURY GOING WEST   196
14 OLD KIT BAG   213
15 MACKENZIE KINK   230
16 TRYING TO STAY ALIVE   247
17 NUCLEAR AND UNCLEAR   264
18 CHANGE THE WORLD   281
19 INDEPENDENCE AND BACK   298
20 WHOSE CENTURY IS THIS?   314

   Bibliography   329
   Index   332

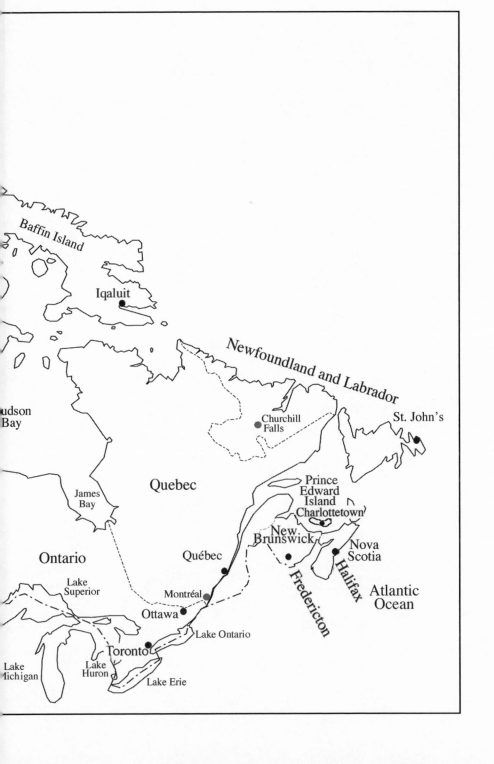

BEFORE EUROPE

Tyrannosaurus and triceratops
(IMAGE #35827/AMERICAN MUSEUM OF NATURAL HISTORY)

The popular view of the universe is that there must be other life forms out there, somebody who at least appears quasi-human. But when it comes to this planet the popular view is that all human life evolved out of Africa. If something like human life could evolve at different rates all over the everything, why do we suppose that the first people in North America came over the bridge from Asia? If some Darwinian accident could make humans in Africa, why couldn't a similar thing happen in North America?

If you have any curiosity at all, you can be enticed by studies like a recent one at the University of Michigan, which proposes that the

Iroquois peoples are descended from the Ainu of northern Japan. But until the human genome is explored to everyone's satisfaction, let us assume what the North American Aboriginals assume, that they have always been here.

We rely on the archaeologists to tell us what happened before the historical period in North America. "The historical period" is a phrase meaning whatever happened after the white folks got here. Hello, said John Cabot's men to the brown folks they found working in their front yards along the big river. Hello. We are bringing history from across the great water. History went on to kill most of the brown people.

So the archaeologists have to tell us what was happening here before the historical period. They do this by digging up arrowheads and pipes and costume jewellery. Most of the archaeologists think that the brown folks came over from Asia, starting about twelve thousand years ago. They keep finding arrowheads and so on, but they have a big problem. They can find arrowheads in Oklahoma and British Columbia and Labrador, but they can't seem to find any up in Alaska—where the land bridge was supposed to be. Maybe all the brown people's leaders said, "Okay, everybody, remember: no shooting arrows at anything till we get way to hell and gone south or east. If you see an arrowhead on the ground, pick it up. That goes for pipes and costume jewellery, too."

Whatever happened, for twelve thousand years or a lot more, the brown people of North and South America had to get by with no help from the Europeans. Some did better than others. The archaeologists admit that the people of central Mexico have been around for at least twenty-five thousand years. Tenochtitlan, the Aztec capital, was two hundred years old when the Spanish arrived with their history. It was a city built in the middle of a lake, with a sewer system that brought fresh water to the island and took the bad stuff away. Hernando Cortés reduced the city to ruins, something he could recognize.

In 1520 the European world view was Christian, or so the Europeans said. But Church doctrine was not prepared to handle a whole new continent with humanoid creatures in it. They weren't covered in the Bible, and Socrates had not said anything about them. There were competing views about the creatures. You could say that they were some kind of animal no one had seen before. Certainly there were lots of new animals over here. If they were animals, there would be nothing wrong with killing them off—like passenger pigeons or bison. But maybe they were devils, a whole continent of devils. They seemed very friendly, but then so did Satan when he was after souls. The jury was out on whether you could kill devils. But maybe they were some kind of human beings. If they were human beings they would have souls, and these souls could be reaped if Europe were to send in lots of priests to convert their owners. In 1537 Pope Paul III declared that the Indians were human beings. That made for another problem, though. If these were indeed people, it would be impossible to say that the continent was empty, that unclaimed land was there for the taking. The Church might be after souls, but the Church was not paying for all those transatlantic ships.

There were two ways of handling the people problem. You could give them beads and iron pots for land in trade. Or you could say that the Indians were cruel and warlike and would respect nothing but extermination. You could put a bounty on them, just as you did with pests that were threatening your livestock. You could change the word "savage" so that it would mean not just uncultivated but murderous. When the USAmericans came up with their Declaration of Independence, it was largely a list of complaints against George III. Among them was this: "He . . . has endeavoured to bring on the inhabitants of our frontiers, the merciless Indian Savages, whose known rule of warfare, is an undistinguished destruction of all ages, sexes and conditions."

The fact that the Native people had shown the greatest hospitality in the history of the world to the first boatloads was conveniently forgotten, and visions of tomahawks danced in a lot of heads. How would you like your wife and daughters to be carried away by those savages with their unspeakable appetites?

Canadians like to believe that while the US army and civilians were massacring Indian wives and daughters, the Natives north of the border were being enfolded in an enlightened social security system. They should have been in Newfoundland in the early nineteenth century, when English fishermen and settlers were finishing off the last of the thousand Beothuks who had lived year-round on the island.

Still, once Canadians started spreading out into the West in the nineteenth century, they did not ride into Indian villages and slaughter everyone, and certainly individual farmers were discouraged from taking target practice on Aboriginal persons. Pro-US business journalists are always talking about the gap between US and Canadian enterprise and its relationship to the Canadian restriction of personal initiative. The restriction on shooting Indians was an early example.

But the fact that the Catholic Church and some radical leftists argued that Indians were people and thus deserving of some human rights made it a little trickier overcoming guilt while grabbing Indian land. Then along came the Church's great nineteenth-century nemesis, Charles Darwin. Enemies and supporters of Darwin did not read his ponderous texts, but they summarized and simplified his principles. They also applied them to areas of life that Darwin had never thought of, just as the Marxists would do in the twentieth century. They applied them socially, for example. They claimed that Darwin called for the "survival of the fittest." This meant that you could read any historical event backward and say that the victors in some struggle were meant to be the victors. You could now add Darwin to the Bible in your justification of black slavery. Or you could say that it was obvious, after all the shooting and all the smallpox, that the Indians were not the fittest. They were on their way out as a species. This would leave a lot of land for the fittest.

Native populations plummeted from the time when they were discovered by the Europeans, until the early twentieth century. Then they began to grow slowly, despite new diseases such as heroin and pulp mills and provincial lotteries. The old wisdom that the Aboriginals were a doomed race was beginning to look wrong. So if the Aboriginals are not going to disappear as a people, how can we shuck the guilt of taking away their lands? Fortunately, in the twentieth century the archaeologists came up with the Siberian-Alaskan land bridge.

That would mean that the Natives were not natives, after all, but really just earlier immigrants. We could call them First Nations. That still left us with a little guilt—if they were on the land first, how were we going to take it over? On the prairies that problem was settled with "treaties" written in the Europeans' language. In British Columbia matters would become quite dicey.

So the descendants of landgrabbers and racists and litethinkers who had been happy with all the laws and customs that excluded Native peoples—the liquor laws, the voting laws, the school systems—looked around in the late twentieth century and saw that British Columbia was making land deals with Native nations. Wait, they said: we think that there should be one law for all! We do not think that there should be any special considerations based on race. No one could explain to them that the new treaties were not made between races but between nations.

Swamp giants

Dinosaur fossils and footprints have been found in Europe, Asia, Africa and the Americas. But they were unknown to scientists until 1824, when some fossils were found in England. No one mentioned them to Noah, it appears. Paleontologists tell us that the "terrible lizards" lived on this planet as early as 230 million years ago until as recently as 65 million years ago. There were lots and lots of varieties, and they shared the earth with bugs and birds and fish and snakes and reptiles and mammals.

Dinosaurs have never gone out of fashion. Comic strips have always shown human beings riding around on dinosaurs. They share the notion with the recent leader of a large Canadian political party that humans and dinos lived at the same time.

The dinosaur centre of Canada is in the Red Deer Valley of Alberta. During the Mesozoic era, the climate on the Prairies was warmer and moister than it would become. People say that it resembled present-day

Florida. Dinosaurs stood around with their feet in the water or stomped on wet ground that left the footprints we enjoy today.

Then something unusual happened sixty-four million years ago. Either gradually or suddenly most of the big creatures died off, along with a lot of other animals. Some of the smaller dinosaurs survived and after a while learned to grow feathers and become birds.

Elephant hunters

The Cenozoic era (mammal times) saw some pretty large animals on Canadian ground, too. Schoolboys such as I used to draw pictures of dinosaurs and planets and pyramids in scribblers called "Mammoth" that had pictures of huge hairy elephants with long, bent tusks on the covers. Mastodons and woolly mammoths showed up in North America during the Pleistocene epoch, 1.6 million years ago till ten thousand years ago. Formerly lush prairies were now covered with ice a kilometre thick. Elephants in our part of the world had to wear thick hair and grow specialized teeth to chew up whatever leaves they could find between the icefields.

Some people say that we are still in the Pleistocene. Why not? We do know that by the end of the ice age there were people with spears hunting woolly mammoths. The earth had gone around the sun sixty-four million times since the last dinosaur fell down beside a river near Drumheller, Alberta. Sometimes a mammoth would fall into an ice crevice and lie frozen for thousands of years, only to become dog food for sled teams in the nineteenth century A.D.

The last cold snap ended around thirty-five thousand years ago, and stone-age folks spread out and hunted small game in the treeless expanses of Eastern Europe and Western Asia. They made houses out of mammoth bones. A great deal of the Northern Hemisphere was an enormous continental glacier, and until it started melting no one knew that it really covered two continents. The people who had always lived down south did not even know that there was a continental glacier. Those that went back and forth across the North welcomed the eventual melting, and noticed with pleasure that edible animals were more plenteous south of the glacier.

Eleven thousand years ago the edge of the continental glacier ran pretty well along the forty-ninth parallel of latitude, just above Lake Michigan. Most of the eastern prairies was made up of gigantic shallow Lake Agassiz, which would become rich grassy soil surrounding some still pretty big lakes. As the edge of the glacier moved northward, so did some folks called the Clovis Culture.

Clovis is a town way to hell and gone up in the high country in New Mexico, near the Texas border. It was named after three Frankish kings of the Middle Ages, and set up as a railway town in 1906. There in 1932 archaeologists started finding a lot of ancient missile heads stuck in old mammoth bones. These weapons were shaped like a leaf with parallel sides and a concave base. Some were found later in a site in Texas, where they were lifted from a hearth that was radio-carboned at twenty-seven thousand years. Eventually Clovis points were discovered far to the east, at the Debert site in north central Nova Scotia, where eleven-thousand-year-old points were dug up.

The archaeologists have long liked that figure of eleven thousand years, and they are having a hard time of it with that old site in Texas. In fact, for a long time, they said that the Clovis people were the first immigrants to North America, and that they came eleven thousand years ago and kept coming till the Siberian "land bridge" was engulfed by the melting ice. But there was a part of the Yukon that was not covered with ice, and some pre-Clovis people left signs that they were living there at least thirty thousand years ago, if not forever. Eventually the Clovis folks arrived in the Yukon, and now the archaeologists are discombobulated again. They don't know whether the Clovis spearmen chased the older crowd out, or whether they assimilated them, or killed them, or somehow even recognized their ancestors in them. The story I like best is that the original folks packed up and headed for South America, looking for a cool climate in the Andes. Alpacas and llamas and vicuñas offer better wool than hairy mammoths, anyway.

The archaeologists, who for some reason persisted in classing ancient peoples according to their weapons, noticed that in a few thousand years the people of the west began using different tools, tools that were more useful than Clovis points for the killing and skinning and tanning of bison. Now the archaeologists called the western folks the Plano culture, to distinguish them from the late Clovis culture in the east. The border appears to be around Western Ontario, just as it is for curling tournaments today. The Plano people had quarries along the north shore of Lake Superior and on Manitoulin Island. The mine on Manitoulin Island was used for ten thousand years by Plano people and Clovis people. With stone hammers, the ancient miners dug four feet deep into adamant quartzite bedrock.

Meanwhile, in Northern British Columbia, the local miners spent ten centuries making beautiful blades out of a jade mountain. They stood in the deep jade dust that their great-grandparents had left.

Stone. The ancient peoples did not wear stone shoes. They did not eat stone salad. They did not build stone houses. Over the eons the winds of time and the acid in the earth finished up all the clothing and food and domiciles. They were living in a broad stone country, and along the spine of that country they left stones that they had banged together in order to make sharp points. This is why the archaeologists refer to the people by their spears. Once in a very long while they will get lucky. In August 1999 the snow on a high glacier in Far Northern British Columbia melted and exposed a man who had died untold years before. My gosh, he was wearing a hat, said newspaper readers when they saw the pictures, and it looks a lot like a hat you might see on Denman Street today. My gosh, he was not a Clovis man. He was a woven hat man, a human being. He was not a dinosaur. People did live hereabouts.

Yeah, but he didn't own the place, said the logging barons.

So it was amazing to find soft things that were really old in Canada. It was as amazing as it was to open the graves of the doomed English sailors of the Franklin expedition and see their well-preserved naval jackets and their permafrozen faces looking skyward after a century and a half of Canadian history. It was as amazing as Kennewick Man, the body discovered in 1996 under the water behind a dam on the Columbia River. Some white people offered the opinion that he looked a lot like a European, so maybe Indian land claims were not as watertight as they might be, after all. So it goes.

North American free trade agreement

The archaeologists like to talk about something called the Archaic period in Aboriginal populations, and then split the country in two, with the Shield Archaic culture covering the ground from Lake Huron to the west, and the Laurentian Archaic culture from Lake Huron to Quebec and New England, at least. The nomadic hunters began to settle and increase in numbers during this period, usually given as 5000 B.C. till 1000 B.C. Hunting and butchering tools had for centuries been coming from the west and the southwest, and now the people in what would come to be known as the "centre of the universe" were seeing more and more interesting objects brought from the south and east. More and more, too, the makers of these objects were immigrating into Ontario and Quebec.

Archaeologists cannot tell you exactly when the Laurentian culture got going, nor even why they should make a vague boundary between the Archaic folks and the people that were there before them. The terms are handy to signify a time from which we have evidence of pre-agricultural settling into place. Our diggers have found burial sites and can thus make suppositions about the religious ideas of the Laurentians. They have noted that the Laurentians placed objects made of stone and bone and copper beside the corpses of their adult male dead, then sprinkled or painted them with ochre. Sometimes their hunting dogs would be found in the same graves. As the centuries progressed, these decorations were increased and variegated, suggesting that burial was becoming more cult and less simple disposal. Except for women and children, that is.

While we have found graves from six thousand years ago, we have not found houses. We presume that the Archaic people lived in temporary houses in the summer, and winter houses that would have been destroyed by centuries of weather. But our diggers have found the hearths on which fish and game were slowcooked. The farther north you looked, the more likely you would be to see people eating caribou, and if you have ever eaten caribou, you know how good eating meat can be. It was probably after their first feed of caribou that the European explorers decided to gobble up as much of northern North America as they could get their mitts on.

But thousands of years before those pushy people came from the east, there were peoples travelling north and south, trading items and showing each other how to do things. Five-thousand-year-old graves in Southern Ontario contain conch shells from the Gulf of Mexico, as well as other fancy shells from the Atlantic Coast and metallic doodads from around Lake Superior. People living at the foot of the Rockies liked to wear tubular shells from the Pacific Coast, while people on Vancouver Island showed off their grizzly claws from animals who had used them to scoop fish far to the northeast. Along the lower reaches of the Columbia there were people who told their jokes in an Athapaskan language usually heard in the land of the midnight sun. The folks on the Aleutian Islands learned their crafts from their connections to the west in Siberia.

We can be pretty sure that when flints from the Dakotas turn up among the artisans of the far north Shield people, they had been passed from hand to hand along a route that did not include any tariffs or border checkpoints. But we also know that, contrary to European observations, the inhabitants of the huge land mass were not all one people. There were more than forty nations in British Columbia alone. The profession of translator was an important one, whether in trade or peace negotiations.

Translation is an act of poetry. Canada's first poems evaporated into the air. But our first stories would pass down through the families that owned them. And free trade could not touch them.

A thousand

Anthropologists are fond of the date 1000 B.C.

When they talk about Central Canada, they say that the Woodland Period went from 1000 B.C. till the "Historic Period." The Woodland

Period started when the people changed the way they made bowls. Until 1000 B.C. they made bowls out of stone. After that they made bowls out of clay. The anthropologists are grateful, because there were a lot more bowls being made now, and anthropologists really like potsherds. The potters of Central Canada learned pottery from their trading partners down south and started making clay pots that looked just like the stone pots they used to make there. Later they experimented with beakers and rope and so on.

The people of the Arctic Pacific also began making pots around 1000 B.C., but these looked more like the cord-impressed pots being made in the Northern Orient. They also started to make oil lamps and fishing settlements, as hunting in the interior for some reason became less popular.

At Head-Smashed-In Buffalo Jump, Alberta, the plains people continued their ancient practice of herding bison over a cliff. On foot and carrying spears, they would induce large supplies of meat to take the last leap. They had long ago learned the value of a communal workplace. Now they were fooling around with smaller spears that they could attach feathers to and propel with a curved limb and twine. They learned how to get up close and shoot between ribs.

In 1000 B.C., Europe was greatly diversified. There were lots of different peoples speaking lots of mutually incomprehensible languages. In the Southeast they were learning how to make little cities because they were close to the civilizations of nearby Asia. Their artisans had been in the Bronze Age for ten centuries. In the Northwest they were making utensils and weapons out of stone. If there ever was such a thing as Celtic culture, it was the largest group around, but the Celts in Scotland did not know the Celts in Portugal.

When the Greeks or ancient Lebanese went to sea, they liked to keep the shore in sight, and they did not sail very far westward because there were barbarians out there.

So on both sides of the North Atlantic any sense of cultural progress was going to begin in the south, where the ice age had not even been a rumour, and spread northward. Three thousand years after 1000 B.C., the farther north you went, the more civilized both continents would be.

Seeds of time

Anyone who went to school back when they taught something about "ancient man" remembers that we made a giant step when we changed from hunters and gatherers into farmers. This was the kind of progress that would lead to making villages, which would give rise to cities, which would need infrastructures and defences and writing to aid the development of commerce, and eventually to trade unions and entertainment multiplexes.

A long way south of Canada, the people had been growing corn since about 3000 B.C. Sometime in the first millennium A.D. the people of Ontario were growing it, and corn would lead to those folks we now call the Iroquois and Huron. Sometime late in the second millennium it would lead to the Kellogg. Nowadays the white experts of Canada know more about the Iroquois and Huron past than they know about any other Aboriginal nations. Native people, with a different way of knowing and telling the past, if it is the past, know things they never told the Récollets and Jesuits or anyone since.

On the Prairies, and in British Columbia's interior, the nations did not go in much for agriculture until the European fur merchants and God merchants arrived to show them the advantages of hacking at the ground.

Anthropologists and prehistorians really like corn. The development of the Iroquois culture depended on food and stories created by the harvesting of corn. There was still fishing, and still hunting, but now, by 1000 A.D., people lived near the corn and went on trips for meat. Villages got bigger and bigger, maybe four hectares in size. Longhouses were put up. Dogs roamed around and sometimes served as a domestic foodstuff.

As in Europe, the development of villages and tribes led to competition for resources. Villages were fitted with palisades, and men started looking for conquests. If they suffered too many casualties during a war, they would adopt the women and children of their enemies in great numbers. The proto-Iroquois also brought about the first confederation on Canadian soil, as military operations grew in scale.

Interior of Iroquois longhouse
(NATIONAL MUSEUM OF CANADA/PN76024)

None of them ever called themselves the Iroquois. Some Frenchman heard someone speaking some Aboriginal language and saying some word that he mispronounced while not understanding that it did not refer to the people. This sort of thing was always happening. In the late eighteenth century on the west coast of Vancouver Island some Englishman asked a Native where he was from, and the Native said, "Around the corner of that big rock." The Englishman heard something that sounded kind of like "Nootka," and promptly called the town and people after that word.

European prehistorians and anthropologists see the switch to agriculture as a step in the progress of a culture, because that is the way it seems to have worked for Europeans. You can see their point of view. The monumental cities of Aboriginal Mexico were erected where corn and beans and other ground crops had been cultivated for many centuries, even though the people there had not thought of domesticating animals other than their cute little dogs.

But sometimes the earth is too bountiful to urge farming, and sometimes the earth will not permit the plow. The Innu people of today's
Quebec and Labrador would have starved if they had had to stay in one
place and plant gardens. In the nineteenth century A.D. the Métis of
Manitoba would have been the skinniest people in the world if they had
given up the buffalo hunt and tried to live on the agricultural program
of the Red River Settlement.

But the good soil around the eastern Great Lakes was another story.
Between 1000 and 1500 A.D. the population soared as sunflowers were
grown for oil, tobacco for smoking in pipes, beans and squash added to
corn in the vegetable market. Protein galore. Some of the latter was also
supplied by the application of cannibalism, according to the gnawed look
of some bones in Ontario and New York middens. Here we had the basis
for romantic scare stories in France and the United States. Nutritionally
self-sufficient, the Five Nations of the Iroquois Confederacy, the
Mohawk, Seneca, Cayuga, Oneida and Onondaga, could build walled
towns and raise families in social groups, in longhouses. Long before
the Europeans arrived, they were a complex of horticultural societies.

Things were not as comfortable in Northern Ontario. There the
basic unit was the single family. Food was scarce, so there was a lot of
hunting, and information about useful animals had to be shared among
brothers or lads and uncles. With all the work that went into understanding the local animals, there was a motivation for the men and boys
to remain in their areas. Women, on the other hand, were occupied with
childrearing, potmaking, fishnetting and general housekeeping. They
were a lot more mobile than the men were.

Here are three young brothers living in a nice camp on the north
shore of Lake Superior, between Nipigon and Thunder Bay. They are
smoking some pretty awful stuff that someone brought from the
southeast and watching their wives making pottery.

"Look at them," said the oldest brother. "They look as if they were
sisters."

"They all have their own way of making those pots, but we will never
be able to tell one serving of moose from another," said the middle brother.

"They haven't stopped talking since they met," said the third one. "I had no idea how many ways there are to speak Algonquian, but they chatter away as if they were all brought up in this town."

"When I got my wife down in Wisconsin, I could make out about half of what her father was saying."

"Same with me in Manitoba."

"Ditto with me at Lake Nipissing."

"This is truly a dull conversation," said the youngest brother.

A millennium and a half later the same conversation would take place among three other brothers, except that they would be fixing a truck at the time.

The Algonquin people would hear quite a bit from the Huron people, too. The Algonquin showed the Huron how to make birchbark canoes and fish-camp houses. The Huron traded corn and nets for meat and furs. It was a trade practice that was to become more and more familiar as the centuries went by—the Algonquin people learned to speak Huron, and when it came to influence, well, the Iroquoian people lived in the centre of the universe. All the strong cultural forces originated in Southern Ontario.

Big country

Alongside the Fraser and Thompson and Columbia Rivers in British Columbia, the people had been harvesting salmon since the beginning of time. Since 3500 B.C. they had been living in big pit houses during the winters, architecture introduced by folks from the south. When it came to trade, the people down at the coast already had enough salmon, so the folks from the interior swapped jade and rattlesnakes and willow baskets and copper and slabs of obsidian for seashells and cedar boxes and oolichan grease and stories about whales.

As the ice grew deeper and moved southward, the Dorset people of the High Arctic had been moving south and making small settlements along the coasts of Labrador and Newfoundland, where they piled the harp whale bones for the anthropologists to find two millennia later. The Dorset people liked to hunt animals they could walk to from their homes, and they harvested the prey that was plentiful and easy to kill. They were not much interested in trade, and they had their own ideas. When the climate relented toward the end of the first millennium A.D. most of them headed north again and tried to keep to themselves.

When the Europeans arrived in the "New World," most of the Dorsets did not know it, and the few who found out did not care. They would not trade their beautiful stone carvings for foreign metal. They reached the height of their culture around 1000 A.D., but then they began to disappear. Unless there are a few hiding somewhere around the Canadian-Danish border now, the last ones disappeared in an epidemic on Southampton Island at the turn of the twentieth century.

But most of them disappeared when the Thule people from the west arrived after 1000 A.D. The Thule were a lot more energetic about hunting than the art-loving Dorsets. They grabbed up every animal they could find, and travelled great distances to do so. They also brought diseases that had originated in Eastern Asia. The Dorsets started to disappear. They knew that whatever came from outside was bad news. The ones that survived hunger and disease went to hide in High Arctic coves. A few hung on in Northern Quebec and Labrador.

In the twentieth century A.D. the Canadian poet Al Purdy wrote a poem titled "Lament for the Dorsets." Here is the way it ends:

Did they ever realize at all
what was happening to them?
Some old hunter with one lame leg
a bear had chewed
sitting in a caribou-skin tent
—the last Dorset?
Let's say his name was Kudluk
and watch him sitting there
carving 2-inch ivory swans

for a dead grand-daughter
taking them out of his mind
the places in his mind
where pictures are
He selects a sharp stone tool
to gouge a parallel pattern of lines
on both sides of the swan
holding it with his left hand
bearing down and transmitting
his body's weight
from brain to arm and right hand
and one of his thoughts
turns to ivory
The carving is laid aside
in beginning darkness
at the end of hunger
and after a while wind
blows down the tent and snow
begins to cover him

After 600 years
the ivory thought
is still warm

2
THERE GOES THE NEIGHBOURHOOD

Leif Eiriksson Discovers North America *by C. Krohg*
(NATIONAL ARCHIVES OF CANADA/C-232227)

A reader will not be much blamed if she makes some remark about giving a whole chapter to prehistorical stuff that looks more like footprints than a story. But think of this: at least 98 percent of the time that human beings have been walking around in this country belongs to those ages before Europeans floated over here. We could let a couple of hundred centuries go, I suppose, but certainly we should at least give a nod to the last twenty centuries of pre-European civilization.

A lot of that civilization is still shaping the country. You can buy a canoe at Canadian Tire. People working for the Provincial Forest Service get around on snowshoes. If you are smart you regularly eat beans and squash and corn. If you are not so smart you might have a smoke after dinner. Later you might pop some popcorn into the microwave.

In various parts of the country judges are sending lawbreaking Native kids back to their communities to undergo Aboriginal legal sanctions rather than another trip to the slammer.

In the Okanagan Valley, where I grew up in the middle of the twentieth century, white people used to live in pithouses. Orchards did not make people rich quick, so it took years and years to build a family home. First you would build the concrete foundation. Then you would put down the floor above you, and live in the basement for a few years. That was not a bad idea, given that the summer temperatures were often in the forties Celsius.

Everybody was first

Like long poems and war songs and parental advice, history books are generally about myths. The primary myths are about origin. Where did we Greeks come from? Why do we humans have to die? Where did you get my baby brother? Where and when was the first baseball game played?

In places where white people used not to live, the white people always want to know who was there first. How did the Aboriginal people get there, and then who was the first European to get there?

When I was a kid the first European to get to the New World was Christopher Columbus, and somehow my province got his name. Well, his name was Colón, but no teacher was going to tell that to elementary-school boys with their cloacal humour.

We were told that the first European to get to Canada was an Englishman named Cabot. The first time I heard of him his name was pronounced Cabeau. Then it was Kabbitt. It turned out that he was as Italian as Cristobal Colón (which is Spanish for Cristoforo Colombo), and his name was Giovanni Caboto. When we got to Champlain, I was sure you had to have a name that started with *C* if you were going to get anywhere in the exploration business.

So in the USA the Italian Americans celebrate Columbus Day, and in Canada the Italian Canadians celebrate Thanksgiving.

But sometime after I left school, the news came that the first European visitors to the New World were some Scandinavians who kept going after they had seen Greenland, built a house or two in Newfoundland and maybe kept going south till they came to Delaware.

Then it was some Irish monks who came over in a pea-green boat. I once read a Soviet magazine that suggested that the Phoenicians were responsible for some of the pyramids in Mexico. In recent years we have heard about South Sea Islanders fetching up on the western shores of South America. There are followers of Erich von Daniken who believe that North America was first explored and settled by people from somewhere else in our galaxy.

You have to pick your myth of origin. Or you have to mention that everything you say should be considered to be within quotation marks. Everything I have to say here should be understood as lying between quotation marks.

Take the Scandinavians, for example, the people we call the Norse. A couple of millennia ago they began to write heroic epic prose in a genre called the saga. Sagas were always about great adventurers and their families. Two surviving sagas tell stories about our country—in a way. These are *The Saga of the Greenlanders* and *The Saga of Eirik the Red*. The stories are fragmentary, vague, contradictory, probably exaggerated and written at least two hundred years after the voyages described. In other words, they are a lot like most history books.

Eirik the Red grew up in Iceland, where his father had been exiled from Norway for killing people. Iceland was populated by Norsemen who had fled the iron rule of a king named Harald the Blond. But Eirik the Red killed some people, so he had to leave for farther west. He talked a lot of farmers into going with him to the west side of Greenland, where they established two agricultural settlements. Amazingly, these places grew over the centuries, and became bases from which brave Vikings sailed off to see what they could grab and whom they could kill.

According to the sagas, the first Europeans to reach our continent were some brave traders under the command of a man named Bjarni Herjolfsson, who got lost in the fog of Davis Strait and wound up at a low forested coast that faced eastward. He looked around there, and farther north where there were mountains and glaciers, before pointing his craft eastward and finding Greenland at last.

Eirik the Red's son Leif Eiriksson knew this story, of course, and sometime around 995 he decided to have a look at the coasts that Herjolfsson had seen, and go farther. Imagine his ship. There were lots of different kinds of Viking ships, but all of them were long and narrow. They had evolved from the canoes of the stone-age north men. The Vikings had a lot of success against other European warriors and traders because their long ships and their trading knorrs did not need a harbour. They could enter rivers. They could be sailed or rowed and were fast and manoeuvrable.

Leif Eiriksson's long ship was probably a little over twenty metres from end to end, about the distance from home plate to first base in a softball game. A good base runner can cover that distance in three seconds.

Leif's thirty-five Norsemen landed in a place that Leif would call Vinland. For the past century people have been trying to figure out where Vinland was. It may have been on the New Brunswick–Maine border, or a place where wild grapes grew. It may have been in Northwestern Newfoundland. Maybe Leif was lying about the wild grapes in order to encourage Scandinavians to come and start farms. In any case, Leif never went back himself; his kid brother, Thorvald, went on a two-year expedition, having a look at the Bay of Fundy, they say. He never came home—some local people objected to his manners and killed him. The next Scandinavians to have a look at Vinland were Thorfinn Karlsefni and his sixty men. They were also unpleasing to the residents, and more European blood seeped into the mossy earth around Vinland. But the Norsemen kept coming to Vinland over the next three hundred years. For one thing, there weren't enough trees in Greenland, and these seagoing people needed trees to turn into ships and houses.

North America is full of legends and fanciful sites of ancient European settlements. Scandinavian Americans have found stones with runes on them in places like Minnesota and Ohio. But the archaeologists pooh-pooh all such places except L'Anse aux Meadows. L'Anse aux Meadows is on the tip of that long peninsula that reaches north almost to Labrador. "L'anse" means "inlet," but it also means "handle," which is kind of neat.

In 1961 a team of archaeologists from Norway, armed with the sagas, went poking around in a nice little bay and found an ancient Viking settlement that started around 1000 A.D. If you visit the museum there now you can see some iron rivets excavated at the site and see the shape of the smithy where they were made. There are several holes where sod houses used to be, the remains of cooking pits and so on. The starring role goes to a soapstone flywheel used for spinning wool. It is the oldest official European artifact in Canada.

But this was way out on the inhospitable edge of the medieval world, and there were not enough Norse people with good reasons to leave home and dig holes in Newfoundland earth. It did not look as if there was a lot of gold to pick up, and life in Norway was not that bad. By 1500 the Vikings had quit North America and even Greenland.

The residents of the continent had a few curios to show their grandchildren—a bit of chain mail on Ellesmere Island, a Norwegian penny on the coast of Maine.

Hello, sailor

Maybe some of the Basque whalers from Northern Spain took on water or timber from our shores while they were hunting in Greenland waters around 1300. But the Basque whalers did not write sagas. St. Brendan the Irish monk did write an adventure story, in Latin. He visited some very strange lands before the Vikings got there, and he did it in a coracle, a little round boat made of reeds covered with animal hides. Brendan's story is a little like Gulliver's story, filled with marvels never seen by anyone else on this continent.

What really got the Europeans going for the lands to their west was the Renaissance. When you mention the Renaissance, a lot of people think about Italian paintings with perspective in them. There was a good reason for perspective, and I will mention it in a bit. The Renaissance, some people think, means Michelangelo's sculpture of *David* and Leonardo's painting in which Jesus and twelve other men sit at only one side of a long table for some reason.

It is not easy to fix an event that brought the Middle Ages to a halt and started the Renaissance. There was no equivalent to the fall of Rome, for example. But the fourteenth century seemed to do the trick. That was not a good time to spend one's short life. The poor people of France and Britain and elsewhere started the biggest peasant revolts yet known, and they had to be slaughtered by the nobles and kings. The Hundred Years War between the monarchs of France and Britain spread ruin across both lands and outside them. But worst of all was the Black Death, the bubonic plague. In the fourteenth century it killed twenty-five million people, a quarter of the European population.

People became obsessed with death. They wondered why they should bother to be loyal serfs if the end of the world was coming anyway. The medieval system of landholding and hoe swinging had been around for a long time, but the fourteenth century gave it a great challenge. By the end of that horrible century all the ties were in doubt, the ties between bondsmen and nobles, between peasants and priests, between landowners and kings.

Another term for the Renaissance is capitalism. There had been guilds and merchants in the century before 1400, but they were pretty well local institutions, just as the agricultural system had been. In fifteenth-century Italy, some businessmen became capitalists—that is, they were making such big profits from luxury goods brought from the East that they had surplus capital, and what could they do with it? Why, they could reinvest it. Reinvestment meant expansion. Expansion meant partnerships. Merchants in Italy acted as middlemen between the East and Europe. In the north of Europe, merchants created the Hanseatic League to play ball from end to end of the Baltic Sea. In Holland there were Italian ships tied up at the docks, and the merchants began getting the noblemen in debt.

There were still kings and dukes and bishops around, but the new dispensation had begun with the creation of the capitalists, the bankers and the working class.

What does the capitalist system need? It needs expansion, constant expansion of markets for acquiring and selling goods at a profit. In the fifteenth and sixteenth centuries it could really use a New World, a couple of continents filled to the rafters with natural resources. Leif Eiriksson had found a New World, but he was not a capitalist.

An Italian world

Two centuries earlier Marco Polo spent years hobnobbing with Kublai Khan in Beijing, and even now the Italian merchants were satisfied to get rich on the Asian trade in silks and spices. But the Spanish and French and Portuguese and British were on the lookout for treasures beyond the control of the Italians and outside the reach of the Musselmen along the Silk Road. The great jumping-off place of Constantinople had been in Muslim Turk hands since 1453.

This meant sailors with the nerve to reach Asia by sea. There were two possible routes. The Vikings had never found anything but ice with a few grassy bays up north. Ships would have to go around the bottom of Africa, which at least was on the maps, or head westward across the Atlantic. China was probably over there, but there were no maps.

Venture capitalists like to talk about taking risks, but when it comes to risks as large as the Atlantic, they always go to governments for help. The kings and queens of Europe had a lot of resources that they had not had to work very hard to get, and they liked to see themselves as the most interesting things in the history books. They also had the navies to defend anything that might be found. They were glad to help.

The upper classes of the Catholic Church also had a stake in this great adventure—there were Asian heathen to convert.

Now if you were going to go into business with a merchant seaman, who better to sign a contract with than an Italian? But when Christopher Columbus tried to do business with the Portuguese king he was told that his projections did not compute. So he went to see the Spanish queen, who was busy moving the Muslims and Jews out of her country. She too told him to get lost. But when he announced that he was going to make his proposal to the French king, she called him back for further discussions. The rest is geography.

The French, having missed on Columbus, would get their Italian, Giovanni da Verrazano, and he would look at the coast from Labrador to the bottom of South America, searching for a water passage to the Orient. A few years earlier the English made a deal with an Italian to try to find a Northwest Passage. This was Giovanni Caboto, and the year was 1497.

John Cabot did not cost Henry VII much. The Italian had to raise all his own money and supplies. But he was not a bad businessman; he was going to have first dibs on a lot of what he would find over here. He was forty-eight years old in 1497, when he sailed from Bristol with three of his sons and eighteen crewmen. Of course he was looking for Asia. Everyone was looking for Asia. People dreamed that China was festooned with silk and pearls and ivory. Cabot landed at Labrador or Newfoundland or Nova Scotia. Wherever he was, he poked a flag into the hard ground and claimed everything for England. Then he sailed back to England for further talks with the king's people.

Cabot probably thought that he was in some part of Asia unknown to Europeans and maybe unknown to most Asians. He did not run into any human beings. But he saw an enormous number of fish. The codfish were so thick that his keel was always rubbing their backs. Europeans had probably been fishing off the banks of Newfoundland for some time, but what did they know about kings and charters?

John Cabot was a year or two older than Chris Colombo, but we don't know whether they knew each other when they were children in

John Cabot and His Three Sons
by Abbé Francesco Griselini
(COPYRIGHT © CORBIS/MAGMA)

Genoa and Venice. Chris went to sea when he was only fourteen, and now in 1498 he was on his fourth voyage to the New World, where he would become perhaps the first Jew to set foot in South America. John Cabot, meanwhile, was headed back to Newfoundland, this time with five ships and three hundred English sailors. This time, too, the king was kicking in some funds.

Cabot was not so sure that he was in Asia now, but wherever he was, he wanted to find something worth picking up. He cruised the coast as far south as Virginia, and he found some deep and enticing bays, but they did not lead anywhere, and their banks were not littered with gold. In the Europe of 1498 there were a lot of stories about strange lands with irregular human beings and emerald trees. But supplies were running out. John Cabot and his ships turned back north and then east, and then we do not really know what happened to John Cabot and his fleet.

You don't have to consider the essential fictionality of history to talk about the haziness of exploration records. Explorers lied and exaggerated and often didn't know what they were looking at, and the businessmen that made deals with them were not meticulous record keepers when their own purses were not involved.

So maybe John Cabot died aboard ship off the coast of Newfoundland in 1498. Maybe his ships never made it back to Bristol. Or maybe he was still sailing the North Atlantic several years later.

Henry VII didn't care. He now claimed ownership of a lot of forested land that was impeding his attempt to get to Beijing before the Spanish and French.

Another solitude heard from

In the beginning of the sixteenth century the French heard about England's claim to these "new" lands, but the French did not throw up their hands and hope for better luck next time. Verrazano traced Cabot's path from Virginia to Newfoundland and claimed the whole coastline for *his* sponsor, calling it Nova Francia. The English could read Latin. In the Hundred Years War they had lost all their possessions in France except for Calais. They got ready for another hundred years over here.

It looked as if the French, as usual, would be their one big obstacle. In 1493 Pope Alexander VI, reasoning that his religion was the only proper world order, chose a neat way to keep peace between the Portuguese and the Spanish. At the Treaty of Tordesillas the following year, a north-south line was drawn sixteen hundred kilometres west of the Azores. Spain was to get all overseas trade west of the line, and Portugal all overseas trade east of the line. No provisions were made for the Protestants or the Iroquois.

It happened, of course, that Newfoundland and all that stuff west of Newfoundland was Spanish trade territory, but the Spanish fishermen would be on their own—the Spanish military would be busy in South America and Mexico, showing off their bright armour in the Latin-American sun.

In the 1530s, the French king, François I, was looking for an adroit seaman who could go across and pick up gold and jewels and spices, find a passage to Asia and remind everyone that those were French lands, as established by Verrazano. He had a good look at a forty-three-year-old Breton seaman who had been from Brazil to Newfoundland with the Italian. This was

Jacques Cartier, a name that every Canadian schoolchild would know until the avalanche of USAmerican popular culture. Cartier did not think that they would find any spices, and he was not expecting a lot of gold, but a commission is a commission. Off he went with two ships and sixty-one men. It was spring of 1534; the Spanish had been killing people in Peru for three years. After fifteen years of designing and carving, Michelangelo was putting finishing touches on the Medici Chapel.

A long time before that, God had told the fratricidal Cain that he was sending him to a land that he would find difficult: "When you till the ground, it will no longer yield you its produce." We are told that Cain then headed east. Nevertheless, when Jacques Cartier had a look at the north shore of the Gulf of St. Lawrence, he wrote, "Along the whole of the north shore I did not see one cart-load of earth and yet I landed in many places. Except at Blanc Sablon there is nothing but moss and short, stunted shrub. In fine I am rather inclined to believe that this is the land that God gave to Cain."

Cartier was often this droll.

But he should have reminded his followers and successors that God put a mark on Cain, that anyone who killed him would be in for it.

In his 1534 voyage Cartier looked around PEI and Anticosti and headed home to Brittany. He had two kidnapped young men with him. A year later he brought them back to America and with their help he headed up the great river, and named a little bay he put in at after St. Lawrence, whose feast day is August 10. It is a good thing that he did not arrive four days later: we would be sending ships and pollution down the St-Arnulf River.

In his 1535 voyage he sailed his three ships to Stadacona, where he moved in next to a Native village and told the locals that a great day was coming. Then in September he sailed as far as Montreal's island, to a village called Hochelaga. There the Natives gave him a warm welcome, but he didn't stay long. He and some of his men climbed to the top of the hill that people in Montreal would later call a mountain and jammed a cross into the ground. He was always jamming crosses into the ground, but this was the highest one yet.

From the top of this hill, which he called Mount Royal, he could see that his ships would never get through the Lachine Rapids. This was too bad, because the local people told him that if you could keep going that way, you would find a great sea with no salt in it.

"Is there any gold up there?" the French asked.

"The place is crawling with gold," the Natives replied.

"What about spices?" asked the Frenchmen.

"Lots of delicious spices," they were told.

"Thanks. We'll be back," said the Frenchmen, and coasted down the river to Stadacona, where they had decided to spend the winter. After all, Stadacona was more or less on the same latitude as St-Malo. How cold could it get? Well, it was just a normal Quebec winter. The Frenchmen contemplated suicide. The river froze solid. There was not much in the way of fruit and vegetables alongside the wide St. Lawrence River, and the Europeans began to die of scurvy. The Iroquois showed them what bark and root to chew on, but a quarter of Cartier's 110 Frenchmen died, and a lot of the living had teeth falling out of their gums. As soon as the ice was finished breaking up in May 1736, they were ready to brave the Atlantic again.

But first they had to establish good relations with their Iroquoian hosts. They decided that they would take ten of them back to meet the King of France. The Natives did not want to go, but Cartier reasoned that once they had learned French and seen the land that God gave to Adam, they would be grateful. Among them was the Stadacona chief, Donnacona, who had thought that it might be possible to form a trading alliance between his people and the toothless ones. When he met the king he told him about his great trading country of the Saguenay, a place where gold and diamonds littered the ground. He and his entourage were eager to get back there, he said, but they never did. The king had European problems and was not about to send any more ships to New France for a while. Donnacona was the first Canadian politician to die in Europe. François was preoccupied for a few years in his squabbles with Carlos V of Spain. Carlos V was the master of the warmer places in the New World and got really angry at the French king for his encroaching on Spanish territory in Northern Italy. François was also conspiring with the Protestants in the German dukedoms and, they said, maybe even with the dangerous Turks. It was all very complicated. Europe was made up of various states in which the people spoke languages incomprehensible to their rulers. Jacques Cartier wanted to go back across the Atlantic to gather gold. His Indian hostages began learning French and Christianity and then dying.

Finally, in 1541, François I decided that it would be a good idea to lay claim to all of North America and keep the Spanish out, no matter what some dead pope had decided. He would require one of his noblemen, Jean-François de La Rocque de Roberval, to set up a colony somewhere along the great river that Cartier had found. Cartier would act as Roberval's advance supernumerary. He arrived at his old Quebec base in the late summer, and took another trip to Montreal. The Iroquois were not as happy to see him this time. They had yanked his cross off the hill, so he had to put up another one.

It was another horrible winter in Quebec. If you have ever been to Quebec in the winter, try to imagine camping there in January. Try to imagine that you do not have a clue about fishing and hunting. Then imagine that the locals hate you because you took their chief and nine other people away to another planet from which they would never return. Cartier built a little fort at a place he optimistically called Cap-aux-Diamants, and everyone began getting skinny. The Native people and the French sailors started killing each other. When the snow had gone and the ground got a little softer, the Frenchmen loaded their ships with gold and silver and diamonds, and when the ice was reduced to rotting floes in the great river, Cartier's ships headed east.

They were supposed to wait for Roberval and his colonists. They were supposed to have prepared a settlement that the intrepid settlers would inherit. Cartier ran into Roberval's ships at Newfoundland. Roberval said that Cartier should turn around and escort him to Cap-aux-Diamants. In the middle of a foggy night, Cartier slipped away and headed for France, his hulls deep in the water.

It took about five minutes for the king's geologists to determine that Cartier had brought over a pile of iron pyrites and other shiny junk minerals. Thinking of Carlos V and his mountains of Peruvian and Mexican gold, François was dejected. He was ready to forget about French colonies.

"What do the pagans over there call their country," he asked the hangdog Cartier.

"When they were on board my ship they pointed to the shoreline and said 'Canada,'" replied the explorer.

"Maybe the Spanish have been there," said the king, trying to summon a smile. "In Spanish *aca nada* means 'nothing over there.'"

"I don't think—"

"Maybe the Portuguese have been there. In Portuguese *canada* means 'a little bit of water.'"

"I don't want to think of those miserable people in that miserable place," said Cartier. "You should see them. Half the time they are naked. The other half they go around in clothing made from the hair of the beaver. There is no future in that place."

These two men could have used a translator. The word the shipboard Indians were using was something like "Kanata." It meant something such as "the place where we live." Now it means a suburb of Ottawa.

What happened to Roberval and his colonists? They spent a Quebec winter and headed back to France as quickly as they could. Now there is a town called Roberval on the southwest shore of Lac St-Jean. There they have an annual festival called *Huitaine de gaieté*.

So Jacques Cartier was too scared to try the Lachine Rapids. He created really bad relations with the Native people. He hauled tons of fool's gold back to his king. He spent the rest of his life going over his account books. But he did stick a French cross on Mount Royal.

MAKE WAR, 3 NOT COLONIES

Sir Francis Drake
(PROVINCIAL ARCHIVES OF VICTORIA, BC)

It was never easy to get settlers to start life anew in unfriendly nature. When it came to settling that furnace called Australia, the British had to ship out loads of Irishmen who had been convicted of the kinds of crime that poor people engage in. You have to tell prospective settlers that they will find religious freedom, or diamonds and gold, or the fountain of eternal youth. What was there in the forests alongside the river that Cartier had sailed? A lot of hard work with few tools. There were no oxen or horses or plows until 1627. There were Native people who could not forgive Cartier for murder and kidnapping and self-satisfaction.

The French government did not think much about colonies after Cartier dumped his worthless rocks on the king's floor. Fishermen continued to scoop up the cod around Newfoundland and to treat the foreign fishermen as interlopers. There was the odd landing on North American soil, where a European might trade something worthless for something to eat. The only people with colonies in their eyes were the French Huguenots, who had their reasons for living somewhere other than Europe. But after looking at the St. Lawrence country they decided to settle a lot farther south. Unfortunately, there were a lot of Spanish and Portuguese Catholics down there, and those people decided to kill the Protestants before the virus spread through the New World.

Every ruler in Europe was involved in making war on someone all this time. The monarchs of England, for example, offended the pope, who had armies all over the continent. But Queen Elizabeth I was the smartest ruler in Europe. She was the daughter of Henry VIII and Anne Boleyn, but she was no zealot. She would not throw in with the Catholics or the Protestants. Philip II of Spain persuaded the pope not to excommunicate this queen, because Spain needed her friendship against their normal enemy France. She was equally clever at keeping peace inside Britain, encouraging the House of Commons, but putting gentle limits on freedom of speech, slowing down the onslaught of the Puritans while demonstrating that she was no friend of Rome.

But in the second half of the sixteenth century England and Spain drew apart. This happened because the Spanish market in Antwerp collapsed, and Britain had to go and trade with someone else. Why not China? Elizabeth began sending sailors north, telling them to find a channel to the Orient. In 1553 an expedition tried to go northeast and did not get all that far, but it would lead to relations with the Russians, who were not Catholics or Protestants. In 1576 Martin Frobisher came back to England with a kidnapped Inuk man and a shipload of black ore with shiny stuff in it. I have found the Northwest Passage and a lot of gold, he said.

However, his rocks were no more valuable than Cartier's, and his Northwest Passage was just a dead end in the Northeast of the New World.

The queen's explorers would keep looking, of course, but she also had her pirates. They worked on commission, penetrating Spanish territory in the Caribbean, for instance, trying to set up their own trading posts. When the Spanish reacted with cannon and cutlasses, the queen hired the greatest English pirate of them all, Francis Drake, and Drake tore into the Catholics, burning their ships to the waterline, raiding their warehouses, getting them really angry at their former ally. Drake laughed and sailed around the Horn, then destroyed the little Spanish depots along the Pacific Coast of America. He went as far north as he could, and said that he went farther. He was the first English captain to look at the tall trees on the coastline of British Columbia. He went ashore for water and may have said something there about claiming this otherworldly place for the red-headed queen.

When he got his ship, *The Golden Hind,* back to Blighty the little queen came aboard and put a garter on his leg. She liked this Sir Francis Drake. He brought real gold home, and better than that, it used to be Spanish gold.

Not that the Spanish were going to go away. By 1580 Philip II was King of Spain, King of Portugal, King of Naples, King of Sicily, Duke of Milan and ruler of the Netherlands. He was the personal ruler of a world that stretched from the edge of China to the mountains of Peru. The Spanish Inquisition never had to get any approval from the Vatican. Philip knew in his heart that he was the real leader of the Christian Church, and that he had to extirpate Protestantism and Islam and heathen practices throughout the world. It was a calamity beyond comprehension when the Armada's harbour at Cadiz was torn to bits by Francis Drake and his outlaws. In 1588, when the Spanish ships went north to even things up, they lost half their vessels and had to bring the rest home.

Still, though they had demonstrated that Spain's military could be embarrassed, the English did not really go into the colonial business. In 1585 Walter Raleigh sent some people to try their first colony on Roanoke Island, but by 1590 all the people had disappeared. There were rumours that they had been eaten by Indians. After that it was impossible to find English people who wanted to be colonists.

Also in 1585 some English pirates did their own Armada sinking, destroying the Spanish fishing fleet along the south coast of Newfoundland. In the following years some small groups of English settlers built homes in the little coves along that shore where there were so many codfish that they could never be fished out. Any French fishing folks, or fishers from other European countries, would have to find somewhere else to lay their nets. The French tended to go right past the south shore and try the wide part of the St. Lawrence.

The skins game

These French fishermen would often meet some Algonquin people at Tadoussac, where the Saguenay River slips into the St. Lawrence. For fun the Europeans would slide down the immense sand dunes. To fill their spare time they would trade with the Native people, handing over iron tools and cloth in exchange for fur cloaks. Thus began the fur trade that would pretty well define Canadian economics and history for the next three hundred years.

Monarchs and other rich people had always liked to line their fine clothing with fur. Even if they lived in warm climates, they would sport fur to show how well off they were. When hatmakers discovered that the undercoat fur of the waterproof beaver could be made into very good felt, the Canadian beaver was doomed to sit atop the heads of European noblemen and merchants until the silk hat became the vogue in the middle of the nineteenth century. Have a look at all those European paintings, or read Gerhart Hauptmann's 1893 satire, *The Beaver Coat*.

There were some beavers building their little dams along creeks flowing into the Rhone, but they would never be able to keep up with the amazing demand for felt hats. Besides, their king, Henry IV, had managed to put an end to his religious wars and could now turn France's attention back toward New France. The French merchants, hearing stories of far forests densely populated by fur-wearing animals, were eager to make deals with the king. Henry IV was big on privatization.

He would offer trading rights in New France if the traders would take care of colonization and converting the Indians to Catholicism.

In 1602 Henry gave the first contract to a businessman named Aymar de Chastes, and the latter would gladly hire the king's man Samuel de Champlain. Champlain had fought in the king's wars and then become a sailor. He had gone over to have a look at Cartier's country in 1599, and when he came back he wrote a wonderful report on what he had seen. The king was so well impressed that he made Champlain his royal geographer. Now Champlain saw his main chance and got permission to join Aymar de Chastes's expedition.

He sailed with de Chastes's partner, Pontgravé, up the St. Lawrence to Cartier's dreaded Lachine Rapids. All the way along he listened to Native people, hearing about a great bay to the northwest and some big water to the southwest. Some of the latter was supposed to be salty. This made Champlain prick up his ears. He was an explorer working for the bourgeoisie, but he was also a very curious man. He would spend a lot of time in this new country, and he would eventually be called the Father of New France.

Champlain was a pretty good politician, and he understood the relationship between colonial economics and political alliances. For example, at Tadoussac he made friends with the Montagnais, an Innu people, telling them that if they would round up a lot of fine beaver pelts for the French merchants, he would see about helping them in their wars with the Iroquois.

But when he got back to France he found out that de Chastes had died and that the king's people had passed the Royal Permission, the licence to reap riches in the king's newly explored lands, on to one Pierre de Monts. Champlain joined his outfit, and was a little disappointed to hear that de Monts did not think much of the St. Lawrence. He had seen Tadoussac and thought it was too damned cold. He was going to make his first settlement in the Bay of Fundy.

Pierre de Monts had about as much sense as the Marquis de la Roche, who stranded fifty convicts on Sable Island in 1598. He also dumped his colonists on a sandy island with no source of fresh water.

This was at the mouth of the St-Croix River at the Bay of Fundy. A hundred unfortunate French people spent a winter at that unlikely place, some dying from scurvy, some almost freezing to death, partly because the businessmen had used all the timber to make nice homes for themselves. In the spring the ill survivors were moved to the mainland to found Port Royal. There the weather was a little nicer, and by 1607 the first European settlement north of St. Augustine was growing decent crops and starting to create Acadian music.

These first colonists were not really idealists and social climbers. Many of them, and the later colonists around Tadoussac, were petty crooks and roustabouts, who made a deal that meant that they belonged to the company for two years at least. As the Natives were exploited for their furs, the settlers were exploited for their labour. And they were not allowed to do any fur trading themselves. Because there were very few women from Europe, most of the first workers took Native companions. Thus were the exploited joined, and thus began the history of New France as seen by Quebec nationalists in the twentieth century.

Port Royal had a checkered career. Pawns and kings contended for that little habitation until 1940, when the Canadian government created Port-Royal National Historic Site. In 1607 de Monts moved the whole population back to France, because more aggressive businessmen had managed to get his monopoly rescinded. In 1610 another merchant, who had been horning in on de Monts's trade earlier, set up business at Port Royal. In 1613 some English visitors from Virginia wrecked the place. Pretty soon there were Englishmen and Frenchmen claiming chunks of land. Both kings made official grants of land—often the same land. In 1621 Britain's James I granted the entire region from the Gaspé to the Bay of Fundy to a fellow Scotsman, and they decided to call it New Scotland. As the habit was to write charters in Latin, the place became known as Nova Scotia.

Champlain's town

In 1604 Miguel de Cervantes published the first part of *Don Quixote*, which would soon become popular all over Western Europe. In 1605, led by Spanish soldier Guy Fawkes, a bunch of Catholic gents in beaver hats conspired to blow up London's Parliament Building. In 1606 the great painter Caravaggio killed a man in Rome in a dispute about the score of a tennis game. In 1607 the English captain Christopher Newport founded Jamestown near the mouth of Chesapeake Bay, thus establishing the first English colony in America. In the early summer of 1608 Samuel de Champlain, who had never thought much of a colony on the Atlantic, started building a habitation at the foot of the high rock at Quebec.

Here would be the capital of French America from then on.

Champlain's boss, de Monts, had managed to get a monopoly for one more year, hardly time to establish a French nation in Indian territory. Over the summer and fall Champlain saw his weird conglomeration of buildings somehow adhere to the steep earth. Twenty-eight colonists had come with him to this potential home. It was no new Eden. All the new Edens were down south where the weather was more conducive to gardening. When the winter was at last over in 1609 only eight of his colonists were still alive.

But Champlain had a dream about a kingdom of fur and generations of French people spreading their religion and language throughout the continent, no matter how far it might be to Asia. Meanwhile he planted seeds in the soil defended by cannon, and talked to the Native people about animal skins and Jesus.

These people were his old friends, the Algonquin, the Montagnais and the people who called themselves the Wendat and whom the French called the Huron. "Huron" was a French slang word for undercivilized bozo. This alliance had been fighting against the more southerly Iroquois alliance for years, and in 1609 they asked Champlain to come south with them on a war expedition. They proceeded up a river called the River of the Iroquois (which Champlain would rename the Richelieu) and past the long Lake of the Iroquois (which Champlain would rename the Champlain) and finally encountered a bunch of the enemy. They had a good fight and won a manly victory but set in motion the process that would lead to British North America. The powerful Iroquois Confederacy would never forget whose side this Frenchman was on.

But what could he do? He was a businessman, and his business was furs. When de Monts's monopoly ran out, the smaller outfits moved in, and for three years Champlain had to exercise his political skill with the Indians and with the authorities at home. Like all businessmen he much preferred monopoly to competition. It was no wonder that a couple of years of disorder transpired: Henri IV had renounced his own personal Protestantism and married a Medici, but the Jesuits had a policy against any king who went easy on the Huguenots or foreign infidels, and they hired a fellow to knife the king to death in his coach. It was 1610, and Marie de' Medici would run things for a while until young Louis was old enough to kick her out of the country.

But in 1612 an ugly little priest named Armand du Plessis de Richelieu told Marie of the Medicis that France needed the St. Lawrence River because there were getting to be too many Protestants on the high seas. If they did not look out, the perfidious Britons would send pilgrims across the sea and try to set up something they would probably call "New England." So the lady regent gave Samuel de Champlain his fur monopoly and the title of lieutenant-general of New France. It would have sounded grander if there had been more than a couple of dozen French people along the big river.

Champlain sent out associates to explore the Great Lakes area and navigate the beaver rivers. His Indian allies resisted taking the Europeans very far because they did not want to introduce them to any new suppliers, but they had to take them some distance if they were going to continue raids on their enemies. Gradually, the lieutenant-general was learning the lie of the land. The Orient became more and more distant.

Meanwhile, in these first years of the seventeenth century the other Europeans were snooping around. A rather unknown captain, Henry Hudson, went to work for the Dutch and found a river to name after himself and some friendly suckers to trade with. Then Hudson went to work for the British and discovered a wide strait that would lead from the Atlantic to the great western sea that would become Hudson Bay.

After a terrible winter, and after listening to Hudson say that he would
rather continue exploring than return home, some of his men mutinied,
set Hudson and a few others adrift and headed home. No one knows
what became of Henry Hudson, except that it could not be anything
good. When the mutineers got to England they were put on trial, but
no one went to prison. They had information that some businessmen
could put to use.

When they found out that there were some nice rivers that debouched
into the western shore of Hudson Bay, their eyes lit up and their hearts
shut down. The beavers of Western Canada did not have a chance.

Champlain must have felt as if he were the only person in New France
who had a dream. Between 1612 and 1627 the manoeuvring and back-
biting among the French royalty and nobility were accompanied by a
similar mixture of greed and chaos in the fur trade. Every few years
Champlain would have to put up with a new company, and each one,
reneging on its contracts, was more interested in gathering furs than
in settling a continent. By 1627 there were still only sixty-five settlers
and about fifteen administrators. In 1620 the *Mayflower* had banged
up against some rock a little way to the south. English people were
pouring in. Champlain's bosses told him to quit begging for colonists
and concentrate on exploring for furs. They wanted a trading post,
not a civilization.

Champlain perhaps thought that if his damned bosses were not
going to bring him Frenchmen, he had better try to turn the savages
into Christians. Two Benedictine priests had come over with Cartier
on his second voyage, but in 1615 you did not see any Christian
Huron or Algonquin around town. Champlain got the first four
Récollet priests to come over in 1615. Récollets are a branch of the
Franciscans, who were known for having a lot of branches. Their view
was that the Indians did not have any religion and could use some
instruction. The Native people thought that these white guys had a

hard time understanding what religion was. Any Franciscan priest with a grain of sense could see that four men would have to work long hours for centuries to turn these forest people into Papists. In 1625 they turned for help to the Jesuits.

The best thing about the Jesuits was that they liked to write. When the *Relations,* their reports on the strange lands that they had entered, reached Europe, they became best-sellers, and remain the most exciting first-hand history we have today.

Before the Jesuit *Relations* it was next to impossible to interest French people in the New World. All they heard was how cold it was and how hard it was to get a decent pair of shoes. Still, Champlain's pleading did result in a few immigrants. The most famous among them, these four centuries later, is a man named Louis Hébert. There are many Louis Héberts in Quebec today, and most of them are descended from this first one.

M. Hébert had seen the New World in Nova Scotia, and though this former pharmacist was enjoying an early retirement in Paris, he could not sit still once Champlain had sent someone to whisper in his ear. He packed up his wife, Marie, and his offspring and sailed to Quebec, where he got first dibs on the available land. There were no horses and no oxen and no plows in Champlain's colony, but the Héberts set to work clearing the land and planting European seeds. Every day the Native people would pass by and shake their heads, wondering why these pale people did not make use of the foodstuffs this land was willing to offer to them.

The cardinal and the king

By 1617 Louis XIII felt grown-up enough to chase the dissident princes—and his mother—out of the country. Richelieu had to skedaddle, too, but three years later he was back, now getting next to the son rather than the mother. Louis probably did not like this situation, but he was smart enough to know Richelieu's power and connections— they could be useful to the establishment, and they could be dangerous to anyone that Richelieu did not like.

Here was a homely little man who had become a bishop at age twenty-one, secretary of state for foreign affairs at thirty-two and a cardinal at thirty-seven. He had strong supporters at the Vatican, a network of secret agents all through France and other states and a growing fortune in real estate. He married off the king's sister to the English crown prince. His armies kept winning victories against foreigners and domestic upstarts. He rebuffed the Hapsburgs and zigzagged his alliances whenever it seemed like a good idea. He was a Catholic and a Royalist, and he said that disloyalty to either was treason against the other. And he made money from both sources. It was no wonder that Louis XIII was a little afraid of him and glad to have him run the country.

Richelieu was a busy man. He had to help demolish the German countryside in the Thirty Years War, root out rebels and execute them, change international agreements when it became financially advisable, collect expensive works of art and *maisons* to keep them in, explain why sometimes he made alliances with Protestants to fight the Hapsburgs and save souls for a Catholic heaven. It is a wonder that he had any time to think about Champlain's little town on the St. Lawrence.

But there were savages over there, and if they were not gathered into the Christian fold, they might never have a chance for the afterlife, or worse, they might decide to become Protestants. There were also millions of beavers over there, and most of the Frenchmen gathering them were Huguenots. Prime Minister Richelieu came up with a plan to save Church and Country: France would give a fur monopoly for the whole continent to a new company, and the company would be headed by Armand du Plessis de Richelieu.

The Company of New France, created in 1527, would have the franchise for all the territory from the Atlantic to Lake Superior and from the Arctic to Florida. The CEO would be Richelieu, and the investors would be a group he called the One Hundred Associates. Richelieu reasoned that with him in the front office, the fur traders could no longer ignore directives to move Catholic immigrants onto the land. Sure, he and his ninety-nine friends would make a tidy profit, but the most important thing was to cover the continent with French-speaking Catholics. Richelieu did not need his spies to know that the Brits were hauling pilgrims across the Atlantic. With France at war against the English for the umpteenth time, it would not do to be outnumbered in lands that looked as if they might be almost as big as Europe itself.

In fact, the Brits won the first battle of Quebec before the Company could make its first quarterly report. Three brothers named Kirke, acting as freelance buccaneers for King Charles I, set sail for the St. Lawrence in early 1628. Charles was peeved at Richelieu because he had been shortchanged in the dowry when he took the French king's sister off his hands. Captain Kirke and his brothers were waiting for the Company's ships full of provisions and settlers when they appeared downstream from Tadoussac. A lot of the immigrants regretted their adventurous decision when British shot tore into the masts and sails over their heads. After a day and night of terror, the French vessels belonged to the Kirkes.

This was bad news for Champlain and his fort. David Kirke sent Champlain a gracious letter outlining the hopeless position of the French settlers, who could expect no supplies or reinforcements that year. Would the lieutenant-general not desire to hand over the fort, if only to save the lives of its inhabitants? Champlain had been building his dream too long to hand it over to some foreign pirates. At least a man ought to show some backbone before giving in. He replied that he and his people would fire their cannon if Kirke's ships approached.

The Kirke brothers thought about it. They had a treasure in their hands already. They could always come back and take Quebec. Why not haul all this stuff and people back home and spend the winter in a nicer climate?

Their decision was to be of huge consequence for the course of Canadian history in centuries to come.

The One Hundred Associates would have to get through the winter with no return on their investments. Champlain's settlers were nearly crazy from starvation by the time shipping season started in the spring of 1629. And the ships were not coming. Every bark sent from France was demolished or forced to make a U-turn. The only ships to appear before Quebec belonged to the Kirke brothers. They sent Champlain another polite letter, and this time the unhappy explorer ceded his buildings to the British louts. With a limp that was a reminder of an Iroquois arrow, he led three-quarters of his people aboard the Scotsmen's vessels. Thirty French speakers were left to maintain the grounds.

What a surprise when the Kirkes got back to England and dumped off their prisoners! The French and British had ceased their hostilities three months earlier. When Champlain heard this, his dream was alive again. If the Kirkes had captured Quebec after the truce, his town was not a prize of war; it was simply an unlawful home invasion. He went to see the new French ambassador to London. I just work here, said that functionary. Champlain got a new suit of clothes and went to see his prime minister and king. He was aghast to find that the palace was tired of Canada. What had they managed to do in a hundred years? At this rate there would be five hundred French people over there in another four centuries. Champlain kept talking. He mentioned fur and souls to Richelieu.

Eventually the prime minister talked to the English king. We will give you the rest of the dowry we owe you, he said, if you will give us back those funny-looking buildings in Quebec. In 1632 King Charles decided not to lose his head over a bit of frozen ground he would never see. He signed the Treaty of St-Germain-en-Laye, and Quebec and Acadia on the Atlantic Coast were back in French hands. Champlain hobbled back to Quebec in 1633. He groaned when he saw what was left of his town after the Brits had finished their work. But the old man limped around and tried to inspire his little population.

He had a partner in his dream. This was Jean de Brébeuf, the most determined of the Jesuit priests. Father Brébeuf had been in Canada since 1625, learning languages and trying to make Christians out of Huron fur traders. The Kirke brothers had sent him to France along with Champlain, but in 1633 he was back, trying to make a Huron dictionary. He had news for the Indians: if they would change religions they would get into the best heaven going.

In Quebec Samuel de Champlain was getting more and more interested in heaven, too. He hardly had any time for furs now, as he thought about his citizens' souls. He was the lieutenant-general of God's colony on the edge of the world. He announced that attendance at Mass was compulsory. He had been born to a Protestant family, and he had the ardour of the convert. When it came time for the father of French Canada to die, he did it on Christmas Day of 1635.

Jesuit and other relations

Jack Kerouac, the great twentieth-century Franco-American novelist, liked to boast about the Indian blood in his veins. It came from the Mother of French Canada. When we talk about the small numbers of Europeans along the St. Lawrence River in the early seventeenth century, our calculations are vague. Marie Hébert, the hard-working wife of the first permanent settler, was in a minority in those days. Among the adventurous or desperate who signed aboard Champlain's ships, not many were Frenchwomen. There were not enough of them to go around, so the unattached white men who did not choose to be chaste or too tired or homosexual had to look elsewhere, and that meant finding Native women whose husbands had been killed in battle or whose fathers were in financial straits.

So there were not a few youngsters with mixed European and American backgrounds. The coureurs de bois, in the later seventeenth century, went upcountry to bypass the Indian traders, and probably deposited lots of informal families in the forest. The "legitimate" fur traders back at the St. Lawrence did not approve of these woods runners, and neither did the Jesuit order. The Catholic Church, as Jack Kerouac could tell you, has always had a lot to say about your sex life. Here are a few sentences from a letter of advice to young Frenchmen who might want to be missionaries among the savages. It was written by Father le Jeune, who had arrived immediately after Quebec had reverted to French control: "Here we have nothing, it seems, which incites toward good; we are among Peoples who are astonished when you speak to them of God, and who often have only horrible blasphemies in their mouths. . . . I pass over the small chance of seclusion there is among Barbarians, who scarcely ever leave you, who hardly know what it is to speak in a low tone. Especially I would not dare to speak of the danger there is of ruining yourself among their impurities, in the case of any one whose heart is not sufficiently full of God to firmly resist this poison."

It was really for the armies of Jesus that Montreal was founded in 1642. Champlain had decided that there should be fur-trading posts at Trois-Rivières and Montreal, and before his death the work had started at the former. The annual *Relations* written by le Jeune and Brébeuf inspired religious readers to imagine a kingdom of God among the redskins. There were enough of these pious people to raise the funds for Ville-Marie, a new settlement on the island of Montreal. The first shipload comprised fifty-four people—soldiers, nurses and handymen. It was led by Jeanne Mance, a zealous nurse who relied on deep funding and the occasional miracle to build Hôtel-Dieu, the first hospital in New France. And Paul de Chomedey de Maisonneuve, a military officer who, like Jeanne Mance, was chosen by the Société Notre-Dame de Montréal to bring salvation and obedience to the challenging wilderness.

But Ville-Marie de Montréal would always be a place to fight over, from the time of de Maisonneuve to the time of Mordecai Richler. The mid-seventeenth century was a time of picturesque and violent rivalries. The Iroquois nations who had been driven upriver sometime after Cartier's visits were now powerful and united enough to counterattack. Europeans were alarmed by the military superiority of the Iroquois Confederacy.

In the 1640s the Iroquois were demonstrating their superiority over the Wendat and other neighbours. For a while the "Huron" people had enjoyed the support of Champlain's soldiers, but now the Iroquois were enjoying the support of the Dutch fur traders, who had set up a fort at Albany, and it would not be long till the Iroquois became the allies of the English. The Dutch were unfriendly with the French all over the world, and while the Black Robes were offering European religion to their Huron, the Dutch were offering firearms to their Iroquois.

Ville-Marie en 1642 *by W. Decary*
(NATIONAL ARCHIVES OF CANADA/C-7885)

Two historical patterns would be established: rival peoples would contend the island of Montreal, and there would be a lot of guns to the south of us.

So the Native people became client warriors for the European capitalists. The Iroquois warriors went to Huron villages with Catholic missions in them, and wiped them out—St-Joseph, St-Ignace, St-Louis and Ste-Marie. The surviving Huron went for safety to Quebec, and the Iroquois owned the rivers around Jeanne Mance's town. Now Montreal became the target. For the first two decades of its existence the town would be under siege. Anyone swinging a hoe at the ground outside the stockade had to keep a long-gun handy. Maisonneuve kept petitioning France for more soldiers, and once in a while a few might arrive. The fur trade around Montreal continued, but the French settlers were not permitted to get in on the action.

What did Louis XIV care? He had enough lovely fur to trim his royal wardrobe.

Marie de La Tour

After Acadia had come back to French control in 1632, the spacious area from the Gaspé to what would become Maine was split between two avaricious businessmen and lieutenant-governors, the unbearable Charles de Menou d'Aulnay and his socially inferior rival, Charles de Saint-Étienne de La Tour. It was not long till the two entrepreneurs were at war. Aulnay had the advantage of greater wealth and more influence at the French court. But La Tour had the advantage of Françoise-Marie Jacqueline, his wife.

In 1642, while her husband was holed up at his fort, Françoise-Marie sailed to France and argued the family's case. She came back with a warship and 140 fighting men. La Tour's business connections in Boston lent him four more ships and more soldiers, so he went to battle against Aulnay, chasing him back onto his half of Acadia. Aulnay griped some more to the French authorities, while Mme de La Tour headed back to France for more help.

But by this time the French authorities had been persuaded to support their buddy Aulnay, ordering the intrepid lady to stay in France while her husband was dealt with in Acadia. She disguised herself as a Brit and slipped over to England, where she hired another ship and headed west. In Boston she amassed weapons and ammunition and returned to her husband's fort at the mouth of the Saint John River. There was a standoff and relative quiet until one day in 1645 Charles de La Tour went to Boston on one of his normal business trips.

Hearing that Fort La Tour was defended by forty-five men under the charge of a mere woman, Charles d'Aulnay loaded a sixteen-gun warship with fighting men and parked in front of the fort. Surrender, was his advice. Françoise-Marie showed herself on the wall with a sword in her hand and announced that she would show resistance. Artillery was hurled at the fort for three days to no great effect, but then a traitor helped Aulnay's forces through a gap, and the two sides began a ferocious small weapons battle.

The lady's soldiers were in desperate straits. As a French gentleman, Aulnay offered a deal: if she would surrender the fort, he would spare the lives of all. She surrendered the fort. As soon as he got inside Aulnay had all the living defenders seized and ropes put around their necks, including that of Françoise-Marie. Then he forced her to watch while he hanged them, all but two.

Three weeks later she died of shock. The king made Aulnay the governor of the whole region. La Tour fled to Quebec, where he remained in the fur business there. In 1650 Charles d'Aulnay drowned when his canoe capsized in white water, and La Tour came back to Acadia to see what he could get. As fate would have it, Jeanne Motin, widow of the late Charles d'Aulnay, was laying claim to the empire. Faced with terrific debts, she announced that she would share her fortune with any man who helped her fight off the creditors. Along came Charles de La Tour. In 1653 they were married, and spent part of their connubial life in Fort La Tour, where their spouses had met in arms.

4

BRAVE NEW FRANCE

Jean Talon as intendant in New France, 1665–72
(NATIONAL ARCHIVES OF CANADA/C-8519)

When I was a schoolboy in the south end of the Canadian part of the Okanagan Valley in British Columbia, our history classes were usually about the Picts and the Jutes, or the War of the Roses. Once in a while we would get a little bit of Canadian history, but it was about New France every time. We never heard about anything that happened in Saskatchewan, and not a word about British Columbia, for example. We did not know how Oliver got its name, but we knew what Montreal means. We might, if there were ten minutes left in June, hear something about Confederation, and perhaps the CPR, but our subject was New France.

Our history book was decorated with pictures of Jean Talon and the lot, but for me the most romantic picture was an action scene—Adam Dollard des Ormeaux and his sixteen companions snugged behind some old logs, fighting off hundreds and hundreds of hysterical Iroquois bent on tomahawking and scalping any white person they could get their hands on. I imagined myself as Dollard, though I could not speak a word of French and was too far down the social scale to have a "de" attached to my name. Now, of course, I cheer against him.

By 1660 it began to look as if New France's goose was cooked. There were just too many Iroquois. The fur trade had dwindled to a few beavers and the odd muskrat because the Indians and the Dutch were cleaning up. The colony was entirely dependent on the home country for its supplies, and not much was arriving from France. These outside problems quite expectedly led to squabbles inside the community. Priests yelled at one another when they weren't yelling at the civil authorities. The common people often proved to be a disappointment to both Church and administration. If the Dutch or English had been as much interested in geographical politics as they were in animal hides, they could probably have sent in a thousand troops and won the whole shebang again without a how-do-you-do to Louis XIV.

There was the occasional moment for celebration or at least hope. One of these was provided by those two men whose names are a delight to idle schoolboys across the country: Radisson and Groseilliers. Pierre-Esprit Radisson knew the Huron and the Algonquin as well as any European could, but he was also for a while a prisoner of the Iroquois. He and his wife's brother, Médard Chouart des Grosseilliers, were not sticklers for the law. Not bothering with the formality of a licence, they got themselves some birchbark canoes and travelled deep into Indian country, accumulating great mountains of high-quality furs from the region of the western Great Lakes.

When they arrived in Montreal in 1660, they were welcomed as French heroes by a populace that was aching for good news. But the governor of New France, Pierre de Voyer, Vicomte d'Argenson, said that he would not put up with any freelance fur boys. Everyone in New

France laughed behind the governor's back. The priests and the merchants and the farmers liked the outlaws a lot more than they liked the governor. But d'Argenson said that Radisson and Grosseilliers needed a licence to go trading, and they would not get one unless they took a couple of the governor's men with them to count the furs, and then gave half their profits to him. Ha ha, said the brothers-in-law, and took off without a licence again.

When they returned in 1663 with an even higher mountain of furs, they were heroes again, to everyone but Governor d'Argenson. He nabbed 60 percent of their profits and suggested that if there were any complaints they should be directed to France. The rebellious coureurs de bois complained to France. Take your complaints to God, they were told. Radisson and Grosseilliers decided that they had no future in New France and went to bargain with the people in New England.

Another father of New France

It was probably a good time for the intrepid fur heroes to look for their fortunes elsewhere. In 1663, twenty-five-year-old King Louis XIV said to hell with the businessmen and declared New France a royal colony. The French look upon their colonies as overseas versions of their *départements*. The governor was responsible for defence and security, and had to report to the defence ministry in Paris. The intendant was in charge of trade and economy, and reported to his superiors back home. Neither one could boss the other around, though in those first days they often wished they could. To make matters even more complicated, there was a third bigwig on the ground, this being the bishop. He, of course, said that he was the representative of a very high official indeed. In the late seventeenth century there were three robust and egoistical men in the three positions in New France: Intendant Jean Talon; Governor Louis de Buade, Comte de Frontenac; and Bishop François de Laval.

Louis XIV had the biggest ego in the known world. When he was nine, he wrote in his diary that fame was more important than life. As king he often reminded people that he was a kind of visible divinity. He was going to rule absolutely, and forever. *"L'état, c'est moi,"* he reasoned. He got Molière and Racine to write verses to praise him. He caused monuments to be raised all over France, and then he ordered the building of his palace at Versailles. If he was going to be the most illustrious monarch in the world—the Sun King, after all—he would have the most expensive house ever seen.

This fat man in the priceless wardrobe was not going to go down in history as the loser of North America to some rabble mixture of savages and Englishmen.

A lot of it was going to be named after him: Louisiana, Louisbourg, Louisville. By virtue of the fact that he was heaven's special human being on earth, he was really the owner of New France, and if he could make the whole of the New World French, well, that might be a pretty good monument to his life if things went wrong and he was not really immortal.

Still, the scraps of land along the St. Lawrence were not a big deal; the country was not as desirable as Spain, for instance, which the Sun King wanted to acquire. When he proclaimed the royal colony, he sent out some civil servants to administer the rough place, and soon he sent out eleven hundred soldiers called the Carignan-Salières regiment. These worthies built forts in former Iroquois land, and then rode south into remaining Mohawk land. There they burst into villages and killed all the people they could, and in order to discourage the making of more people, they burned the crops in the fields.

In 1667 the Iroquois people signed a treaty with the invaders, and the Carignan-Salières regiment went back to France. There was peace; now for prosperity.

The daughters of the sun

The invaders were supposed to be converting the heathens to French Catholic ways. To the Church's dismay, things had for a century been going in the opposite direction. Despite Champlain's pietistic rules, a lot of the fur boys who penetrated the forests in search of skin were finding lots of reasons for acquiring Wendat or Algonquin girlfriends or "wives."

One of the reasons was that by doing so one could create good relationships with the women's relatives who were in the fur business. Well, why not? It was for similar reasons that Louis XIV married Marie-Thérèse of Austria, daughter of the Spanish king.

In 1660 and 1661 a couple of hundred colonists had been killed by unfriendly Natives, and many others decided to go back to France where there were not as many tomahawks. When the royal colony was proclaimed there were about 3,000 French people on the river, a third of them children. There were already 100,000 settlers in New England and plenty more were arriving farther south. What the king needed was a population explosion. And neither he nor his Church officials wanted dark-skinned French Canadians.

He decided to send over his daughters.

When I lived in Montreal in the late 1960s there was a nice expensive restaurant in Old Montreal called Les Filles du roi. It was named after Louis XIV's daughters. These were the young women who volunteered to get aboard sailing ships and go to New France to become wives and mothers. Most of the single men in New France were country bumpkins, and most of the king's daughters were city girls. A lot of them could read. Most of them had good reasons for emigrating—they were poor, or they were without family, or they dreamed of adventure. Perhaps they did not believe what they had read or heard from the Jesuit *Relations*, that the new land was a place of snowbanks and tomahawks.

Upon arrival they would find quarters in the nunneries until they had managed as good a marriage as possible. This meant checking to see whether the man in question had a decent cleared farm and some ambition. Once married, the women would live a life of hard work and constant childbearing. The birth rate in Quebec is now the lowest in Canada, but in the last part of the seventeenth century it was double the normal rate of increase. Those Protestant Puritans to the south had better get into bed more often if they wanted to win the continent. To help matters along, in 1671 Intendant Talon issued a rule that any bachelor who was not married two weeks after the bride ship arrived would get no licence to hunt or fish or engage in any trade.

Between 1663 and 1673, 770 daughters of the king landed on the shore of the St. Lawrence. Only thirty of them went back home. They commenced having grandchildren of the king as fast as they could, and the Church started to keep such good records of these crops that the average Quebecker today can trace his family clear back to one of those brave women. For example, Jean Chrétien, golfer and prime minister of Canada for several terms, is descended from a king's daughter who arrived in 1669.

Lights along the river

No one was going to build a Versailles on the St. Lawrence. But this new department would grow to resemble the rest of France as much as its leaders could make it. Along the shores the Native people could see narrow strips of farmland reaching back up to the forest. In school we orchard kids were fascinated with the picture: each landholder should have access to the water, so the farms would be ribbons rather than squares of soil. If you go now to the Île d'Orléans, just downriver from Quebec's heights, you will see a great example of the system. In the early days, at least, those strips did not work all that well, because farmers, understandably, worked as close to the water supply as possible, so that the riverside soil became overworked, and the higher parts tended to see little agronomy at all.

Churches got built along the river, so there were hamlets, villages and soon three little towns—Quebec City, Trois-Rivières and Montreal. Two of them would make it to the National Hockey League three hundred years later, and the other would host a Grand Prix automobile race.

These were company towns and the company was France, otherwise known as Louis XIV. We call the business the mercantile system. France controlled all trade and industry, set prices and taxes, tolls and percentages. There was no room for free enterprise or free trade—English goods were better made, of greater quantity and cheaper. In any trade war the English would swamp the people of the river. So while the farmers were making babies as fast as they could, the state would control their economic life.

The mercantile system was joined with the seigneurial system. A seigneur was hardly ever a real nobleman, just someone of more elevated status than a forest runner or hoe swinger, usually a military officer or merchant's son. He made a deal with the governor—he would erect a big house that could withstand Indian raids, build a flour mill, provide a chapel and pay a priest to tend to his tenant farmers, and organize a court to settle disputes among the hoi polloi.

The tenant farmers also had to make a deal with the seigneur. They paid an annual rent on their land allotments, worked the seigneur's own land when it became necessary, bought their flour and stuff from his store and promised to help fight the Indians. Some of the more paternalistic lords tried to introduce a newfangled concept called *droit de seigneur.*

Kings and beavers

The intertwining of agricultural, religious and economic systems made for a closed society except for those restless souls who jumped into canoes and headed westward.

They had to go west because to the south of them were the five nations of Iroquois with long memories, and to the south of *them* were enormous numbers of Protestants. In a sense, this was a lucky circumstance, because the more northerly beavers had richer pelts and would raise better prices in Europe. Unfortunately, every silver lining has a dark cloud inside it. The French were not the only Europeans in the area. Radisson and Groseilliers, you will remember, were cheesed off at the governor of New France, and had sold their services to the British, who admired the furs they found in rivers leading to Hudson Bay. King Charles II, similar to his Spanish and French counterparts, liked to grant enormous stretches of land to business people in his bailiwick. So was born the Hudson's Bay Company.

At the beginning of the twenty-first century, everyone's mother and grandpa shop at the Bay or its modest subsidiary, Zeller's. The HBC is the oldest joint-stock merchandiser in the world. It was chartered by

Charles in 1670, and on its three-hundredth anniversary its headquarters were moved to Winnipeg. When we were kids the Hudson's Bay store was the biggest deal in Winnipeg. All those Western cities—Edmonton, Regina, Calgary, Vancouver—had big square HBC stores on the main intersection of town. People met in their cafeterias for a bargain on standing rib roast.

The Hudson's Bay Company had more to do with Canadian history than any of the US invasions or any of the confederation treaties. On Vancouver Island it would become the government. Its very founding would lead to a war for control of New France.

The French were packing canoes with skins and making the arduous combination of portage and rapids-skimming all the way to their familiar St. Lawrence. The British just sailed ships into Hudson Bay and loaded up. They didn't have to win the Huron away from the French. They just made deals with the Cree and heard stories about the unbelievable immensity of this new claim the king had laid on them. How could they imagine that the HBC claim would eventually amount to an area that would make Genghis Khan's conquests look like a walk across town?

Yes, there were French names showing up all over the Great Lakes, and even down the Mississippi. But New France was run by French people—in France there was Paris and then there was the rest of the country as a kind of front and back garden. In New France there was Quebec, and there was a big green garden filled with luxurious furs that just had to be removed from their owners and brought back to the source of light.

To understand the French attitude, one need only listen to the words of Quebec's most famous governor, Count Frontenac. Here he is, addressing a gathering of Iroquois at the instant erection of a new French fort at Cataraqui (present-day Kingston):

Children! Onnontagues, Mohawks, Oneidas, Cayugas and Senecas. I signified to you the other day the joy I felt to see you arrive here with all the proofs of submission that children owe their Father. . . .

I invite you to give me four of your little girls from seven to eight years old, and two of your little boys, whom I will have instructed with all possible care, and taught French. . . .

I shall adopt them . . . and place the girls with the Nuns at Quebec, and I shall frequently visit them. . . .

What a swell guy!

Seventeen years later these "children" would overrun their "father's" fort at Cataraqui. So much for submission.

Meanwhile, the HBC traders were forming alliances with more Western Natives, starting bush families with their women, building forts at river mouths and getting into the habit of government. There was a governor of the company back in England, another governor at the Bay, and factors with councils at its stations in the wilderness. It was a trading company, but the longer the traders stayed in one place, the more likely they would have a farm and a notion of property and a mill and a civil service.

The Hudson's Bay Company was a logical step from the capitalism that preceded it. A corporation has voting stockholders, and these people were interested in profit, and profit came from expansion and development, and it had nothing to do with church missionaries and settlers. Not yet, anyway.

If the English had managed to get into the great bay to the north first, Frontenac would send his men south. More trading posts were established on the Great Lakes. In 1673, a year after the great governor's appointment, Louis Jolliet the fur trader and Father Marquette the soul trader were paddled down the Mississippi River as far south as the confluence of the Arkansas River. According to their calculations, they had found the way to the Gulf of Mexico. This was going to be complicated:

there were Spanish people around; there were even some English people around. There were Native people around, but they did not count, did they? The fur man and the priest reported to Quebec, and eventually Quebec talked with the enormously rich Robert Cavelier, whose business name was Sieur de LaSalle. His nickname was Sieur de la Chine, because he was always talking about his hope of finding a river to China.

Robert Cavelier de LaSalle, a key agent in French expansion, in front of a map of fur-trade domains in North America
(P. GANDON/NATIONAL ARCHIVES OF CANADA/C-5066)

LaSalle had many grandiose hopes. He charted the great river country west and south of Lake Erie. He wanted to build a fleet of trade ships that would patrol the Great Lakes. He even built the first one, the *Griffon,* loaded it to the max with pelts and sent it on its way to Niagara,

while his men traded more brandy for skins around Green Bay. East of
Beaver Island the first ship on that great lake went to the bottom. As
Frank Davey writes in his poem "Griffon":

> The furs in her hold
> float upward to enfold the white
> corpses of her six
> crewmen. Breathing
> strings of glass pearls
> to the wave tops.

The *Griffon* thus became the archetype of Canadian poetry. From
the beginning, this would be the difference between US literature and
Canadian literature: US literature would be about great sailing expeditions across the surface of the waters; Canadian literature would be
about ships and people lying far under the surface.

The Sieur de LaSalle was Frontenac's loonie. Early in his life he had
started his training as a Jesuit, but the priests soon saw that he was
demented and let him go. Once into the river system of the North
American Midwest, he did make some terrific discoveries, and he did build
forts and ships. But he was not all that attached to the truth. If a governor
or king or banker needed to be told something, LaSalle would tell him.

Still, he went most of the way down the Mississippi River and when
he thought he was near the complex mouth of that stream, he claimed
the whole shebang for the French king, naming the territory Louisiana.
He had a column raised, a cross erected, a lead plate with the French
arms engraved on it buried in the moist earth. And he joined his worn
group in the hymn that begins:

> The banners of heaven's King advance
> The mystery of the Cross shines forth . . .

Now in control of the two great rivers, France looked like a permanent force in the New World. This would be a good time to send out a

couple of hundred thousand citizens, to surround the English. But in 1682 there were only ten thousand white people in Canada, despite the high birth rate.

Did this victory satisfy LaSalle? Did this thin population deter him? Did he care at all about reality? For one thing, he was still looking for China. For another, he figured that it was time to conquer Mexico in the name of the French sovereign. To persuade the sovereign that his scheme was viable, he situated the mouth of the Mississippi way over in Texas and headed that way with his few Frenchmen and loosely attached Native folks. Waving his sword at a complex fantasy of hope and peril, LaSalle amazed his followers with his duplicity and lack of judgment. Eventually they used up their supplies, staggered around in the Texas heat, and forgot about Mexico. A mock-heroic LaSalle decided to hike to St. Louis for help, but he never got out of Texas. His starving companions assassinated him and turned to face the desert waste.

At least LaSalle had claimed French dibs on Louisiana, and by the turn of the century there were French traders all over the place. Notable among them were the Lemoyne brothers, Pierre and Jean-Baptiste, who founded settlements here, there and everywhere. For a twenty-first-century Canadian it can be fun to look at all the French names on the USA map, and to hear how the USAmericans pronounce them.

The wars

For simple amateurs like me, the period 1688 to 1763 has always seemed a confusing three-quarters of a century. In order to provide a clear setting for the events of that important period in French-English relations, I will list the wars between the two countries. These wars took place in Europe and America, sometimes simultaneously, sometimes not.

The years 1688–97 saw the War of the League of Augsburg. William of Orange had come over to reign in Britain and brought his mono-maniacal hatred of the French with him, as well as his desire to form a great alliance of anti-French monarchs. Meanwhile King William's War was waged from 1689 till 1697 around Hudson Bay and along the border with New England. The English grabbed Port Royal and held on to it till the Peace of Ryswick. Four years later we had the War of the Spanish Succession (1701–13), which began after Britain's James II finally died in France and his hosts recognized the Old Pretender as James III, king of England. A year later we had the beginning of Queen Anne's War, during which the Brits again took Port Royal, which they had handed back at the end of the previous war. At the Treaty of Utrecht, these two wars were brought to a close. But then in 1740 the War of the Austrian Succession began. In this one, just about every country was at war with someone, from Turkey to Sweden. An Austrian woman was ensured a throne, but the French and British spent most of their time smiting one another, with no gains in territory. In 1744 we got King George's War (the French had their own name for it), in which French troops from Louisbourg attacked the English and the English turned around and captured Louisbourg. Everyone got their stuff back in the Treaty of Aix-la-Chapelle in 1748. Of course, this peace was just a rest time before the French and Indian War in America (1754–63) and the famous Seven Years War in Europe (1756–63). Over there England sided with Frederick the Great of Prussia against just about everyone else. In the colonies and on the seas, the English became more and more powerful. At the Treaty of Paris in 1763, they got Cape Breton Island, Canada, Florida, the settlements along the east bank of the Mississippi and the whole Great Lakes area. France got the islands of St. Pierre and Miquelon as long as they did not place guns on them. Even today, when Newfoundlanders want a good loaf of bread and a little red wine, they head over to St. Pierre or Miquelon.

Now that that is all clear, you should commit it to memory.

It was hard to figure out what all the wars were about in Europe. In the New World, they were mainly about animal fur. Even the internal squabbles were about fur: Bishop Laval and Governor Frontenac were at odds about the propriety of trading brandy for furs. Well, said Frontenac, look at the English; they trade rum for furs. At least we are offering a superior product. How can I offer salvation if all my dark-hued parishioners are intoxicated, asked the bishop. He then threatened excommunication for those who sold wine and brandy to the Native people. Banning booze is bad for business, insisted the governor of New France.

For the next two hundred years white people all over North America would be eager to deliver strong drink to the indigenous population. Their fervour was equal to that of the men trying to deliver the Word.

So Frontenac and Laval accused each other of exploiting the Native people for their own purposes. Neither of them seems to have taken the time to condemn the use of slave labour on the farms and in the towns. By the time that Frontenac had established his rule (1672) there were sixty-seven hundred white people in New France, and four thousand slaves. A third of these were African, and the rest Natives. When the English took over the place a hundred years later, they raised the percentage of Africans, and when the United Empire Loyalists fled the vengeance of the victorious USA upstarts, they brought their "darkies" with them. In Quebec the Church owned as many slaves as did anyone else. The Ursuline order of Marie de l'Incarnation and later the famous Grey Nuns could not have created their empire without slave labour. These slaves had to spend most of their time working and the rest of it learning Christianity.

While the Church was offering everlasting life in exchange for unending labour, the military were using the brandy-and-firearm-supplied Huron as surrogate warriors in their battles against the English military's rum-and-firearm-supplied Iroquois surrogate warriors. A great deal of the fur war between English and French was done by indigenous people who were now encouraged to shoot each other with weapons they could not have dreamed of a few decades past.

At the end of Queen Anne's War, the Iroquois were declared British subjects.

Forts on the Prairies

The turn of the century brought good news and bad news for New France. Frontenac had died in 1698, thus avoiding an investigation seeking to account for his unlikely personal wealth. In 1701 the French signed a treaty with the Iroquois, who told them that they had had it with the English. Farming was becoming a bigger concern than the fur trade, but the fur trade was more romantic, and the new century that would be known for classicism and reason did not lack for romantics. Take the family La Vérendrye. They noted the fact that canoes were hauling lighter loads to Montreal and Quebec and Trois-Rivières, and they began to entertain the thought that the trappers might soon outnumber the beavers in the Great Lakes region. Pierre Gaultier de Varennes, Sieur de La Vérendrye, decided that he would head north and west, out into whatever land would take him to the ocean that just *had* to be on the other side of this bounteous continent. He was a kind of LaSalle with sanity.

The sieur (a title for minor nobility) and his sons were Patriotes, of course, but they also had the hearts of businessmen. They did not know how damned wide this continent is, but they kept building forts and hiring people to protect them. By 1743 they had a string of forts stretching from Northern Ontario to the eastern end of the Saskatchewan River. What was to stop French traders and soldiers and their Native friends from scampering across these plains and grabbing the territory the HBC hadn't got to yet? The answer was the old problem. There were well over a million white people living in New England, and about seventy-five thousand in New France.

Still, if you looked at the big picture from a legal point of view, France would seem to be running the whole North American show. New France included the whole St. Lawrence valley, swatches of the Atlantic region, the Great Lakes and the Midwest and the Mississippi valley. If the Great Plains were to be added, every person in France would be able to wear ermine underwear. But how many *filles du roi* could the *roi* conceive to populate this land?

THE ENGLISH ARE COMING, THE ENGLISH ARE COMING!

View of Louisbourg, Nov. 11, 1762
(NATIONAL ARCHIVES OF CANADA/C-005907)

That huge population of English Protestants would not be contained forever. There were more English arriving in America all the time, and the phenomenal birth rate in French America would never be able to keep pace. There were French forts over a very wide area, but there were not a lot of Frenchmen around them. The English were bound to expand westward, and because there were French fur people out there, there would inevitably be a war for the continent.

But for a few decades, and over the course of four conflicts, the capture and surrender of land went on in the East. For a century, Port Royal had been sacked and captured over and over, becoming Annapolis

Royal once the English grabbed it for the last time in 1710.

After Queen Anne's War, the French decided to build a more impressive fort, this one on the tip of Île Royale (later Cape Breton). Louisbourg, a great stone fortress, had the job of protecting French interests in all directions. To the east and north it would protect the fur trade in the St. Lawrence and the fisheries around Newfoundland. To the south it would harass the English pirates and businessmen.

Louisbourg in the north and New Orleans in the south would be relied on to keep New France out of foreign hands.

If only there were a few more French people on the ground.

In the next war the English captured Louisbourg, but in the next peace they had to give it back. However, it wasn't long till the next war.

The Treaty of Utrecht in 1713 had split the Maritimes between the two great rivals. France got Île Royale and Île St-Jean (later PEI), but Britain now held the rest of Acadia. They also held just about all the Acadians. What were they going to do with these Acadians?

The Acadian farmers had had a grindingly difficult beginning to their existence at the start of the seventeenth century, and after a century and a half of farming and fiddling and dancing and church-going, they thought of themselves as a people. For much of their existence they had worked their farms and spoken their language in a land occupied by the English. When the French officials came back into the country, the Acadians were still the Acadians. While a century and a half of war was waged off their shore and on their ridges, they tried to present themselves as neutrals.

Still, they went to Catholic churches and spoke a dialect of French. This made them suspect in the eyes of English colonists. Their position was like that of the Japanese Canadians around Vancouver in 1941. But maybe it was also a little like that of the Doukhobors in the Kootenays in 1941. The English authorities demanded that the Acadian people swear an oath of loyalty, promising military aid against France. The Acadians said leave us alone. The governor of Massachusetts, then a colony including what is now Maine, insisted that the Nova Scotians do something about the vipers in their midst. The English navy was also worried about these dangerous folks. When the French and Indian War broke out, the Acadians were given one more chance: swear loyalty or else. We are not English and we are not French, said the Acadians. You're out of here, said a nervous acting governor. And in 1755 the English began the expulsion of the Acadian people from the only lands they had ever known. There were seven generations of Boudreaus and Thibaudeaus in the graveyards, but now ten thousand of the thirteen thousand Acadians were pushed aboard ships and dispersed, dumped in various English colonies of North America, families scattered willy-nilly.

Six years earlier Lord Edward Cornwallis had brought twenty-five hundred shoeless English folks to Nova Scotia, to start a new capital at Halifax. The new fort would have a citadel to rival Louisbourg, and more and more British Protestants would arrive to make sure that the remaining Acadians would be forever outnumbered. A year into the new town's life, an anonymous ballad appeared in *The Gentleman's Magazine* back in England:

Let's away to *New Scotland,* where Plenty sits queen
O'er as happy a country as ever was seen;
And blesses her subjects, both little and great,
With each a good house, and a pretty estate.
Derry down, down, down, derry down.

The exiled Acadians languished in prison camps. They died in large numbers from epidemics. They were surrounded by English-speaking Protestants. But those that survived survived. After the fall of New France and the Treaty of Paris, many of them found their way back to their homeland and won permission to toil on its earth again. Some went to an island off the northwest coast of France, where they consider themselves Acadians to this day, reading the Moncton newspaper and the writing of Antonine Maillet. Some keep their names but speak English in Maryland and upstate New York.

The most famous part of the Acadian diaspora is southwestern Louisiana, where the Cajun people play a music that sounds like

something you might hear around Grand Pré, Nova Scotia, and cook
food that resembles Acadian cuisine that has fallen into the hands of a
demented chef with hot sauce in his veins. When you are around
Lafayette, Louisiana, go to the old bakeries if you want to hear grand-
mothers speaking what's left of Évangeline's tongue.

There are now about 400,000 Acadians in New Brunswick, Nova
Scotia and Prince Edward Island. Not all of them speak Acadian French.
Only a few of them can sing songs that are two hundred years old. But
they will still tell you this: they are not English Canadians, and they are
not Quebeckers. They are another community, and they have been here
as long as any other white immigrants.

Thinking

All the while the monarchs of Europe were waging wars to see who the
next monarchs would be, the thinkers were at work wondering whether
there should be monarchs at all. The two most influential books of
the seventeenth century were René Descartes's *Discours sur la méthode*
(1637) and Isaac Newton's *Principia* (1687).

The medieval thinkers had said that knowledge should be pursued
via induction—they would assemble all "known" material about a
subject and seek a pattern. Descartes argued for deduction—one starts
by doubting everything, and then searching for a self-evident truth to
begin a system of thought. Newton argued for an understanding of
fundamental mechanical laws that could be expanded to perceive the
coherence of the universe.

The Divine Right of Kings is not a logical conclusion of either system.

Kings and Churchmen had mixed feelings about the great scientists
and philosophers of the seventeenth and eighteenth centuries. They were
proud to claim them but edgy about their social and political effects. In
1633 the Inquisition had shut Galileo Galilei up, but the rational cat was
out of the bag that had been so nicely shut up in the Pandoran box. The
monarchs and Churchmen hated to see a rift between faith and reason.
Even when they got a good conservative thinker like Thomas Hobbes to

support absolute state power, they had to attack him because he based his argument on material bases rather than the model of God.

Boy, the seventeenth century in Europe! William Petty invented political science. Christiaan Huygens caught time on a pendulum. William Harvey noticed the circulation of the blood. John Locke cleared the human slate. Blaise Pascal invented the scale of probability.

With so much materialism and reason going on, it was no wonder that the basic tenets of Christianity would become subjects to analyze. The Bible, for example, might be subjected to literary criticism rather than revered as supernatural. If the Church were going to withstand the Age of Reason, it had better see to it that the masses remained unread.

So by the shores of the St. Lawrence River you were not supposed to read Voltaire's *Candide*, which arrived in Quebec about the same time that the English did. Voltaire did not hold a high opinion of the place. In *Candide* a smart guy says of Britain and France, "You know that these two nations are at war for a few acres of snow, and that they are spending more than all Canada is worth."

The Church owned two million of those acres, a quarter of all the land granted in New France. No wonder, then, that when the first volume of the great *Encyclopaedia* was published in 1751, the spiritual leaders of New France tried to prevent its being read in their fiefdom. The *Encyclopaedia*, which would be completed in 1772, was the first great compendium of human knowledge, and it was a threat to the clergy because it denounced Christianity as example and supporter of privilege and absolutism. The editor was Denis Diderot, and some of its most famous contributors were Voltaire, Jean-Jacques Rousseau and the Baron de Montesquieu. Molière's plays were written for the amusement of the nobility and the bourgeoisie, but they incurred the wrath of the Church, so Molière, too, joined the ranks of the writers feared and hated by the official Christianity.

What about the couple of million colonists in New England? Well, most of them were Puritans. They didn't read secular writing. They were waiting for Walt Disney.

Not thinking

Someone must have looked at the North American situation around the time of the Aix-la-Chapelle Treaty of 1748 and told the French authorities that the best thing they could do was hole up along the river from Montreal down to the islands at the mouth, to have babies as fast as possible and try to preserve a French-speaking enclave that would seek to be a good neighbour of the infidels.

But oh no: in 1754 the new governor, Michel Ange Duquesne-Menneville, Marquis de Duquesne, decided that the top priority would be the control of the Ohio River; he needed it to keep his connection between Louisbourg and New Orleans. He told his military to build a dandy structure to be called Fort Duquesne, of all things, at the forks of the Ohio, where Pittsburgh now stands. Now the governor of Virginia considered the Ohio country to be his backyard. He sent some militia and Natives under the command of baby-faced George Washington to expel the French and their Natives and habitants. The Northerners counterattacked and captured Washington and his fellows. Then, unfortunately, they let them go with a talking-to.

A lot of people say that this was the first skirmish of the Seven Years War. It was also the first time the Canadians defeated Washington.

It was still all about furs, though there were getting to be more and more farmers, and eventually they would need more and more land. While the French and Brits were bruising each other about animal hair in the East, the Russians were putting sticks together on the West Coast. The brave Danish captain Vitus Bering had sold his expertise to Tsar Peter II, and though it was an enormous distance from St. Petersburg to the Sea of Okhotsk, and though it was really hard to say "the Sea of Okhotsk," messages did get through to the handlers of the young tsar that Bering had left Petropavlovsk with the ships *St. Peter* and *St. Paul*, which found a nice big continent to the east, replete with Native people who knew where all the sea otters were.

It was a momentous and historical and commercially interesting voyage, but things did not turn out well for all the voyagers. While the

St. Peter stopped for just one day at the sixtieth parallel and then headed home, the *St. Paul* landed farther south, and several of its crew headed up a creek, never to return. Vitus Bering never got home, either. In December 1741 he died of scurvy on a frozen island off the Siberian coast.

The crewmen who made it back to Petropavlovsk took some furs with them. Eventually some of these furs got back to St. Petersburg, and the usual pelt lust occurred. Rubles were found, and by the middle of the century there was a string of Russian forts along the Alaskan coast.

But France was not distracted by the Russian fur trade. No one could quite figure out whose side Russia was on in all the European wars, and in North America France had enough problems to occupy its politicians and soldiers. The population of Canada had reached more than fifty thousand by mid-century. There were new farms along some of the other rivers, the Ottawa, the Richelieu, the Chaudière. There was a larger militia now, and it was ensconced over a more developed terrain.

Still, a military strategist from Mars would have had one look at the continent and advised the French to settle for the St. Lawrence system. The frontier they had traced from Louisbourg to New Orleans was very long and very thinly garrisoned. They would have to depend on the unwavering support of their Indian allies against any incursions from the East. Sure, there were fifty thousand Canadians, but there were more English Americans than you could shake a flintlock at—and they had *their* Indian allies. If New France were to call up its entire militia, the English colonies could call up a tenth of its militia and still amass a horde that would scare the pants off a fifth-generation habitant. Then there was the problem of feeding these soldiers. Not only did the English have a lot more farms, but they had a longer growing season.

How much is this snow worth, anyway? a French soldier recently arrived from Rouen might ask himself.

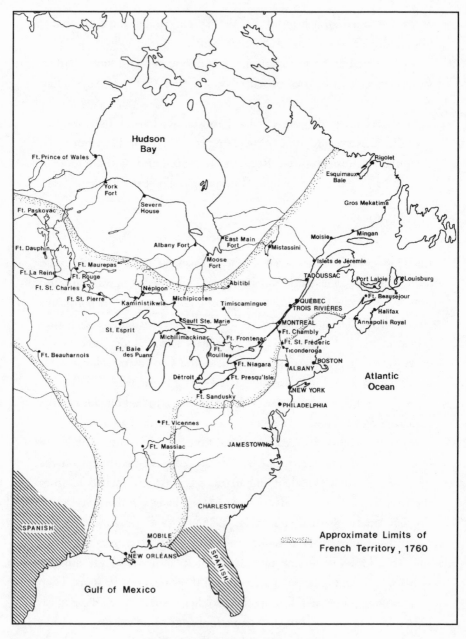

Hudson
Bay

Ft. Prince of Wales

Rigolet

Esquimaux
Baie

Gros Mekatima

York
Fort

Ft. Paskoyac

Severn
House

Moisie   Mingan

Ft. Dauphin

Albany Fort

East Main
Fort

Mistassini

Islets de Jérémie

Ft. Maurepas

Moose
Fort

TADOUSSAC   Port Lajoie   Louisburg

Ft. La Reine

Ft. Rouge

Abitibi

Ft. Beauséjour

Ft. St. Charles

Népigon

Michipicoten

QUÉBEC
TROIS RIVIÈRES

Halifax

Ft. St. Pierre

Kaministikwia

Timiscamingue

Annapolis Royal

Sault Ste. Marie

MONTREAL
Ft. Chambly

St. Esprit

Michilimackinac

Ft. Frontenac

Ft. St. Fréderic
Ticonderoga

Ft. Beauharnois

Ft. Baie
des Puans

Ft.
Rouillé

BOSTON

Ft. Niagara

ALBANY

Détroit

Ft. Presqu'Isle

Atlantic
Ocean

Ft. Sandusky

NEW YORK

PHILADELPHIA

Ft. Vicennes

Ft. Massiac

JAMESTOWN

CHARLESTOWN

SPANISH

MOBILE

Approximate Limits of
French Territory, 1760

NEW ORLÉANS

SPANISH

Gulf of Mexico

French and English Territories, ca. 1760
(*THE STRUCTURE OF CANADIAN HISTORY*, 3RD ED., BY J. L. FINLAY
AND D. N. SPRAGUE, PRENTICE-HALL CANADA, 1979)

Fighting

At first the English military fouled up, and a silly hope rose in the French breast. They had chased young George Washington home with no blood on his sword. Now the great British general Edward Braddock planned a dramatic simultaneous attack on four major French forts from Niagara in the west to Beauséjour in Nova Scotia. What a lesson that would be for the expansionist French! Braddock himself commanded the attack on Fort Duquesne. It took him and his twenty-five hundred soldiers two months to make their way over the hills to the Ohio forks, because they were building a road as they went. At last they reached the highland over the Monongahela River and looked down at their easy way to the fort. Unfortunately the French and their Native allies did not believe in wars; they liked surprises among the foliage. In the great ambush on the Monongahela, they shot the great general Braddock to death and wiped out his army.

How did the other attacks go? Hearing about the bad luck at Duquesne, the British called off the contest at Fort Niagara. At Fort St-Frédéric they fought to a draw, and at Fort Beauséjour the English routed the defenders, thus taking Acadia and making it possible to go after Louisbourg.

Okay, the Brits had the east coast. But everywhere else in 1755 and 1756 the French were whipping them. Part of the reason for this was that the English had decided that the American colonists had to take care of matters themselves. If the colonies wanted to annex western valleys such as the Ohio, they were free to try.

What to do? What to do? Should the French take heart from their successes and knock off all the British forts all the way down to Boston and New York? Or should they retire to the St. Lawrence valley and protect their major towns and their growing civilization? The governor, Pierre de Rigaud, Marquis de Vaudreuil-Cavagnal, wanted to attack. He did manage to get his general Montcalm to take Fort Oswego, at the northeast end of Lake Ontario, thus controlling the Great Lakes. Then he sent him south from Fort Carillon, and after a very tough campaign,

Montcalm grabbed Fort William Henry on Lake George. Next in line was Fort Edward, which would be even tougher. Go get it, the governor told the Marquis de Montcalm, but Montcalm wanted to stay home and make sure that the British could never take Quebec. I am the governor here, said Vaudreuil, and I say go. But Versailles sent a message: in matters of the military, the general would outrank the governor.

This was particularly galling news for Vaudreuil. He was born in Quebec. He was the son of a governor. He had a lot of friends in business and politics who resented France's disregard of their aspirations and the officials that France sent to keep control of the wilderness. If he had cared more for Quebec autonomy and less for adding to his own fortune, he might have beaten George Washington to the punch.

Still, 1757 had been a pretty good year for the French. Unfortunately, it was followed by 1758.

Pitt and the penetrant

William Pitt the Elder came from an extremely rich and cranky family, and he could not sit idly by and watch England get pummelled the way England was getting pummelled in the first two-sevenths of the Seven Years War. So he shunted all the slowfoots aside and formed a group of governmental types to take over the conduct of the British Empire. He made himself the prime minister and set about pouring money into the military. He thought that if Britain could wipe out French interests in India and America, that would be a pretty good lesson for France itself.

So he made the big navy bigger, and he employed an awful lot of foot soldiers who would carry rifles and bagpipes into battle on three continents. The navy would be used to make sure that French supplies did not make it to Louisbourg or the St. Lawrence. The foot soldiers would start by retaking the forts lost to the French and end by conquering everything in sight.

Some forts had to be fought for, and others were left as fire-blackened logs. At the forks of the Ohio River, Fort Duquesne's wreckage fell into the hands of the English troops, who built it anew and called it

Fort Pitt after their prime minister. In the summer of 1758, the English scooped up Fort Frontenac and now held the connection between the Great Lakes and the great river. One end of the French river was theirs; now the English could go after the other end. First business was Louisbourg again.

Now, the way to protect a place such as Louisbourg is to have a fleet of warships on hand. Unfortunately for the French defenders, the English navy was not allowing French ships to hang around North America. The idea was to knock off Louisbourg overnight and head on to Quebec. Unfortunately for the English soldiers, they were trained to fight like chessmen in Europe, and Cape Breton is not Europe. It took the British commander, Lord Jeffery Amherst, and his young general, James Wolfe, seven weeks of constant bombardment to capture the fortress. They captured it, but now it was too late in the year to advance on Quebec.

The Brits were doing well on the left flank and on the right flank, but up the middle they ran into trouble. Montcalm had decided to make his stand along the Champlain-Richelieu corridor. He had his greatest success at Fort Carillon, which the English insisted on calling Ticonderoga, at the southern end of Lake Champlain. There the commander General Abercromby sent in the Scottish Highlanders with bagpipes, and Montcalm's men, behind a huge pile of trees, killed fifteen hundred of them before Abercromby decided to try something else. Then winter came, and it was time to rest up for the spring melt.

Seventeen fifty-nine is the year that saw half the North American continent fall out of French hands into English ones.

When I was a kid in school we were encouraged to sing the catchy words of a song that some people called the Canadian national anthem:

In days of yore
From Britain's shore

Wolfe the conqu'ring hero came
And planted firm Britannia's flag
On Canada's fair domain . . .

We had no idea that there were people back East who looked on our "Maple Leaf Forever" as something to be disapproved of. When I was a schoolboy there was a war going on in Europe, and King George VI was leading against the foe. So foes were people to be defeated and defeated good. Besides, Abraham was in the Bible. It was all very patriotic and religious and romantic, the Battle of the Plains of Abraham. The most famous paintings in Canada were the death of Montcalm in a blue outfit and the death of Wolfe in a red outfit.

Who was this conqu'ring hero?

He was thirty-two when he died so picturesquely, high above the wide St. Lawrence. A member of a military family despite having almost no chin, he got his commission at the age of fourteen. He fought England's battle in France and then acted as one of the Duke of Cumberland's officers at the Battle of Culloden, on a moor in north-eastern Scotland. There Wolfe learned some valuable lessons of war. One should far outnumber one's enemy. One should get the battle over in less than an hour. And one should be persistent enough to destroy one's enemy's most remote and smallest sources of support. At Culloden Bonnie Prince Charlie's supporters were finally defeated. Those that survived the cannon and bayonets fled every which way, and for several weeks James Wolfe's men hunted them down and killed them, along with their families and anyone else who gave them shelter.

It was under Wolfe's grim leadership that the English had taken Louisbourg against a smaller French force. Wolfe then spent the winter in England, eating well in preparation for Quebec. Appointed commander of the English forces, he led enormous numbers up the St. Lawrence, looking forward to another British victory in what was so far the Three Years War (five in America). Montcalm's defenders were defending their home. There were ten thousand French Canadians in his army of fifteen thousand men. In other words, just about any habitant male who was not a child or a geezer was in the armed defence of his home.

So when Wolfe made his first attack at Montmorency, he was repulsed by the determined Canayens. Now Wolfe was known to his officers for three things: (1) he dithered a lot, finding it difficult to settle on a plan of attack, (2) he did not suffer from an active imagination, and so plugged away at what had worked last time and (3) somehow he had a lot of charisma.

After his attack at Montmorency failed, Wolfe thought and thought about creating a new plan. In the meantime he used up his foot soldiers' time in a version of the technique that had been so much fun in Scotland. His men went up and down the river on both sides, ruining crops, burning outbuildings, killing chickens and pigs. They destroyed over a thousand buildings along the South Shore. The French Canadians would have no harvest in 1759. Here is the pronouncement that James Wolfe made to them on the Île d'Orléans, June 28, 1759: "The King of Great Britain wages no war with the industrious peasant, the sacred orders of religion, or the defenceless women and children: to these, in their distressful circumstances, his Royal clemency offers protection." So Wolfe was in the protection business. He went on:

> The people may remain unmolested on their lands, inhabit their houses, and enjoy their religion in security . . . but if, by a vain obstinacy and misguided valour, they presume to appear in arms, they must expect the most fatal consequences; their habitations destroyed, their sacred temples exposed to an exasperated soldiery . . . should you refuse these terms, and persist in opposition, then surely will the law of nations justify the waste of war, so necessary to crush an ungenerous enemy; and then the miserable Canadians must in the winter have the mortification of seeing the very families, for whom they have been exerting but a fruitless and indiscreet bravery, perish by the most dismal want and famine. In this great dilemma let the wisdom of the people of Canada shew itself; Britain stretches out a powerful, yet merciful, hand. . . .

This document, more than any other words that have come down to us, offers the basis for two and a half centuries of mistrust and misunderstanding between English Canada and French Canada.

The French, for some reason, had not thought to set up defences on the South Shore, so it was an easy thing for the English to set up cannon across the river from Quebec and blast away at the city all summer. Meanwhile, English ships could sail right up past Quebec, and have the city pretty well cut off from Montreal and Trois-Rivières. Farther inland, French garrisons fell one by one to the English. Anyone could see what was going to happen. There was no help coming from France. Montcalm was a smart general but all he had was the heights of Quebec.

"What should I do, what should I do?" wondered General Wolfe.

He had to take Quebec before the river turned to ice.

Well, everyone knows what happened. Wolfe's ships went upstream past the fortified front end of Quebec, and eased into a little cove. In French it is called L'Anse au Foulon. In English it is called Wolfe's Cove. From the cove there was a steep footpath that led up to a grassy area on the unfortified west (people from BC would say south) side of town. There were about three French-Canadian militiamen guarding the cove.

"Who goes there?" they inquired in French.

"We are a group of French relief troops," said an English soldier in French.

"Pass on by," said the militiamen.

And two by two, up they went, four thousand crack English troops, to the Plains of Abraham.

Really, there is nothing biblical about the Plains of Abraham. Here was a nice flat grassy field that had been granted to a ship's pilot named Abraham Martin in 1645. If it had been granted to his brother, the great battle would have been fought on the Plains of Claude. Nowadays it is a historic site, owned by the Canadian government. When I finally got to see it in 1968, after a leisurely climb, I was disappointed to see that the Plains of Abraham take up less space than the boys' playground at my old elementary school in Oliver, BC.

But our boyhood battles did not produce such a heavy casualty rate. At daybreak on September 13, Wolfe had forty-five hundred veteran musketeers lined up, and Montcalm attacked them with about as many soldiers. Unfortunately for Montcalm, a lot of his soldiers were habitants who loved their land but did not know much about military tactics. Montcalm was partly to blame. He should have waited a little, because Colonel Bougainville was on his way with three thousand more men.

The English waited until Montcalm's men were about forty metres away. That is about the distance from corner to corner on a baseball diamond. In twenty-five minutes there were thirteen hundred dead people, and General Wolfe had taken Quebec.

But he was dead. Twenty-four hours later Montcalm was dead.

New France was on its deathbed.

Canadian art was alive and well.

It would be a terrible winter. Every important winter in Quebec history seems to be a terrible winter. The English inside the walls of Quebec were ravaged by scurvy, and when fighting season returned in the spring, there were only four thousand of them left. There were seven thousand French troops under the command of the Chevalier de Lévis approaching from upriver. James Murray, the English commander now, led his troops out past the Plains of Abraham to Ste-Foy, and met Lévis. This time the French won, and killed eleven hundred of the English. Murray called for a retreat to the garrison, and the French and Canadiens laid siege. They took turns firing cannon and praying for a French fleet.

But there wasn't any French fleet. In November 1759, just off the coast of Brittany, where so many Canadiens' families had come from, the English navy demolished the French fleet, finishing off what the Brits called "the year of miracles." Now India and Canada and Martinique would become red on the maps. The Plains of Abraham make for a nifty story about the fall of New France, but New France was really at the bottom of the ocean near a Breton town called Quiberon.

Every spring there is a competition to see whose ship can be first up the melting St. Lawrence River to Montreal. These days it will be a commercial hull from Russia, maybe, or Panama. In May 1760 the first ships to arrive at Quebec were all British. By this time, Lévis was so low on supplies that his men were pegging stones over the walls of the city. When he saw the British ships he retreated to Montreal. But he knew that it would be only a matter of time until he would have to surrender the island.

Lévis had and still has a reputation for gallantry mixed with the peculiar insanity expected of a career militarist. By the end of the summer he had two thousand soldiers with which to defend the fur capital of the world. Unfortunately for him, the enemy had almost ten times that many. They came from all the territories recently fallen into English hands—from the Great Lakes, from Quebec and from the forts along the Champlain-Richelieu system. Lord Amherst sent a message to Lévis, suggesting that he hand over the remaining *arpents* of Canada. The riverfront from Quebec to Montreal was darkened with the ashes of farms and villages. Don't make us burn down this beautiful provincial French municipality, Amherst pleaded.

Lévis wanted to go down in flames. But Governor Vaudreuil prevailed, and Montreal surrendered on September 8, 1760. New France would become British North America. Seventeen days later King George II died, and his grandson, twenty-two-year-old George III, began his long reign. What could be better?

6
THE YANKS ARE COMING,
THE YANKS ARE COMING!

General George Washington
(ANNE S. K. BROWN MILITARY COLLECTION,
BROWN UNIVERSITY LIBRARY)

The Seven Years War was not over. It would be another three years before the Treaty of Paris. In 1759 there was a new king in Spain, and he was stupid enough to jump in as an ally of the French. So in the last years of the war, the English took Guadeloupe, Martinique, Cuba, Manila and all the French slave posts along the Atlantic Coast of Africa.

They knew that the war was approaching an end, and they knew that there was going to be another complicated peace treaty. Over and over the British had taken French settlements in America, only to give them back during the confusing allotment of territory at the peace table. Just to be careful this time, the British took Louisbourg apart piece by piece. The French, hoping to hang on to something until the bargaining began, mounted an invasion of Newfoundland in the spring of 1762. About a thousand French and Irish Catholics grabbed a fort in St. John's harbour and, using that as a base, went about getting revenge for Wolfe's depredations, burning fishing boats and breaking windows.

Lord Amherst sent his kid brother with seventeen hundred English and German Protestants to prove that Anglo-Saxons could still climb. They climbed 150-metre Signal Hill, told the French defenders to hand over the guns and started pummelling the French positions. The last skirmish of this war in North America was over, and all the French would hang on to were two little islands off Newfoundland.

The spoils of peace

Yes, the British navy was now the ruler of the seas, all the seas known to European sailors, anyway. In the last half of the eighteenth century there were a lot of British naval officers who would become famous and remain famous a couple of centuries later. Among them was a former farm boy, James Cook. As a youngster he got lots of experience handling ungainly commercial ships in the North Sea, so he knew a lot about danger. He studied mathematics and joined the navy, and in the Seven Years War he saw action in the Bay of Biscay. There he was given his first naval command, of a captured ship.

On the west side of the Atlantic, Cook took part in the siege of Louisbourg, and when Wolfe got going, the assault on Quebec. He was thirty years old, and enjoying his favourite occupation, exploring and charting the St. Lawrence and its feeders. In the winters he sat at his table in Halifax and learned all there was to know about surveying and making charts. After the Treaty of Paris, he spent five years surveying Newfoundland. There was a complicated map for you. He was becoming famous as England's chartmaker.

And he didn't even have a commission yet. He was the smartest Master in His Majesty's Navy.

In 1768 the Royal Society was the most interesting non-military outfit in Britain. The scientific revolution had been going on for a hundred years. Everyone who could read had a little laboratory in the drawing room. And look at the navy—it was now the biggest thing afloat. What could make more sense than to have the Admiralty and the Royal Society get together and try to figure out the far side of the globe? So at the age of thirty-nine, James Cook finally got his first commission. He was given a converted coal hauler and sent to Tahiti with a bunch of curious idlers from the Royal Society. What a life!

English rules

Now, according to English politicians and writers, the habitants of Quebec were the luckiest defeated people in history. Formerly they had been ruled by the minions of a king with absolute power. Now they would be guided by a people who had shown that kings can be deposed, beheaded, exiled or subjected to the people's Parliament. They were being invited to share in the Enlightenment. What a blessed conquered colony the former New France would be!

There were, of course, rules. But all the rules were laid down in the service of a liberalized *communitas*. Civil rule, it was called. In 1764 James Murray, the military governor, became the first civil governor general of Canada. There was a bit of a contradiction, though. Call it a glitch. If you were going to convert a military occupation into a civil administration, you should have a colonial constitution fabricated by Parliament. Until the Quebec Act of 1774, what Murray had was the Royal Proclamation of 1763.

Imagine that—Canada was going to be governed by a contradiction.

And really, the Royal Proclamation was not made so much to fill the gap caused by the Treaty of Paris. It was issued because of Pontiac's revolt. Or as it was often called by politicians in the Thirteen American Colonies, "Pontiac's Conspiracy."

Pontiac was a great chief of the Ottawa, whose seat of government was at the edge of Lake Huron, on the Detroit (strait) River. He was not

happy about the destruction of the French by the British. The French
fur people and armies had been accustomed to giving the Native people
presents every year for the use of their lands and waterways. The British,
though, were more interested in getting signed deeds and buying the
place for good. More recently a lot of them thought they could just pick
up a parcel of land free.

Pontiac discussed this threat with other Native leaders, and wound
up convening the largest Native confederacy anyone had ever seen.
Still, the white people kept arriving from the colonies east of the
Alleghenies, just wild about the wonderful soil in the Ohio and
Mississippi valleys. So the Native people spoke French to one another
and set to war against the British. Thus began the period that would
inflame the imaginations of book-reading boys for two centuries. It
was tomahawk time for sure. So powerful and dedicated were the
Amerindians that in 1763 they took every English fort west of Niagara,
except Fort Detroit and Fort Pitt. Blood flowed down stockade walls.
New farms hacked out of the forests were captured by the Natives. Two
thousand white people became part of nature. Often the victorious
"red men" would enjoy some scalping, the practice introduced to them
by the white man as an accounting measure.

For a fanciful portrayal of Pontiac's war, and especially the action at
Fort Detroit, readers with patience and a taste for gore might want to
read *Wacousta*, a gothic romance published by John Richardson in
Scotland in 1832. It tells the story of a wronged lover from Scotland
who becomes simultaneously a Red Indian and what appears from all
description to be a giant penis in his search for revenge against the man
who stole his love. There are enough tomahawks to keep one awake
despite the ridiculous dialogue. I loved it, at least the version that is
available in the New Canadian Library paperback.

Suffice it to say that the ubiquitous General Amherst was kept busy
for five years, learning how to fight Indians in the wilds. But as early as
1763, the English knew that they would have to try to make some kind
of peace with the Indians. Most of the rich and titled French went to
France rather than remain under an English military or civil rule. But

Chief Pontiac
(© BETTMANN/CORBIS/MAGMA)

most French Canadians had nowhere in France to go to. The Royal Proclamation of 1763 tried to outline a way to handle both potential problems. It also had something to say about Grenada and about Florida, which today is the winter home of a lot of Quebeckers.

The proclamation was meant to define the new colony and set some kind of boundary for awhile. First, the king and his administrators wanted to outnumber the French speakers, so they offered land to immigrants from England and from the southern colonies. Hardly anyone took them up on it. Everyone by now had heard how cold it was along the St. Lawrence, and how many wolves and bears there were. The king also said that settlers were not allowed west of the Appalachians or anywhere near the Great Lakes. The only Europeans allowed into Indian territory would be trappers and traders with licences from the authorities, including the Hudson's Bay Company.

The province of Quebec

British North America was always changing shape. On the Atlantic, the former French areas were gathered together to make a larger province of Nova Scotia. But in Britain there were a lot of business and government people who were not all that hot on Canada, despite the big fur business. Some people said that at the peace table the English should have given Canada back and held on to the sugar islands of Martinique and Guadeloupe, even though the black slaves in the former had been armed and fought against Britain.

For some reason, people were always dissing the northern colonies in the eighteenth century. There was that character in Voltaire, of course. But what about this unmelodic song from the American War of Secession?

Of all the vile countries that ever were known,
In the frigid or torrid or temperate zone,
From the accounts I have heard there is not such another;
It neither belongs to this world or the other.

A kind of Limbo, then.

In Quebec, Governor James Murray outlined the kind of province the authorities wanted to see. As soon as things had settled down somewhat, there should be an assembly of freeholders, like those in the southern colonies. As stipulated in the Peace Treaty, people should be permitted to belong to the Romish Church, but these people had to submit a list to the authorities of all their firearms and ammunition, and there could be no priestly order. Nuns were all right, because they were only nurses or lacemakers. The Anglican Church and English schools would be set up, and the people would be gradually converted. Here is what Murray said about the situation: "The Canadians are very ignorant and extremely tenacious of their religion [that is, they were a lot like the Irish], nothing can contribute so much to make them staunch subjects to his Majesty as the new government giving them every reason to imagine no alteration is to be attempted in that point."

He went on to advise two particular measures. As the Jesuits were not all that popular, they could be sent packing, thus removing a threat of militancy. And the great church in Quebec, which had been shelled badly in the war, could be rebuilt, thus showing the ignorant masses that the new administration could be trusted.

Actually, Murray's main trouble was not with the conquered French. It was with the Scottish merchants. As of 1760, these, along with some English opportunists, had hurried into the newly won cities, especially Montreal, and set up shop. In no time, the habitants were relegated to the rural and agricultural world, while the Scots and English took over trade, including furs and shipping. English money became valuable while French piastres turned into waste paper. In fact, the French farmers, whose farms were still black from Wolfe's fires, made do with playing cards for their promissory notes.

The Scots, or the "Montrealers," as they began to call themselves, were more interested in profits than politics, and they found a way to make friends with the veteran coureurs de bois, joining money to expertise. In very few years the new company was gathering pelts all across the prairies and into the semi-arctic regions, where the furs were very luxuriant indeed. They built trading forts across the huge continent and raised the attention of the HBC, which had to reconsider its policy of staying with the rivers that ran into Hudson Bay. Now the HBC had competition in the form of traders who would combine as the North West Company in 1783.

These opportunistic businessmen in Montreal got under the skin of Governor Murray and his successor, Sir Guy Carleton, 1st Baron Dorchester. These gentlemen did not appreciate the boisterous hucksterism of the merchant class, the striving for monopoly, their hope that they would be able to control the promised assembly. Murray and Carleton, therefore, went easy on the French Canadians. Rather than implement the Proclamation to the letter, they allowed the continuation of French law, the seigneurial system and the Catholic clerical system. As to the idea of an assembly—Carleton had seen what happened with assemblies in the seaboard colonies, where business more and more equated with power. As for the habitants, what did they care about an assembly? They never had one under French rule, and if there was one now it was just going to be a debating club for the conquerors.

In England they noticed that while the Proclamation of 1763 might be working all right in East Florida and West Florida, in the province of Quebec the governors had had to ignore some of its stricter applications in order to keep peace and forestall the kind of uncontrolled enterprise the businessmen favoured. So in 1774 the British Parliament passed a Quebec Act.

It was a bold move. It made the province about four times as big as it had been in 1763. Imagine the thinking of the British Crown. No one knew just how much land there was out there in that seemingly endless continent. But except for the part loosely held to be Spanish, all of it was somehow vaguely British property. Therefore Parliament, in the name of George III, could slice it in whatever way they liked their pie. The new Quebec expanded in several directions. To the northeast it stretched to the Labrador border, or if you are listening to Quebec historians, it stretched to include all of Labrador. It went westward to take in the

Great Lakes and a buffer zone. To the southwest it absorbed the Ohio country as far south as the joining of the Ohio and Mississippi Rivers, in what is now the Old South.

This really made the fur traders and real estate agents in the Thirteen Colonies angry. The proclamation had first given their natural western garden to the Indians; now England was reneging and giving it to the Catholics. The society in colonies tends to be more conservative than society in the Old Country, holding on to prejudices and customs that prevailed when their grandfathers emigrated. So while Catholics in England were slowly winning some civil rights, they were still damned papists in Rhode Island and Massachusetts.

It is unlikely that the Native people were overjoyed about the way that their land grant had been taken back after eleven years. They appreciated the wisdom in giving it to Quebec rather than to the Thirteen American Colonies, but from this time forward they would be confused about the nasty epithet "Indian giver."

But it made good business sense to the merchants in Montreal. Now the hunting and trapping country was inside the colony. The middleman would have to make out as best he could. The whole deal did not interest the habitant much. The only difference was that now he was paying taxes to both his French and his British masters. There was a Legislative Council (appointed by the Crown), and it even had some French speakers on it, but if it did anything the governor didn't like, it had to go back and try again. The legal system was a kind of compromise. French law would apply to matters of property and other civil concerns. Criminal law would be English. The French church would be allowed to continue the soul business, which included behaviour on earth. The priests for the main part liked this, and the highest-ranking ones happily hobnobbed with powerful English gents in Quebec and Montreal.

The merchants were a little less happy. They did have access to the hunting grounds, but they did not have control of an assembly. Merchants like it a lot better when they have control of an assembly.

Birth of a war nation

Meanwhile, what was Captain Cook up to out there on the Pacific Ocean? He did make it to Tahiti with his science-loving passengers, and they did observe the transit of Venus across the face of the sun, and everyone was quite satisfied with that. But Cook had other orders, less scientific, more secret. Since the days of Marco Polo there had been an agreement among geographical speculators that there had to be a great southern continent or two to balance the large earth forms of the Northern Hemisphere. It was usually referred to as Terra Australis Incognita, the great unknown southern land.

Cook was told to explore all the lands he could find, claim them for George III and bring back stuff. In his first great voyage, with the eminent naturalist Joseph Banks on board, he surveyed the whole of New Zealand, proving that it was just a couple of islands, not the great continent, and he surveyed the eastern parts of Australia. He was not the first European in those parts, but he was the first to get along with the Natives, many of whom already had European venereal diseases.

Loaded with plants and pictures of weird animals, Cook and the *Endeavour* went back to England in 1771. In 1772, he took off again, with two ships, *Resolution* and *Adventurer*. This time he looked all along the coast of Antarctica and satisfied himself that Europeans were not going to get rich there. So for a couple of years Cook roamed the Pacific, checking out dozens of islands, gathering lots of specimens and drawings and ironically killing time by reading John Milton's *Paradise Lost*. He came back to England in 1775. The king and the Royal Society noticed that he was staying away longer with each voyage. But they sent him again in 1776, this time to check out the long-desired Northwest Passage from its western end.

Mumbling and grumbling

The 2.5 million people living in the Thirteen Colonies were still British in their prejudices and appetites, but their families had left

England for good reasons. The Catholics had fled Cromwell. The Puritans had wanted to be as far as possible from the Catholics and the almost-Catholic Anglicans. They all had reason to start thinking like Americans and to begin to see the British authority as something like an occupation force.

When the English passed the Quebec Act of 1774, giving all that wonderful midwest land to the province full of Frenchmen, the colonists got really browned off. They had been having trouble with British "meddling" since the fall of New France. When Britain designed the new government in Quebec and saw that it could best manage things without a representative assembly, the notion developed at home that the mother country had let things slip too much toward local control in the southern colonies. Those upstarts were trading goods with other European countries, for example, generating wealth that was never even sniffed by Britain.

So Britain decided to tighten things in the Thirteen Colonies. It levied duties on products imported into the colonies. Britain had spent a lot of money conquering Quebec and the French East India Company, and it needed revenue. Taxes in Britain were high and threatening to go higher to pay for the war. Duties in America might alleviate that condition. About a third of the American colonists decided that the duties were logical and necessary. Another third had no opinion. The last third said that the people of America would not pay those damned duties.

The seas and woods became rife with smugglers of tea, paper and paints. Sailors and excisemen were dispatched to find the smugglers. The woods were full of armed and suspicious men and boys.

In 1767 a sloop belonging to John Hancock, one of the biggest smugglers, was captured by the excisemen. A riot resulted, in which revenuers were forced to swallow noxious liquids and so on. The British army garrison at Boston was strengthened. The guys in the woods started fires and took potshots at government buildings and beat up taxmen in the streets. As affairs grew more and more violent, and as the protests fell out of the hands of merchants and into those of scrappers who called themselves "Sons of Liberty," the future looked more and more bloody.

The Brits eased up on their impositions, removing all duties except a small one on tea. In 1773, in order to prevent the collapse of the East India Company, London allowed them to carry tea to Boston harbour without any duty, thus undercutting the price asked by John Hancock and other smugglers. The politician and incipient revolution leader Samuel Adams addressed seven thousand colonists on the evils of drinking legal tea, and the crowd swarmed onto three ships and stove in all the tea chests before dumping the cargo into the sea.

The British responded by occupying Massachusetts and passing the Quebec Act of 1774.

Now a lot of people in the Thirteen Colonies really thought of the British as "them."

In New England the Puritans began talking about the king's "intolerable acts." The worst of all was allowing French Catholicism to operate in the sparsely populated but geographically large colony of Quebec. It was worse than making deals with the Indians.

In response the smugglers and other sons of liberty sent messages southward and called for a Continental Congress of the aggrieved colonies. Georgia was the only colony to demur. This meeting took place in Philadelphia, and out of it came a "Declaration of Rights and Grievances." The main thrust of the declaration was against the paying of taxes and duties. The signatories also framed an invitation to the people of Quebec, urging them to join in their resistance to British rule. The idea was that the Northerners would have the choice to be with them or against them if there happened to be any, you know, armed clashes.

George Washington was there. He was upset that the British army had not made him a colonel during the French and Indian War.

The first significant clash occurred at Lexington, Massachusetts. A lot of Red Coats were heading for base after an unsatisfactory attempt to seize a smugglers' trove at Concord, and colonists hidden in the bushes opened fire on them. About two hundred Englishmen and a hundred bushwhackers were killed or injured. Warlike words were being heard all up and down the coast, from merchants, preachers, politicians and arms manufacturers. British authority was waning fast. Fellows called "minutemen" worked with firearms within reach. The pattern of American life was being drawn.

In spring of 1775 there was a Second Continental Congress, and this time the colony of Georgia attended. George Washington finally got his promotion and went to Massachusetts to fight against the army he had once sworn loyalty to. The Congress had no basis in law, but it began to act as the government of the colonies. Most citizens were against independence, and there was always a fear of an uprising against the uprising. Something had to be done to provoke patriotism toward a non-existent country.

Blame Canada

Another American pattern would be seen in late 1775. If you want to arouse patriotic support for your political base at home, why not invade someone? The rebellious colonies had been sending messengers to Nova Scotia and Quebec, enjoining the people there to join their cause. But the Nova Scotians and Quebeckers were not all that interested, and hardly anyone knew how to use a gun, anyway. The Nova Scotia merchants would find a way to carry on trade to both sides of the secessionary struggle.

Well, if the people of Quebec would not rise up against their oppressors, maybe a little invasion would win their hearts and minds. So northward along the old war route went the rebels, taking forts along the way to Montreal. A lot of the English and Scottish merchants liked the economic prospects of an American victory. Governor Carleton got out of the city just before it capitulated, and headed to Quebec to prepare for the siege there. He made a mental note to block the steep path to the Plains of Abraham.

The Americans then headed down the river to Quebec City. They tried to gain support of the habitants along the way but had little success beyond a few farmers who wanted to settle some local grudges. These people were not too crazy about the rule of the seigneurs and the clergy, but they were pious, most of them, and the ones who were not were well aware that the Americans would only subject them to whatever regime they would come up with. It would certainly not smile on the idea of independence for Quebec.

The Americans were astonished that the Canadians did not grab the chance to become Americans. They are still trying to figure that one out.

Benjamin Franklin was a war correspondent in the captured city of Montreal. He was greatly puzzled that the French Canadians were not begging to be part of the revolution. He wrote of his amazement that the downtrodden were not offering any aid to their "liberators." If supplies were not shipped from home, he said, the occupiers must "starve, plunder, or surrender."

In Quebec City the American commander, Benedict Arnold, fared even worse. He must have thought that God was on his side—otherwise, why would an army lay siege to a city like Quebec all through a December snowstorm, and then try to invade at the end of that month? You should never attack St. Petersburg or Quebec in the winter. Arnold's troops were weary and hungry, and a lot of them had said to hell with it and deserted. The rest took to looting habitant farms for food. On the last day of the year, the invaders ventured into the snowy crooked narrow streets and alleys of the lower town, where they were fired upon from above and met with surprises at every corner. Hundreds died in the maze. They killed three Englishmen. When spring melted the snow, Benedict Arnold's soldiers appeared along with the customary frozen dog turds of winter.

USA! USA!

Nowadays most of the baseball fans in the Maritime provinces cheer for the hapless Boston Red Sox. In that way they are almost part of the "Boston States." But in Halifax all the history for the tourist trade is about the British heritage, which includes the navy base and the Citadel on the rise overlooking the harbour. The Citadel began as Col. Edward Cornwallis's 1749 fort built to rival Louisbourg. Now, during the

American insurrection, it would protect Nova Scotia against invasion. But the rebel ships did not come to the great harbour. They were content to hassle little towns along the coast.

It was a touchy situation. Half of the colony's population was made up of immigrants from the South. There was a fear that these people might take up arms against the British, as the troublemakers in Massachusetts were advising. But a lot of the settlers, for example, the grandparents of the Canadian prime minister Robert Borden (1911–20) had acquired land in Nova Scotia as a hedge against riotous times to the South. The folks in Nova Scotia were not big fans of the British Colonial Office, just as later they would be largely unconvinced members of Confederation, but they did not really want to shoot Red Coats, either.

In any case, the secessionists removed their last bedraggled troops from Canada in the beginning of July 1776, and then declared themselves an independent country on July 4. The first signer of their Declaration of Independence was the richest smuggler, John Hancock. The declaration begins with the shifty philosophical claim that truths can be self-evident, and that the secessionists have the right view of them. All men are created equal, it announces, and the governed should consent to the powers that be. Some voices might have asked for a definition of the term "men," but with all the noise it was hard to hear them.

Now for the first time the term "United States of America" was used, and the declaration of their unanimity lists twenty-eight complaints that King George III had been acting contrary to the laws of Nature. "Let Facts be submitted to a candid World," it demands. One complaint is against the creation of a larger Quebec. Among the most interesting is the one about encouraging dissenters: "He has excited domestic Insurrections amongst us, and has endeavoured to bring on the Inhabitants of our Frontiers, the merciless Indian Savages, whose known Rules of Warfare, is an undistinguished Destruction, of all Ages, Sexes and Conditions."

In 1776 Carleton was sent a nice big army to resist the uprising, but he wanted to reason with the rebels instead. In 1777 another commander, John Burgoyne, led this army south along the old Richelieu-Champlain invasion route. A dope by the name of Gen. William Howe had been defeating George Washington all over Long Island and Manhattan, but just when he could have sashayed up the Hudson and forced the desperate rebel troops into a Red Coat sandwich, he decided to go to Philadelphia instead. Then when all his Indian soldiers decided to quit, Burgoyne's men were simply abandoned to defeat at Saratoga.

Now the Seven Years War started up again. The English enjoyed an infusion of German troops, but the French thought it might be time to regain their pride, and along with their friends the Spanish, gave their navy to the US cause. By 1780 Britain was at war as well with Holland, Denmark, Sweden, Portugal and Russia. This was the first world war, with English forces fighting in India, Gibraltar and the Caribbean, as well. The US naval chief John Paul Jones was firing at the whites of British eyes along the Yorkshire coast. How could George III concentrate?

The last hope of the British in North America was at Yorktown, Virginia, in 1781. But they faced a French naval and ground force that won France's greatest victory over the British in the past half century. There were some US troops there, as well, and when the British commander attempted to surrender his sword to the French commander, someone went to find George Washington, and he accepted the gesture. After Yorktown, it should have been clear that the French and their US friends were not going to be resisted. George III threatened to abdicate, such was his disappointment. Lord North resigned as prime minister. Brits and USAmericans started secret meetings in Paris, looking for a way to end the war. Benjamin Franklin, the US emissary, had promised not to make a separate peace with the Brits, but he did a deal anyway, and the French looked the other way. The Treaty of Paris II was signed in 1783.

The British could have come out of the treaty with better terms, but they conceded independence, with the Mississippi River as the new western boundary of the US. They also gave the US fishing rights off Newfoundland and Labrador and in the mouth of the St. Lawrence. The new international boundary also left most of the good fur trade forts in US hands. Spain got both Floridas. The French won some islands. In return the States were supposed to pay all the bills and debts of those people who had remained loyal to the Crown. Lots of luck!

7

A LOYALIST NATION

Habitations in Nootka Sound *by John Webber*
(BC ARCHIVES)

"Find me the Northwest Passage once and for all," instructed the king.

"You know," replied Captain Cook, "I am beginning to hold the opinion that there is no such thing, that if there were such a thing we would have found it by now. I have a similar belief about El Dorado and the Fountain of Youth."

"Well, then, go out there and prove it. And while you are there, see how many Russians and Spaniards there are in the northwest part of your great continent."

Captain Cook never did like to spend much time at home. He was for the Pacific, even the portion with no palm trees.

So he sailed the deep inlets of Alaska, looking for the Passage. He sailed north and farther north, right through the gap between Asia and America, along the north coast of Alaska, looking for the Passage. When winter closed in they went south, discovering, as Europeans liked to put it, Christmas Island and Hawaii.

Four summers and four winters Cook's men travelled the great ocean. They never did find the Passage, but they saw a lot of Native people along the northwest coast of America, and they noticed that they were wearing clothing made of sea otter pelts. Once, they put in at a nice cove on the west coast of a long island that would later bear Vancouver's name. What is the name of your home? Cook thought he was asking a Native man. It is just past that small point, said his interlocutor. It sounded to Cook as if he had said something-something-Nootka. From then on the Europeans called the place Nootka. It would become the busiest fur-trading town in the world. Cook claimed it for the English Crown.

Then he went to Hawaii for the winter, where he was considered to be a god. Unfortunately, some moron in his employ killed an important Hawaiian, and in retaliation the Islanders stabbed James Cook to death and separated his body into little parts. George Vancouver went about making peace and gathering as many parts of this eighteenth-century Osiris as he could find.

The first US refugees

The armed rebels in the united colonies did not take kindly to anyone who did not want to fight the British. They called all non-fighters "Tories," and tried to make them understand the revolutionary cause by beating them up and taking away their houses. Some of those damned Tories did not even speak English. So during the war, a lot of people who wished no part in a revolution escaped to Canada or Nova Scotia. These people, and others who fled the US in 1783, were given the title United Empire Loyalists by Governor Carleton. They and their children were permitted to affix the letters UE to their last names.

Some refugees went back South, but when they got there, they found out that contrary to the promise in the Declaration of Independence, their family property was no longer in the family. Some people had stayed home during the conflict, but now found that they could not stand the intolerance and continuing violence after the war, and they left for the North. Some of them went because they were promised land to scrape at north of the border. These people would be given the nickname "Late Loyalists," one of the nicest examples of ambivalence I know.

There are plenty of estimates on the number of refugees. Most recent guesses make the figure around 100,000 men, women and children. Among them were descendants of English pioneers, people who considered themselves citizens of the New World but peaceful adherents to imperfect British government. There were people from other European heritages, German, Dutch and so on. There were black people, some slaves of white Loyalists, some runaway slaves, some free blacks. There were Indians who would rather live among the Red Coats than the minutemen.

The wealthiest and highest-ranking refugees went to Britain. Many from the southernmost colonies went to the Floridas to live under Spanish rule, or to the islands of the Caribbean. About 90 percent went North. They took a last look at the farm that had been in the family for four generations, and got on a ship bound for the fog. The largest numbers fetched up on new land in the Atlantic colony. Others settled along the St. Lawrence. Some went to the shores of the Great Lakes. One of their most beautiful and sad souvenirs is the Loyalist graveyard in Saint John, where the names on the stones have been smoothed out by two centuries of Atlantic mist.

The received wisdom about the United Empire Loyalists is that they had a great influence on the Canadian national character, that they were so many that they came to dominate our style of life, so that we would be polite, peaceful evolutionists in contrast to the hyperemotional militarists to our south.

Perhaps the most famous Loyalist was Gen. Benedict Arnold. He was a very successful military commander in the US forces, though his raid on Quebec had failed. He was wounded badly at Quebec and crippled at Saratoga. But he won many valiant battles against superior forces, employing unusual techniques and inventions. More ordinary officers came to resent his derring-do and conspired to have him passed over when Washington was handing out promotions.

When it got so that he could hardly walk because of his wounds, he was given the command at Philadelphia. Philadelphia was home to a lot of prominent Loyalist families, and they threw good parties. There in 1779 he met Peggy Shippen, a handsome Loyalist woman, and as love grew along with reawakened loyalty, Arnold would become a defender of Canada, first telling the Canadians of a forthcoming Yankee raid, and eventually leading a foray against the USAmericans in Connecticut.

When the war was over the Arnolds moved to Britain, where the general lived out a remaining life pained by his war wounds.

New provinces

After the decisive victory of the French navy and army at Yorktown, Virginia, the Loyalists' homes were looted by their neighbours, their wedding dresses and family furniture carted away by thugs who wanted to act quickly before anyone could pass laws against looting. Now when the widows and orphans and families came to their new lands in Quebec or Nova Scotia, they had not been able to bring anything with them because the thugs had taken it all. They were in for a generation or two of great privation, of hunger and homesickness.

In a poem called "To Cordelia," Joseph Stansbury in 1784 portrayed the ambivalent feelings that a newcomer might harbour. Stansbury emigrated from England to Philadelphia in 1767, opened a china shop and started writing poems and satirical plays. He wormed his way into the same polite society that Benedict Arnold enjoyed, and in fact became a Tory agent, delivering Arnold's messages to the right places. Later, he took his family to the Loyalist town of Shelburne, Nova Scotia, but he stayed only two years before moving them to New York. "To Cordelia" contrasts the Loyalist dream with the pioneer's reality:

But when I see a sordid shed
   Of birchen bark, procured with care,
Design'd to shield the aged head
   Which British mercy placed there—
'Tis too, too much: I cannot stay,
But turn with streaming eyes away.

Canada would benefit greatly from the arrival of these people, just as two centuries later our culture would get a boost from the influx of US refugees during the USAmerican war on Indochina. The image we usually see displays white people in late-eighteenth-century costumes, with the unbroken forest as backdrop.

But a lot of refugees were the descendants of Africans.

The war was a frightening and confusing time to be what was then called a Negro. The English sent proclamations that said there was a place in the English army for black Loyalists and a reward of freedom for those who fought against the secessionists. Black men who did not have families to abandon joined up, and when Cornwallis had to surrender, he had to surrender two thousand black men back into slavery. The freeing of slaves was one of the great fears of the United States. Some of George Washington's slaves managed to get away. When the British said that they would offer haven to whole families, things looked even more dangerous for the US cause. A general African uprising was a US nightmare.

Most of the blacks in the war fought for the British side, but there were some in the Continental army. Many of these were acting as a kind of military version of whipping boys. A white slave owner was permitted to send a slave in his place and to have the black soldier's pay sent to the master.

When the peace was signed, and the Loyalists were boarding ships to sail to their new homes, there was a general disagreement between the English and the USAmericans as to what constituted a black person. The English said that these were people who had earned the right to live in Canada or the Caribbean. The US opinion was that these blacks were property and should be returned to their owners, as provided for in the Treaty of Paris. One can hardly imagine the emotions of the person who had made it as far as the ship, only to see his former owner with armed employees coming to get him.

In May 1783 Governor Carleton met with General Washington in New Jersey to discuss black people. Washington was incensed that the English had not returned all the slaves, including those who had escaped him. Carleton said that there were already a lot of black people in Canada, and that it would be impossible to get them all back into US hands. Washington said that the white people of his new land of liberty wanted as many of their slaves back as was possible.

The English went this far: they compiled a Book of Negroes. If a black person could prove that he had lived behind British lines for a year, he could get onto the ship or otherwise make his way across the border as a free person—as long as he was not a British slave, of course.

Somewhere between a tenth and a fifth of the Nova Scotia Loyalists were blacks. Half of them were slaves of white Loyalists; the rest were unattached. In a few years it would be hard to tell the difference.

This is not to say that the troubles for blacks were over in British North America. Carleton was not a slave owner on a large scale, as was Washington, but he had a personal valet who was of African descent; and his valet was required to stay on after the war. The promises made to black refugees were reneged on in just about every way. They got the worst land available. They got the worst jobs available. They got the lowest pay (i.e., nothing) and lousiest food in the refugee camps. They got the slowest lineups when it came to settling land claims. And as soon as they got to sit down on their claim, there were some white businessmen and lawyers looking at how they could grab it from them.

Some of the blacks went to work for white men. Now these white men decided that the black workers should be paid less than white workers would be paid. Then when the white workers saw that the black workers were working for less, they got mad at the black workers and beat them up and burned down their houses.

A lot of the blacks then in Canada were slaves. The ones who were not slaves were forbidden to vote and forbidden trial by jury. So what if the promises made were not exactly fulfilled, said the Canadian authorities, aren't you glad that you are not in bondage in Georgia? Well, it is a lot warmer there, came the reply.

There was an unusual opportunity presented for ex-slaves who wanted to have a little dignity along with their deprivation. In 1787 an English outfit called the Sierra Leone Company bought a tract of jungle on the West African coast and shipped some ex-slaves and some unhappy white people there to start a colony. Soon there were recruiters in Nova Scotia, and eventually twelve hundred black Loyalists set sail for Africa. Now the white employers were really angry. Before the ships sailed, they tried every dirty trick they could think of to keep their cheap labour pool.

In 1796 some ships from Jamaica arrived in Halifax, carrying five hundred black people who had been called Maroons in Jamaica. Along with them came some money from the Jamaican government, and a letter asking Nova Scotia to supply land and building materials for these people. A lot of them were set to work building the great Citadel overlooking Halifax harbour. The Maroons were known as a fractious people. They were ex-slaves who, in 1739, had been guaranteed freedom and land by the new governor of Jamaica, Edward Trelawney. But these free blacks and the English plantation owners could not get along, and now the Maroons had been invited out. They tried Nova Scotia for a while, and some of them even intermarried or almost did, with local whites and blacks. But in 1800 most of them got aboard ships and headed to Sierra Leone.

The influx of white Loyalists was to have quick political results in their refuge. As early as 1784 the new province of New Brunswick was snapped off Nova Scotia. Cape Breton Island was also made a province. PEI had been separated for fifteen years. When local business concerns are more active than are political overseers from far away, large colonies become smaller provinces. The process was delayed a while in the huge province of Quebec, because the British were still busy ruling a defeated people and highly concerned with the details of control. But the growing English population kept looking for English Law, for habeas corpus and other newfangled ideas.

More and more the English in Quebec became separatists.

How long can this Seven Years War go on?

You will remember that on September 27, 1513, Vasco Nuñez de Balboa climbed a hill in Panama and got a glimpse of sun off the blue Pacific. He immediately claimed the ocean and every shore it would ever lap against for the King of Spain. It took a while for the news to reach the Papuans and Haida. Even when a pope in Italy divided New World waters between Spanish and Portuguese sailors, the folks in Pago Pago and Alaska did not send in change-of-address forms. But the Spanish took their ocean seriously. They established a western command in Peru and large shipbuilding facilities on the west coast of Mexico. When the Russians started hammering boards together in semi-arctic America, the Spanish decided that it was about time to pay more attention to the northern reaches of their big lake.

About the time that the ruffians in New England were tossing tea into the harbour, there were Spanish ships moored off the sixtieth parallel where Vitus Bering had spied an interesting mountain. Just to make sure that no one misunderstood, some Spanish fellows took a boat to shore and planted a big cross on the beach. Beneath it they placed a bottle with a rolled-up proclamation inside. It was written in Latin, the universal language. The idea was that anyone who happened along might open the bottle and read the Latin and say, "Of course! Now I remember! This is all Spanish territory!"

The Spanish had been planting crosses all up and down the coast. In warmer climes they planted priests to speak Latin and keep the Native people from their injurious ways. By the late 1770s there were boats galore, and the most successful of them were commanded by the great Peruvian explorer Don Juan Francisco de la Bodega y Quadra.

But for some reason the Spanish quit coming north for a while after 1779. The British arrived, and somehow missed the news that this was all Spanish seacoast. They had heard about Captain Cook's month at the place he called Nootka, and they had heard about this sleek fur-bearing creature called the sea otter, and what low prices the Native people were asking for its skin. A scoundrel named John Meares, for example, actually named his ships *Nootka* and *Sea Otter*, and stumbled about the north Pacific. He made fanciful claims about the things he had discovered, but that was pretty common behaviour around that time in that place. There were periodic claims to having discovered the western reach of the Northwest Passage, because there was a big cash reward involved.

Capt. George Vancouver was unusual in this regard. What he really wanted to be doing was firing his cannon at French vessels in the Atlantic or the Caribbean, but what he was charged with was showing up at Nootka and explaining to the Spanish that it was a British post. While he was in the neighbourhood he was to look for the Northwest Passage and to check the ground for gold and jewels and the like. King George III was not amused by the fact that wherever the Spanish set ashore there was gold aplenty, whereas the British sailors tended to find coconuts or codfish.

If he could not be blowing French vessels out of the sea, George Vancouver would be the best navigator and mapmaker in the world. He had been along the west coast of North America with Captain Cook, and he had winced whenever Cook told his measuring men "Close enough!" Vancouver would take his little cutter up to the end of every inlet on the most inletted coast there was, and drop a line every few feet in a zigzag pattern, all day, every day, till he had made the naval maps that would be used by the US Coast Guard two centuries later.

In 1792 George Vancouver and his surveyors were rowing across the water that would become Burrard Inlet, when they were espied by some elegantly dressed officers aboard a lovely bark called the *Sutil*. They were asked aboard for tea and sweets, and thus did Captain Vancouver meet

Captains Galiano and Valdés. They became very cordial friends, but Vancouver's great personal and strategic friendship was with Captain Bodega y Quadra. They would develop a tradition of inviting each other over for meals. The Spanish put on a better show, but then Bodega y Quadra was both older and higher ranked than the British commander. They had met in 1779 when Vancouver was twenty-two. Now they would discuss the ramifications of the Nootka Convention.

The Nootka Convention had been signed in October 1780, half a world away from "Nootka." In fact, most of the people who lived there at Friendly Cove would never hear about it. The Spanish were mad at people like Meares, who had built a fur-trading warehouse on land he claimed he had purchased from some Native people. This was the Pacific Ocean, after all, Spanish territory. First come, first served. The English had pointed out to the Spanish that their empire was a little overextended and that their great ally, France, was not about to be much help over here.

So they had signed the Convention, which said, "The officials of the two Crowns shall withdraw, respectively, their people from the said port of Nootka." In the two years since, both sides had been blithely ignoring the Convention, while plunking their surnames on as many nearby islands as they could find. Now William Pitt wanted Vancouver to remind the Spanish that they were the beneficiaries of British politeness. Vancouver did not want to blow his friend out of the water. In fact, he wanted the polite dinner parties to go on for a while. So he would add diplomacy to his many accomplishments.

The courtly Peruvian and the puritanical Brit ate and negotiated and toasted one another and told old naval fibs and fired off twenty-one-gun salutes to each other's king and negotiated, and passed the most important week in the history of Canada's West Coast. Of course these two expert sailors had differing views of the situation. Vancouver was embarrassed to be defending the unruly Meares against the Spanish sailors who had grabbed his building, but he was compelled to point out to his gallant senior that by the Convention any Spanish landing north of Monterey, California, was only a visit, that the British Crown had possession.

"I understand your viewpoint, my friend," said the Spaniard, "but in actuality our claim is prior. This is simply the northern portion of our God-given, or at least pope-given, domain."

"According to the details worked out in Madrid and London, any port between California and here is to be a free port, with neither Spanish sail nor British denied entry. Nootka is to be given into my hands," said Vancouver.

And so it went. There could have been a more lethal use of cannon, and there could have been a world war that rolled smoke all the way back to the European coast. But the two great sailors talked and talked, and agreed to send their reports to their respective courts. Then they enjoyed a pleasant sail around the big island, which would be known as Vancouver and Quadra Island on the former's maps. In 1794 the Nootka Convention would be amended. Now "Nootka" would become an open port, where both nations could compete for the growing sea otter trade. Friendly Cove would become the place from which the elegant skins of otters and beavers departed for China in exchange for the Chinese ivory that would show up in every parlour of any standing in Europe.

The invention of Upper Canada

The Loyalists might have been loyal Tories, but they had also been living in the Thirteen Colonies, where progressive ideas were in print. When they got to the promised land they did not settle easily into what they saw as outdated political conditions. They had been used to the local assumption of power, and began agitating for a representative assembly. Their motives might have been different from those of the merchants in Montreal, but then merchants are merchants. They were pleased to see the formation of smaller provinces in the former Nova Scotia, because the smaller the province the more local the decisions. But Quebec was a big problem. It was very large. It was run by a governor with a rubber-stamp council, and it had a lot of French people in it. The refugees from the Thirteen Colonies had a solution: they would like Quebec to be cut into pieces, and the newly severed pieces should have English common law and a representative assembly. Here is where they departed from the Montreal merchants. The merchants did not want Quebec to be cut up because they ran about 90 percent of the business there, and they would never be able to control the Loyalists as they controlled the habitants.

London decided that it would be a good idea to create—or pretend to create—a new form of colonial structure that would keep the old-time inhabitants happy while appeasing the democratic leanings of the newcomers. The deal was the Constitutional Act of 1791. A lot of school-boys and schoolgirls over the age of fifty remember this one. I know: I surveyed some.

The act cut Quebec in half, creating Upper Canada for the Loyalists, and Lower Canada for the habitants—roughly. A governor general would preside over both Canadas, and he would have a lieutenant-governor for either of them. All three of these men would be appointed by London. Each would be advised by an Executive Council and a Legislative Council, all members of which would be appointed or approved in London. The Legislative Council, which would represent the interests of the nobility, would morph into our present national Senate. Then there was a body called the Legislative Assembly, and they were to be elected! Unfortunately for most people in either Canada, these assemblymen would be elected by the merchants and bourgeois landowners and would represent their interests. Furthermore, these were representative assemblies, not responsible assemblies. In other words, their function was to advise the real power-brokers on the wishes and possible behaviour of the merchants and landlords.

Thus was Canada's conservative future prepared. The old French regime, including the clergy and the seigneurs, was pretty happy with the social control it was ensured. The British Colonial Office was happy that it was able to run things with little likelihood of violent protest. The appointed councils would be made up of both French and English, with the English in the majority as befits an English colony. The Anglican Church was happy with the provision that gave it 7 percent of all future settlements. The people could tell themselves that they were represented in government.

Well, some could. If you were a simple French-speaking farmer in 1792, it is unlikely that you cared much about Legislative Assemblies and Legislative Councils. You were just worried that these English merchants and French seigneurs were working out new ways to levy taxes on the non-voters.

One should not forget that the Constitutional Act of 1791 was a response to events in New York and Paris.

The English merchants and French seigneurs were pretty worried about the French Revolution. If people thought that the American rebels were violent and bloody, they must have been terrified by the events in France, especially the hysterical campaign of Madame Guillotine. The French Revolution was also a lot more theoretical than the US one, and more revolutionary. The US politicians had entertained the idea of making George Washington their king. When General de Lafayette, the hero of the US war, tried to save Louis XVI from the knife, he was forced into exile.

For a lot of people France had been the world centre of culture and thought. When heads were carried around on poles, that illusion was at least muddied. Worse, for the ruling people in England and Spain and the Canadas, was the internationalism of the revolutionaries. Before the revolution the clergy and the nobility had been the only people exempt from paying taxes. They had taxes paid *to them*. When that system was violently corrected, the possibility of revolutionary change would occur to the bourgeoisie and peasantry of any country in Europe. It

Major-General John Graves Simcoe
(METROPOLITAN TORONTO LIBRARY)

might even be discussed along the St. Lawrence River. The clergy and the nobility had better do something to stop it.

What they did in Lower Canada was praise the English establishment for ruling so generously. The clergy told their flocks that they were sitting pretty. From Upper Canada the lieutenant-governor, John Graves Simcoe, pleaded with the British authorities to establish hereditary titles among the British nobs in that underpopulated province.

There were, of course, real possibilities that the French Revolution would be exported. A shipload of muskets bound for Quebec was captured by the Royal Navy. A bunch of unenfranchised Quebeckers tried to storm a prison in Montreal. Rumours and plots and copies of Robespierre's writings circulated. The clergy and the seigneurs were in a panic. Their counterparts in France were fleeing for their lives. Bishop Jean-François Hubert, who had not been the easiest clergyman for the governor general to manipulate, wrote a letter to all Quebec's priests, advising them that from now on there would be no ties to France, that the authorities were here in Lower Canada. A year later he and other notable French speakers signed a Loyalist manifesto, condemning all rebellious thought or action.

We have weathered the storm, said the governor general to his lieutenant-governors. What could go wrong now?

Canoes West

The rugged explorers of Montreal's North West Company were almost all Scots—that is, the people after whom the expeditions were named were. There were a lot of Natives and Métis paddlers who never got anything named after them. In 1789 the darling of the NWC was Alexander Mackenzie. He was quite familiar with the exploits of the Spanish sailors in the North Pacific, and he was interested in finding a freshwater route from the West Coast to Montreal. There were rumours that a great river ran to the western sea, and he left Lake Athabaska in search of it. He kept veering northward, finding very large bodies of water, but they were all freshwater lakes. Eventually he found a nice big river, but it flowed north instead of west. He followed it anyway, noticing that there were a lot of animals with good thick fur along the way. When he got to an ocean it was the Arctic, and he knew that he could never expect to see otter-laden English ships congregated around the mouth of this river.

The river would bear Mackenzie's name, but he was after furs. He went back to England and stared at charts and star maps for a year or so. Then he came back to Montreal, and in the fall of 1792 his group was back in the Northwest. This time he decided to try the Peace River, and by the time the heavy snows were falling, he and his men were huddled in home-made shacks in the Rocky Mountains. In the spring of 1793 he and his men were on the river called Takoutch, bending in a kind of westerly direction. The local Natives told the North West guys that if they stayed on that river for too long they would come to a deep canyon full of rocks and white water, and that it would be a good idea to try some other way to the ocean.

Mackenzie yanked his twenty-five-foot canoe out of this river that would later be known as the Fraser, and started hiking toward the setting sun. He thought he could smell salt. The Natives showed him a path that their people had created hundreds of years earlier during their hikes down to the coast to pick up seashells and copper items.

If you are in the mood for a good strenuous hike, walk up and down the mountains between the Cariboo and the Pacific some time. This is what Mackenzie and his crew did. His crew consisted of his lieutenant, Alexander Mckay, six Quebec *voyageurs* and two Indians from back East, who did all the scouting and, more important, all the hunting for food. One day they met some Bella Coola men, who canoed them down *their* river, introducing them to their friends. The Nor'westers were treated to Pacific salmon feasts all the way down the river.

But at the coast the Native people were not so friendly. Mackenzie did not even try to pacify them with the usual trinkets. The coast Indians had met white men. They had probably been fired on by Captain Vancouver's crew two weeks before. This stupid outbreak of animosities had prevented what would have been a neat meeting of Brits from east and south. Mackenzie might have been heard to say, "Captain Vancouver, I presume?" But no such luck. He decided to head back to Fort Chipewyan, the NWC's trading centre on the south shore of Lake Athabaska, to beat the snows. But before he went he had a big white rock painted with vermilion and grease: "Alex Mackenzie / from Canada / by land / 22d July 1793." The rock is supposed to be around still, but I have never talked with anyone who has seen it. We have all seen a romantic painting of Mackenzie's first sighting of the ocean, though. He looks just like a comic book hero.

WHERE IS LUNDY'S LANE?

Laura Secord Tells Her Story to Fitzgibbon, 1813, *by C. W. Jefferys*
(NATIONAL ARCHIVES OF CANADA/C-9148)

After the passing of the Constitutional Act in 1791, there were a lot of squabbles about borders and western fur country, but the USAmericans did not invade Canada again until 1812. For the meantime they were turning their expansionist eyes west and south. While Napoleon was preoccupied with preparation for more wars with the Austrians, the US managed to buy the huge French territory to its west called Louisiana. Thus for three cents an acre the US doubled its size and had a more solid base from which to advance to the Pacific and make its designs on Spanish-held territories.

With its rambunctious neighbour to the south consolidating, British North America remained a hodgepodge of administrations. Late

Loyalists were streaming into Lower Canada and joining the Montreal merchants as influential minorities in a province with French civil law and a Catholic Church. Upper Canada had English common law and freehold land tenure, and a high Tory sensibility that envisioned the province as a bulwark against the social levelling across the US line. Farther east we had Nova Scotia and its offspring Prince Edward Island and New Brunswick as royal provinces with elected assemblies. Cape Breton Island had been separated from Nova Scotia too. The British had managed to get a clause included in the Treaty of Paris that forbade French ships to approach within fifteen miles of the island. Britain wanted to retain Cape Breton as a kind of Gibraltar, a bastion against French or US hostility. Newfoundland, Britain's oldest holding, would remain a Crown colony.

Then there was the West. Rupert's Land comprised all the river systems draining into Hudson Bay and was governed by the HBC, a chartered company. The North West Company was slogging around in the rest of the space, and ships were sailing up and down the West Coast, but the great Northwest did not have any form of white people's government. The British just said that it all belonged to them.

Unfortunately, President Thomas Jefferson, father of the US revolution and a large number of slaves, got wind of Alexander Mackenzie's trip to the Pacific and asked a couple of adventurers named Lewis and Clark to head west and stick a US flag in the sand, so that USAmericans could celebrate them as the first white men to make it across the continent.

Everyone could see that by the beginning of the nineteenth century British North America had a problem in population when it came to the inevitable rivalries with the US. This disparity is not hard to figure out. There are a lot more people in Italy than there are in Norway. No wonder there were more people in Virginia than there were in Cape Breton. When critics with an eye to thematic concerns look at USAmerican literature they descry the theme of the New Eden and the New Adam. When Canadian thematic critics look at our literature they see an Adam and Eve kicked out of Eden into the snow. So it goes.

By 1806 there were only about 135,000 people in the Maritime provinces. In Lower Canada the French Canadians were raising their numbers as fast as they could, but there were still only 250,000 souls in the province. The fastest-growing province was Upper Canada, but there were only 77,000 folks there. West of there the white population was made up of canoe people.

Lewis and Clark, travelling over relatively easy country, arrived after a year and a half at the mouth of the Columbia River late in 1805. They knocked together some boards, stuck a Betsy Ross flag up in the rain and headed back East. But they did not establish a fur-trading post. The Columbia River had been named after the vessel of Robert Gray, a Boston businessman, and this sounded a little ominous, because Columbia was one of the pet names that the USAmericans had given their new country. There were those alarmists who believed that the USAmericans wanted to acquire all the land they could find. If they were not watched carefully they might start calling their country "America."

The Nor'westers had built the first fort west of the Rockies in 1805. This was Fort McLeod. Their head honcho, Simon Fraser, whose mother had left the US and saved him from being a secessionist, called the area west of the mountains New Caledonia. There were going to be a lot of Scottish names borne by the country and the children of its Native women. In 1807 Fort George was built at the confluence of the Fraser and Nechako Rivers.

People my age, who grew up watching US Westerns, think of forts as stockades from which the army rides to kill Indians. But North West Company forts were simply places where the local company factor and his employees could live, and where furs could be collected until there were enough of them to load a train of packhorses headed east. Simon Fraser was the great fort builder. He was a Puritan, who liked to see work being done and progress made. He was impressed by Mackenzie's discoveries, but he said that if Mackenzie had wanted to find a trade route to the coast, he should have got up earlier in the morning. Fraser thought that he was on the Columbia River, and down it he headed, until he ran into the Hell's Gate that had stymied his predecessor. Clinging to old Indian rope ladders on the cliffs and inching their way high above the churning foam, Fraser and his men knew that this was not going to be a trade route for a while. In fact, Fraser began to suspect that this was not the Columbia, after all.

Fraser sent the Welshman David Thompson to explore the Columbia from headwaters to mouth and to build forts in the Kootenays. Now, Thompson was a very good mapmaker, but he was not in a hurry. He liked to hold long conversations with the Kootenay Indians, and he spent a lot of time writing very good prose about the plants and animals and glaciers and forests he encountered along the way. All through 1808 and 1809 he built forts and drew pictures and wrote reports for the company. Get to the damned coast, said the company. John Jacob Astor's ships are poking around down there. Thompson was terrific on space but lousy on time.

It was not until July 1811 that Thompson and his skinny men arrived at the mouth of the river. When they got there they found four buildings that had been there for four months. This was the new Fort Astoria, named after the future New York slum landlord who would become the US fur mogul of the Northwest. His American Fur Company was also heading north, and had built a little trading fort at Kamloops, in competition with the Montrealers, who arrived within weeks. The Indians had a choice between Canadian goods and Yankee goods. But when war broke out the next year the Yankees went back South and began trade sanctions.

Here they come again

When the USAmerican general William Hull led his army across the Detroit River he handed out a broadsheet in which he welcomed the locals' assistance in throwing off tyranny. No one had checked it for dangling modifiers: "Many of your fathers fought for the freedom and independence we now enjoy. Being children, therefore, of the same family with us, and heirs of the same heritage, the arrival of an army of friends must be hailed by you with a cordial welcome."

USAmericans always tell each other that all other people wish they were USAmericans.

General Hull reminded the locals about US policy regarding Natives: "No white man found fighting by the side of an Indian will be taken prisoner—instant death will be his lot." Unfortunately for General Hull, there were a few English soldiers and French Canadians who didn't mind fighting by the side of their 350 Indian companions, and Hull had to surrender his 2500 men and supplies without firing a shot.

It would not be the last time that the invaders gave up without firing a shot. After Laura Secord, daughter of a Loyalist family, tipped the defenders to a US plot she had overheard, five hundred invaders threw up their hands when they heard some serious Indian yelling. The defenders had already heard rumours of the plot, but Mrs. Secord went down as a typical Canadian hero of the war, getting a brand of chocolates named after her.

They'll never learn

The US has always favoured a real or imaginary attack on its ships as an excuse to unleash its war machine. In later years it would call on people to remember ships that were attacked in Cuba, Tampico, Hawaii, the Gulf of Tonkin, etc. In 1812 it went to war with Britain and tried to invade Canada after a series of incidents concerning US frigates. The Brits and the French were, as usual, at war, and both sides had for years been warning the US against cozying up to the other side. President Jefferson had decided that the way to punish the Brits was to declare a trade embargo against them and their enemies. When this did not work, he saw to the passing of a weaker Non-Intercourse Act. Talk about your Puritanism!

Meanwhile, a group of hothead politicos, mainly from the Southern states, where there was little question of trade with the Canadas, kept pushing for war to protect US honour, etc. Their cause received more attention every time Napoleon would seize a US ship, or the British would board one, looking for Brit deserters and sometimes press-ganging US sailors if they could not find enough Englishmen. One of the most famous events took place aboard the USAmerican *Chesapeake*, where a few sailors were killed in a fight. (In 1813 an English ship would tow the *Chesapeake* into Halifax harbour to great cheers from the shore.) Eventually, in June 1812 the Southerners and Westerners got enough votes to start the war. The Brits had a far superior navy, but the invasion of Canada would be a walkover, partly because the inhabitants would welcome the soldiers of liberty and the gleam of hope that they too could become part of God's favoured nation.

Ironically, the US did pretty well on the Great Lakes, but their invasion of Canada was a disaster. Perhaps they had been made overconfident when they maintained that their battle at Tippecanoe was a victory in 1811. Since declaring independence, the US had been riding around in the West, killing as many Indians as they could, in the territory that the Indians considered home. The great Shawnee chief Tecumseh and his half-brother, the prophet Tenskwatawa, had gathered many Native nations to defend their land against the USAmericans and had fought their general William Harrison to a draw at the Tippecanoe River. Now Tecumseh would join the British general Isaac Brock to fight them again.

But how could the invasion fail? The ordinary people would welcome the advance of freedom, and Britain had gathered its forces in Europe, leaving five thousand soldiers to protect a very long border in North America. Canada would have to depend on US incompetence and overconfidence. General Hull made a good start at Detroit. After stopping them at Detroit, General Brock went back to the Niagara region and stopped them again at Queenston Heights. He received a knighthood for his victory at Detroit, but he never heard about it because he died at Queenston Heights.

In April 1813 a US force managed to make it to York, where they set some fires to government buildings, despite the heroic defence of people such as future prime minister of United Canada Allan MacNab, fifteen years old at the time, and his fifty-five-year-old father, who had received thirteen wounds in the last war with the USAmericans. But US successes were few in the Canadas. They were astonished that the English Canadians did not see the logic of their invasion, they were again disappointed that the French Canadians did not welcome their liberators and they were scared out of their wits about fighting the "Savages." The "Savages" did a lot of the most successful fighting. The Caughnawaga (Kahnawake) of Lower Canada repulsed US advances and chased the invaders back to New York. Métis leaders such as John Brant and the remarkable Cherokee John Norton continued their people's long fight for their ancestors' land. Tecumseh, in an alliance with Brock, saved Upper Canada from an enemy army that was superior in number but inferior in tactics.

Unlike the British army that ran away, Tecumseh and his men fought and died in a Battle of the Thames near Chatham. Afterwards, the US troops went around mutilating the bodies of the warriors they had so feared. Their leader was William Harrison, who had fought to a draw with Tecumseh's brother at Tippecanoe, and lost to Tecumseh at Detroit. Now he was supposed to advance eastward, but the weather and roads were just awful, so his men went around and kidnapped as many black people as they could find to sell into slavery down south, and Harrison became the hero of the only US victory on Canadian soil.

The Quebeckers may have surprised the invaders by refusing to join them, but not all inhabitants were loyal to the British Crown. In the Niagara region there were a lot of Late Loyalists. You will remember that many of these were people who had not left during the runup to the US war of secession, but could not make a go of it in the new republic and accepted generous offers of farmland in Upper Canada. By 1812 they far outnumbered the original refugees. These newcomers were not Tories, and in fact many of them went around stating anti-Tory sentiments, often in the numerous grog shops of the area between the lakes. They were seen by the Tories, of course, as opportunists and traitors.

A lot of them expressed feelings that were not antagonistic toward the US invaders. Some of them raided their neighbours' farms, opportunistically or traitorously. The Tory officials, nervous about the disappointing

support for the defence of British North America, apprehended fifty
of the louts who had been raiding their neighbours' farms, and tried
some of them at the village of Ancaster in May 1814. In July eight of
these traitorous civilians were hanged on Burlington Heights so that
Loyalists and Republicans alike could see a nation's resolve to uphold
law and good government.

Weary of war

In a lot of ways the Brits and Yanks were still fighting the war of the late
seventies. They were also fighting the centuries-long war between
Britain and France. The US had ten times the population of British
North America, and probably twenty times the resources. These are the
kinds of odds that US war makers have always liked. But in this war
there were a lot of New Englanders who would rather trade than fight.
True, there were a lot of US immigrants in Upper Canada who rushed
to join the invaders, but there were others who decided to sit and wait.
And in the spring Napoleon's power collapsed, freeing British troops and
ships for attention across the Atlantic.

By the middle of 1814 the Royal Navy was in control of the whole
Atlantic Coast. On Lake Champlain and the Great Lakes there was a
standoff. Northern New England was in British hands. The US invasion
of Montreal petered out.

But the fiercest battle of the war was to take place on the night of
July 25, 1814. Back when history was taught in Canadian schools, teach-
ers used to like telling their students the story of Lundy's Lane, and
students used to remember it as Upper Canada's finest hour. Lundy's
Lane remains a very important address in the Canadian imagination,
especially the Ontario imagination. The US infantry had left occupied
Fort Erie to conquer the rest of Canada, and they got to about a mile
from Niagara Falls. No one ever tells you who Lundy was, but Lundy's
Lane was a nice little road that went up a little hill toward Burlington
Heights. The two armies skirmished and threatened and feinted this
way and that, before engaging in the bloodiest fight imaginable.

In US textbooks it is said that the US won. In Canadian textbooks it says that lots of people got killed on both sides, and that on July 26 the invaders went back to Fort Erie. Neither side composed songs that lasted long. The textbooks do not mention that some of the invaders had consumed so much whisky that they staggered into the defenders' line. The last battlefield was a terrible pile of dead horses and men, enemies sprawled on parts of one anothers' bodies. Burying them all was out of the question. The British and Canadians hauled trees and started a huge bonfire.

Almost two centuries later the whole region is a combination of very pretty river country and dozens of tourist traps.

A month later outnumbered British troops walked into Washington, sending up the odd rocket in whose red glare they saw the US militia running away. The only casualty was apparently a US militiaman who died from the effort of running so fast so far. The Brits put the torch to James Madison's White House and the Capitol and some other government buildings as a remark about the events at York. The British troops did not engage in any looting, however, leaving that job to the locals who took advantage of the excitement.

After that the British tried their luck at nearby Baltimore, but after a couple of days they gave up and went by ship back to Halifax. A US songwriter composed a song about explosions over Baltimore that would become his people's national anthem. President Madison, riding around on his horse, was not in good health. He wished for an end to all this shooting and scalping and loss of markets.

Everyone was tired of this war. The young hawks from the South were still hollering, but more and more people were looking for peace. The US was in terrible shape and could have been broken in half. There was a great sentiment toward secession in the Northeast. But the British, who had been fighting all over the world, just wanted peace.

So at the Treaty of Ghent, the British did what they would do over and over again—they ignored the Canadians and the Native people and made concessions to the US. They kept the old borders in the East, told the USAmericans that they could keep expanding westward if they wanted to and in 1818 agreed to draw the boundary westward at the forty-ninth parallel of latitude. The US had not managed to pull off a successful invasion of Canada, but they did get the British to agree that they could do whatever they wanted to the Native people south of the border, and they did produce a lot of images to ensure later patriotism.

West of war

If you go to standard histories of the war of 1812–14, such as that by our most famous military historian, George Stanley, you won't find anything about Fort Kamloops, or anywhere else in the West, for that matter. You will remember that the American Fur Company of John Jacob Astor had set up its store at the confluence of the Thompson and North Thompson Rivers, but that when the USAmericans found out about the war back east they had skedaddled back to Fort Okanogan on the Columbia.

In fact, the war was good news for the North West Company. The US fur men were dependent on support from their ships at sea, but the British were making things impossible for US ships. The Nor'westers, though, had a well-established land route all the way back to Montreal. They were not content to watch the Yanks head south; they followed them, grabbing their forts as they went, from Spokane all the way down the river to Astoria. The Astor people might have been able to put up a fight if their ships had arrived on time. Unfortunately for them, when the Company ship *Tonquin* arrived at Clayoquot Sound on Vancouver's Island, where the Nor'westers had been doing business for years, some idiot made the wrong remark to a Native politician. The local people took the ship, but one of the crew members set the magazine on fire, blowing everyone to kingdom come. In the light of the following morning a passerby might discern chunks of wood and American Fur Company personnel floating in the chuck.

Two other company ships that were supposed to arrive at the mouth of the Columbia just didn't show up. Thus was the intrepid imbecile Capt. William Black enabled to seize Fort Astoria. Remember that Fort Astoria was there largely because David Thompson was upriver drawing pictures of butterflies instead of building a North West Company fort at the river's mouth. But when the American Fur Company representatives despaired of seeing any of their own supply ships, they listened as the Nor'westers offered them hard cash for their Northwest forts and the furs stockpiled in them. Thus was the scene set for the silliest action of the 1812–14 War.

William Black was commander of a British sloop called the *Racoon*, and his job was to escort commercial vessels along the coast. But he had heard of John Jacob's fort at the mouth of the Columbia, and he was determined to make a heroic military strike against the damned republicans. He arrived on November 30, 1813, and was aghast to see the Union Jack fluttering above the main building. When he came closer he found members of the North West Company drinking and smoking and yukking it up with the American Fur Company guys who were waiting for their ride home. Captain Black was livid. This was no way to wage a war. He went back to his ship and thought about the situation for five days.

On December 5 Captain Black dressed up in his best uniform and stormed ashore with his little contingent of marines. When he got to the fort he distributed firearms to the Nor'westers and announced that they were for the nonce soldiers of the king. Then he had them lower the Union Jack and raise the Stars and Stripes. The US prisoners of war scratched their heads. Then Captain Black charged the fort and had the Stars and Stripes pulled down. Up went the Union Jack again, and the marines and voyageurs let out a lusty hurrah. A group of Clatsop Indian traders who had expected to drop in for a smoke just kept on going. Captain Black stood with sword in hand, one foot up on a stump, and gave a speech about seizing this strategic spot for the British Crown.

And so valiant British North America set up business at the mouth of the Columbia River.

The only downside of Black's great victory was the Treaty of Ghent. According to the Treaty of Ghent, all property that had been seized by force was to be returned. The fact that the North West Company had purchased Astoria before Black's great victory would simply remain as a tasty irony. In 1818 the Star Spangled Banner was again flying over Fort Astoria.

Cutting down trees

Apparently the land that the Native people had been living on for twelve thousand years and more was unsettled. In the mind of the early-nineteenth-century Europeans they were pioneers who enjoyed a holy opportunity and duty to calm that country down. Here is what Adam Hood Burwell, a poet and Anglican preacher, wrote about the white settler who began the Talbot Settlement near present-day St. Thomas, Ontario:

> Then bow'd the forest to his frequent stroke;—
> There from his hearth ascended hallowed smoke;
> Angels look'd down, propitious from above,
> And o'er his labors breath'd celestial love;—

The Reverend Burwell went on to praise the many whites who followed this intrepid pioneer, and said that the land they took over was "fitted to fair freedom's chosen race." We have no record of the number of Indian war veterans who read his major poem "Talbot Road," but they must have rued the fact that they had never got around to settling the land and that their race had not been chosen for freedom.

The question of whether the white settlers were all that free is open to argument. Here is the way such settlements worked, especially in Upper Canada. Some officer in the British army would be granted a land tract and lots of government help in "developing" it. Col. Thomas Talbot, an alcoholic bachelor, was granted five thousand acres along Lake Erie, where he began establishing townships and roads. He developed the road along the lake from the Niagara region, which is now called Highway 3. Colonel Talbot would rule as a potentate over six thousand settlers, many of them Loyalists. Not bad for an Irish boy who had joined the British army to see the world. His luckiest day was the day that he became Governor Simcoe's secretary. Tourists may now observe some of the belongings of Col. Thomas Talbot, along with Jumbo the Elephant, at the museum in, ahem, St. Thomas.

In the years after the war the US would become more and more USAmerican, and British North America would become more and more British. The USAmericans would clamber into the Midwest and reach for the Pacific. But they would slow their spread into the Canadas and the Maritimes. Britain was pretty sure that even after two failed attempts to invade the North, the US would give it another go. Laws were passed declaring that from now on any immigrants from the US would have to wait seven years before they could acquire land and hence the vote.

Meanwhile, British immigrants were flooding in, coming across the ocean in the holds of sailing vessels, the survivors of the crossing coughing and shivering on the docks of Montreal and Halifax. The first few decades after the Napoleonic Wars were not a pleasant time to be unwealthy in Great Britain. Wave after wave of Brits came to the New World. Between the end of the war and the middle of the century nearly a million British immigrants came to British North America.

In the Europe of the first half of the nineteenth century there was a lot of romantic poetry associated with stirrings of desire for national liberty. In Latin America the colonies of Spain and Portugal fought their way to independence. There were troublemakers in the Canadas, too, but most of the people were obedient Tories. They opened fabric shops and hauled out stumps and taught their children how to be good little English kids in a cold climate. Colonel Talbot would eventually rule over sixty thousand of them in an area nearing a half-million acres. In 1823 John Galt would run a couple of settlements to the north of Talbot's, and to top his father's achievements, Alexander Galt would manage 800,000 acres in Lower Canada, importing Brits by the boatload until they formed a sizable minority in the province.

West of Canada

But the most interesting settlement had been going since 1810. The 5th
Earl of Selkirk was a really rich Scot with a dream of helping Highlanders,
who had been battered around by history, begin new colonies in the New
World. In 1810, he started work on his biggest dream, a vast settlement out
in Red River country. Luckily, there was a lot of land for sale. There had
been a big slump in the European fur business during the Napoleonic
Wars, and the HBC was happy to find a way to cover their operating
costs. Selkirk started buying up HBC stocks and accepting the offer of
land use. The Selkirk Settlement would wind up having the shape and
size of Texas. It stretched from Rainy Lake westward past the Assiniboine
River. It reached from northern Lake Winnipeg to the headwaters of
the Mississippi. While the war was being waged in the Canadas,
Scottish immigrants were being carted into the Red River Colony.

More pioneers. But as usual, there were already people living where
the pioneers were pioneering. There were the Cree and there were the
Ojibway and there were the Lakota. There were the Métis, who considered themselves a people by now, and who considered the eastern prairie
their place. This country called Assiniboia was perfect for the buffalo
hunt and for the trade in pemmican. A lot of this business was done
with the agents and workers of the fur trade, with the HBC people to
the north, and the Nor'westers, who travelled this way to get to the
Northwest. Lord Selkirk's farmers were not about to be welcomed by
any of these people.

"Pemmican" is the white person's attempt at a Cree word. To make
pemmican you get strips of bison meat or deer meat and pound animal
grease and berries into it. Then you dry it and preserve it, and sell it to
other people, including the people in the fur trade. It became the staple
protein in the fur trade, and the means by which a lot of Métis people
made a living, and by 1800 it was being manufactured in England and
carried on Royal Navy ships.

The Pemmican Wars were precipitated by a proclamation about
meat, but they were really about race and religion and land, and they

Church of the Bishop of Rupert's Land, Red River, Manitoba, *by G. Seton*
(NATIONAL ARCHIVES OF CANADA/C-1070)

would go on, in one form or another, all through the nineteenth century. They would result, for example, in the hanging of Louis Riel in 1885 and the rise of Wilfrid Laurier through the 1890s.

When Miles Macdonnell led the first contingent of Highlanders to the confluence of the Red and the Assiniboine in the spring of 1813, he did not seem to understand the feelings of the Métis people for this country. All he could see were the descendants of Scotch and French fur traders and temporary Indian wives drifting around the plains, following the bison. He had no idea that these gypsy-like folks saw themselves as a people, proud of their deeds and their independence, cut off from those governments back East somewhere, and in possession of their own lands. The white settlers, looked upon benignly by the angels, remember, saw these bilingual people as unstructured.

So Miles Macdonnell set himself up as governor of the new settlement, and assumed powers over all the people who lived therein. This would include any Nor'westers who were passing through. Now the Nor'westers had always known how to live with the Métis people. Some of them were family. The Nor'westers whispered to the Métis that this

Lord Selkirk was a big stockholder in the Hudson's Bay Company, which was true, and that this so-called settlement was an HBC plot to close the NWC trade route, which was not demonstrably false. The Nor'westers began whispering to the Métis, reminding them that they were a Great Plains people, and that these interlopers were bad news, and that they would just keep on coming unless something were done about asserting the people's rights and independence. Then Miles Macdonnell obliged by making an assertion about pemmican.

When farming became more difficult than expected, and weather proved difficult to oppose, food supplies ran low. Governor Macdonnell declared that it was forbidden to sell pemmican to people who would take it outside the colony. His reasoning was that this commodity was taken from animals that lived inside the settlement, and was therefore his to control. Now, the main market for pemmican was the North West Company. The Métis continued their trading policy, and Macdonnell's men seized the company's supply of pemmican. The people naturally took this as a hostile act by an invading people. Then Macdonnell informed them that it was forbidden to hunt bison on horseback. He was treading awfully close to religious oppression there.

Two Métis leaders, Cuthbert Grant and Peter Pangman, informed the Selkirk people of Aboriginal title to the land and requested compensation for its violation. The white people said, "Get out of here, you half savages." By 1816 Mr. Grant was captain general of the Métis liberation army. In spring of that year he and fifty men under his command intercepted a Selkirk supply brigade and took some prisoners. In June they seized Brandon House, an HBC headquarters named after an ancestor of Selkirk's. To show their disdain for the newcomers' presumption of power, some Nor'westers grabbed Governor Macdonnell and chased his friends back to Montreal. Selkirk sent out a replacement, one Robert Semple. It was Semple who accosted Captain Cuthbert Grant and his men when they were enroute to join forces with other Nor'Westers in an attempt to capture Fort Douglas. Someone fired a gun, and the war was on. Semple was killed, along with twenty of his men. Grant lost one man, and the Métis captured Fort Douglas.

The battle for Fort Douglas would be remembered by Anglos and HBC people as the Massacre at Seven Oaks; the French-speaking Métis would call it La Grenouillère. Whatever it was called, the battle was a sign that Canada's troubles were not all going to come from across the border. It is unlikely that many of the Métis had read about fights for national liberty on other continents. But they were there to tell organizers back East that the western plains were not *Terra Nullius*.

Lord Selkirk did not give up. He sent in the military and captured North West leaders and jailed them. He got farmers back on the ground. He started a lot of court cases. He was pretty disappointed, but he went down fighting. Selkirk died in 1820, and in 1821 the Hudson's Bay Company annexed the North West Company. Both outfits were really not much interested in farmers, and so the old Selkirk Settlement would not be much advertised in Europe from now on. Fifty years later, according to the census of 1871, a year after Manitoba was pulled into Confederation, there were ten thousand Scotch or French Métis in the old land grant area and sixteen hundred white settlers.

REBELLIONS

William Lyon Mackenzie
(NATIONAL ARCHIVES OF CANADA/C-001993)

When the Europeans first came to Lower Canada and Upper Canada they saw a lot of trees. Just look at their paintings: lots of trees. Now Quebec and Ontario look more like Europe—a few trees to mark the edges of property. For a couple of hundred years the docks of Montreal were piled high with lumber bound for the Old Country. The length of time it would lie there on the docks depended on the vagaries of the lumber market in London. We Canadians just kept piling it up. That was our job.

In the early years of the nineteenth century the northern half of the North American continent was itself arranged in halves. The eastern half was run by the various governors and lieutenant-governors of British

North America. The western half was run by the Hudson's Bay Company. In Arctic reaches and in areas where there were not a lot of fur-bearing critters, pockets of Aboriginal government carried on. As the century rolled westward and upward, the white people would try to put an end to that awkward situation.

The whites in Newfoundland were the most efficient. The Beothuk people were the first North Americans the Europeans met. They were unfortunate enough to live, as the Tasmanian Natives did, on an island. The last Beothuk died in St. John's in 1829.

In the twentieth century white people with a more refined sense of justice and humanity learned as much as they could about the people eradicated by the unenlightened settlers of the nineteenth century. They found lots of artifacts, bows and pendants and paint jars in people's graves. It was all right to get things out of people's graves, because the people doing the getting were archaeologists.

Another eastern nation was the Mi'kmaq, who lived along the water-front in the Gaspé region and all through the Maritimes. With their gorgeous clothing they impressed the first European visitors, but that did not help them escape what one historian has called "early depopula-tion and sociocultural disruption." For a while the French used them as middlemen in the fur trade, but when that was no longer necessary they were useful only as military allies. When the English took over their lands they were forced to leave their hunting and fishing grounds and try to learn how to be wage slaves and unemployed. In the twentieth century the Canadians would force them to relocate more than once. Despite all the efforts of the whites, the Mi'kmaq people have in recent years raised consciousness of the heritage both within and outside their group. The Canadians have even given their famous poet Rita Joe the Order of Canada.

But by the 1820s Aboriginal resistance to the European invasion was pretty well quelled in the eastern half of the continent. While occupied lands were rising against the Hapsburgs in Europe and Iberian rule in South America, British North America seemed to become more and more Tory and quiet. It was fortunate for the English governors, perhaps, that the poems of Percy Bysshe Shelley were published in small editions. In "The Masque of Anarchy," for example, he had the earth itself say:

"Rise like Lions after slumber
In unvanquishable number,
Shake your chains to earth like dew
Which in sleep had fallen on you—
Ye are many—they are few . . ."

Shelley wrote this poem in 1819, and it was published in 1832. We know that people would be reading him in Cuba. Even if people in the Canadas were not reading Shelley's rebellious poems, some of them were reading the people Shelley was reading.

Even in Canada?

If you want to get a good rebellion going, you have to develop newspapers with cranky editors, and well-off students with an egalitarian philosophy. In order to acquire these people you have to get your country developed, creating systems of transportation and communication and education. In 1807 a British North American government got involved in schools for the first time, handing out little operating grants to the small schools in Upper Canada. In Lower Canada the Jesuits had been discouraged from teaching since the 1770s, and the Church was not going to put up with secular schools. Rich people hired poets and other literates to instruct their offspring, and you did not yet have to go to law school to become a lawyer or to tech school to become an engineer.

The Churches got interested in higher education, as they had across the border, and soon there were lots of academies, especially in the Maritimes, where today there seem to be more universities than

7-Eleven stores. The non-sectarian Dalhousie University was founded in 1818, and in the 1820s there would be charters granted to McGill and to the colleges that would make up the University of Toronto. McGill would be used to educate the English-speaking merchants' sons, and U. of T. to keep the Family Compact going. It was not until 1852 that the Séminaire de Québec, founded in 1663, received a royal charter authorizing it to become Laval University.

People such as Talbot and Galt, and Thomas Baillie in New Brunswick, were in charge of building the washboard roads for the rough stagecoach ride that by 1830 could take your battered body from the Detroit River to Halifax harbour. In 1809 the first steamship in Canada started running up and down the St. Lawrence, and in 1816 the first Canadian steamship appeared on Lake Ontario. But how could Upper Canada settle for that? Lower Canada had the St. Lawrence and thus trade routes to the Atlantic Coast and eventually Europe. Upper Canada needed a route to the St. Lawrence, and that would require canals such as the one the USAmericans built to connect the Midwest with New York.

I don't know how anyone could even get up the mental energy to conceive of such a task, even if relations between the Canadas were perfectly amicable. French Canadians had seen what happened when the Hudson's Bay Company swallowed the North West Company in 1821. The fur trade had just about disappeared from Montreal. Now the *maudits anglais* were trying to use the St. Lawrence to grab whatever trade was left. The Upper Canadians would not get their canal from Lake Ontario to the great river until 1843, but they did get the first Welland Canal built to connect Lake Erie to Lake Ontario, and they did dig a swell ditch between Ottawa and Kingston.

All these improvements in transportation made it easier for Canadians to ship their natural resources out of the country, but they also resulted in the creation of local industries, such as the breweries large and small that dotted the landscape wherever there was a source of water. The muddy little village called York was incorporated in 1834. William Lyon Mackenzie, the first mayor, saw to it that its old Indian name, Toronto, was reinstated. Toronto quickly became the commercial and political centre of Upper Canada, on its way to becoming the centre of the universe in the late twentieth century.

While the Canadas were jostling one another for economic leadership, peaceful New Brunswick was beginning to make its claim to be the literary home of the nineteenth century. The timber trade had boomed during England's wars against Napoleon, and a middle class began to gather in each other's sitting rooms. They had lots to read, but now they had the leisure and hunger to get in on the writing. In 1825 the first history of New Brunswick was published, if you can imagine. A year earlier a Loyalist's daughter named Julia Beckwith Hart became the first colonial-born person to have a novel published in British North America (published, albeit, in Upper Canada). This was the usually unremembered *St. Ursula's Convent; or, The Nun of Canada*. She had apparently written it a decade earlier, when she was seventeen. It was filled with shipwrecks and intrigues.

One literary effort from that time and place remains in print and is looked at by university students who are directed by zealots for early Canadian texts. This is "The Rising Village," published by St. Andrews–born Oliver Goldsmith in 1825. It was first published in Britain, and written for an English audience. Of course the audience had read "The Deserted Village," published fifty-five years earlier by the more famous Oliver Goldsmith, our man's great-uncle. The earlier and greater poem laments the disappearance of lovely old villages as mercantilism destroys pastoralism. The later poem celebrates the creation of communal life hacked out of the New World wilderness, and the moral strength needed for such an enterprise. It's very Canadian.

But its beginning will alert you that you are not dealing with a John Milton here:

What noble courage must their hearts have fired,
How great the ardor which their souls inspired,
Who, leaving far behind their native plain,
Have sought a home beyond the western main.

Even in Canada

The families in the Family Compact were quite happy to see such senti-ments spoken and inscribed. So were the appointed officials of Lower Canada, who hung around the governor's château and were thus called the Château Clique. The Family Compact, the Robinsons and Jarvises and Strachans, had all the important government jobs. Anytime that British mercantile families get going in a colony, they play sports together and intermarry. A radical Kingston journalist named Robert Dalton made up the phrase "Family Compact," and rebels such as William Lyon Mackenzie said it as often as they could, until it began to sound like something official. The Family Compact sat in carpeted drawing rooms and recalled the great days of the 1812–14 War, and said "Harrumph" a lot. The Château boys spoke English and tried to keep the French and American revolutions a secret from the habitants.

The British were genially racist or simply Tory. Other human beings might from time to time put up a great building or illustrate a fine prin-ciple, but the British system was the finest achievement of man and had to be conserved. Other kinds of people, such as the Yankees, are riffraff. Ask Mrs. Susanna Moodie, who joined her husband in putting down the unruly. She and her sister Catharine Parr Traill wrote *Roughing It in the Bush* and *The Backwoods of Canada* to tell their readers back in Blighty why they were so disappointed in the Canada of the 1830s, of how awful it was that so many people over here did not seem to under-stand the rules of class and gentility.

Louis-Joseph Papineau did. He was a son of the petite bourgeoisie and since 1808 a member of the elected Legislative Assembly of Lower Canada. He was a lawyer and a hothead and by the 1820s the leader of the *parti populaire*. His second-in-command was a Scot, John Neilson, publisher of the *Québec Gazette*. They offered the sentiments of the French-speaking portion of the Assembly, which made up 80 percent of that body. Often Papineau was heard to suggest that the progress toward democracy in Britain should be echoed in her colonies. In Britain it was getting harder and harder for the king or the nobles to pass laws without considering the opinion of Parliament. Papineau was a fiery democrat—he did not like autocratic rule, whether it came from a governor and his council or from the priests. He and his newspaper buddy said so whenever the opportunity arrived.

As early as 1822 the colonial administrator, Gordon Drummond, complained that as speaker of the Assembly, Papineau was a sedition-monger. Papineau corrected Drummond as often as possible, calling himself a democrat. In 1828 the governor, George Ramsay, 9th Earl of Dalhousie, asked Papineau and Neilson to become members of his Executive Council, but they refused to be compromised. In 1834 Papineau offered the opinions of French Canada in his famous Ninety-Two Resolutions, many of which were thought to be dangerously revolutionary in a Tory country. But they pointed out that they were *British* rights that were being trammelled. The Resolutions are pompously and confusedly written, representing no threat to Thomas Jefferson's eminence as a writer, but over and again they call for reform rather than US-style revolution.

The British government spent its time on more important matters for three years, then issued the Ten Resolutions. Unfortunately for the Lower Canada Legislative Assembly, one British resolution was worth more than 9.2 French-Canadian resolutions. The Brits said no to the idea of responsible government, in which the executive branch is held collectively responsible and accountable to an elected legislature and may retain power only as long as it has the support of the legislature, and announced that all matters of finance would be in the hands of the Château Clique. Unfortunately for the advocates of peace and quiet, there were massive crop failures and outbreaks of infectious disease.

Papineau was from the land-owning class, as leaders of progressive revolts usually are, and while he stood up and lipped off at the aristocratic British governors who passed through the province, he always counselled non-violent resistance. But among his followers there were lots of young people with heads even hotter than his. They had heard of the French Revolution and the US Revolution, and they liked the idea of bombs bursting in air.

Meanwhile the French-Canadian middle class fought its own battle against British lords and French priests. In 1817 the Bank of Montreal had been set up by merchants and pillagers such as Peter McGill and John Molson, the kind of businessmen who were allowed to eat at the Château. Now the friends of Papineau would refuse to enter that bank, setting up their own Banque du Peuple. Papineau's followers promoted laws to limit the power of the Church, but the Executive Council refused to go along. Tensions, as they say, mounted.

In 1832 there was a by-election that featured bullets being fired by army people into a group of demonstrators. Two English soldiers who killed two Patriotes were found innocent, and then-governor Matthew Whitworth-Aylmer, 5th Earl of Aylmer, said that that was dandy with him. The young Patriotes' heads got hotter. Among the rebels there were now factions that were radical and factions that were more gradualist. Neilson was becoming increasingly conciliatory; Papineau, against his predilection, was being moved to the radical side.

Still, he hated to see blood and filth, and when the animosities finally broke out into physical action, he was not on the scene. He was supposed to be the future Father of the Republic, but he was no militarist, and in fact the accidental army of the rebels never did have a strategist or anyone to organize enlistment. The first battles were street fights in Montreal, between gangs of toughs, some political, some not. Fights were usually broken up by British soldiers, who gave no sign of being objective in their duties.

But eventually a bunch of lawyers and atheists and Irishmen and revolutionaries gathered in St-Denis, a little ride outside of Montreal, on the Richelieu River, that old military pathway. There in November of 1837 they were determined to hold a congress, declaring a republic, just as the US plotters had in Philadelphia more than a half century before. Papineau wasn't there—since making a narrow escape from some soldiers who were looking for him, he had been slipping from farmhouse to farmhouse. The rebels, including young George-Étienne Cartier, actually managed to chase the king's army away after its first attempt to break up the proceedings. It was the rebellion's first and last victory. Two days later the army forced its way in. The rebellion's great leader, Papineau, was now in the USA. He did not want a revolution made with guns.

If the rebels had fought a guerrilla war the rebellion might have lasted longer. Unfortunately they had a habit of getting inside a manor house or a church and inviting the soldiers to attack their redoubt. The army destroyed the Patriotes at a manor house in St-Charles. Near the end of November two hundred rebels raided the HBC store at Oka, gathered up rifles and ammunition and one little cannon, and holed up in a new convent and the church at St-Eustache.

On December 5 martial law was declared, and civilians were told to turn in their firearms. Two weeks later the army arrived at St-Eustache. They fired cannon at the front of the church and set the back of the church on fire. As Patriotes leapt from windows the colonial army used them for target practice. Some escaped. Some were burned in the church. After its victory the army burned the town and the farms along the road back to Montreal. A lot of rebels, including sympathetic priests acting against the command of their bishop, went to the USA.

Rebellion in Loyalist country

No one took up arms in the maritime colonies. A lot of Maritimers had left gunfighting country when they came north, and their children had grown up in a Tory environment. There was one great agitator, the newspaperman Joseph Howe. He had a quick temper, and it was almost always the ruling Tory cabal that made him mad. But he never advocated violence. He did not like the US model any better than did the elites, but he dreamed of a more sovereign Nova Scotia. For the rich snobs, talk of freedom was Yankee cant. Their great spokesman was Howe's ex-friend the arch-Tory Thomas Chandler Haliburton, another writer forced upon today's Canadian literature students. He wrote satirical dialogues between a Yankee clock peddler named Sam Slick and whatever citizens he could inveigle into conversation.

Sam Slick made a lot of sly comments that became adages as Haliburton's books became the first best-sellers in British North

America. People who did not know that they themselves were being satirized quoted his sayings as they went about their lives in Halifax. "Speak the truth and feel it," spoke the passionate Joseph Howe. "It's all bunkum, you know."

Two ideas Haliburton derided were responsible government and union of the BNA provinces. They would lead to assimilation by the USA, said this son of Loyalists. He saw the US system as mob rule, and the Nova Scotia system as far superior. When it looked as if British rule was going to be loosened, he moved to Great Britain.

In Upper Canada there were several kinds of dreams being dreamed. The Family Compact, snug in their Anglican pews, wanted to live in a society that resembled the British one of several generations back. There were a lot of non-Anglicans in Upper Canada, however. The Methodists, for example, led by preacher Egerton Ryerson, looked for a gradualist reform. By 1828 the Reform Party, led by Robert Baldwin, had a majority in the Assembly. But then there was William Lyon Mackenzie, whose combustible newspaper writings made Joseph Howe look like a moderate.

Mackenzie kept getting elected to the Assembly, denouncing the Family Compact and getting ousted from the Assembly by the Family Compact. Mackenzie fought Baldwin for control of the Reformists, and by the mid-thirties he felt strong enough to publish a draft constitution for a modern state. It sounded a lot like the US one, partly because much of it was simply lifted from the US one. The first bunch of clauses struck at the Anglican control of Upper Canada, going so far as to pronounce it illegal for anyone connected officially with the Church to hold any political office. He followed this document with a US-style declaration of independence, which included these incautious words: "Up then, brave Canadians. Get ready your rifles, and make short work of it."

Mackenzie wanted a new Jeffersonian republic, but he could not get the anti-Tory sides together. In Lower Canada the rebellion had no

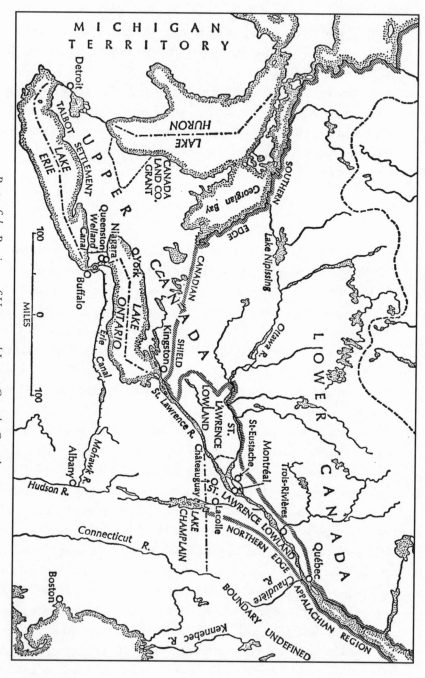

Parts of the Provinces of Upper and Lower Canada Canada, 1830
(THE PENGUIN HISTORY OF CANADA BY KENNETH MCNAUGHT, PENGUIN UK, 1991)

chance of success because the Church and the Patriotes, though they both desired a cohesive and different people, did not care for each other's vision of a people. In Upper Canada the breach was between the radical reformers and the peaceful ones.

In such a situation the smart leaders of the radicals will try to engineer a picturesque example of oppression and violence perpetrated by the authorities against the people, thus radicalizing, they hope, the gradualists. Mackenzie's chance came with the election of 1836. There was a new lieutenant-governor, Francis Bond Head, fresh from England. He scoffed publicly at the republicans, bragging that he himself could do more for the people than the people would ever be able to do for themselves. Then he stole the 1836 election, or so Mackenzie said. The polls had been well attended by agents of the Family Compact handing out free booze, and large hard-fisted men encouraging the undecided not to vote for the radicals.

Mackenzie's side lost the election two to one. He would bide his time, meanwhile uttering his printed description of Bond Head's administration. The perfidious English had lost half of their American lands to freedom and would descend to any foul-doing to retain the rest for the pleasure of their nobles and rich snobs. When news of the Papineau uprising in Quebec reached Lake Ontario, Mackenzie's lieutenants started rounding up farmers and tradesmen, and when all the English soldiers from Upper Canada went to Lower Canada to put down the Patriotes, Mackenzie's gallant few met at a tavern just north of Toronto. Their plan was to march down Yonge Street and bask in the noisy welcome of the grateful citizens, who would then chase the Family Compact out of town.

Everyone had a few whiskies to keep warm. It was December 7, after all. Mackenzie's army of liberation, toting whatever weapons they could lay hands on, including the iconic pitchfork, started their march down Yonge. Unfortunately, Lieutenant-Governor Bond Head was in command of a local militia. These fellows had a few whiskies and assembled on Yonge Street to repel the revolutionaries. When the Mackenzies appeared on the scene, waving old rifles and crosscut saws, the militiamen fired a volley northward. Smoke filled the air. Under cover of the smoke, Mackenzie's men fled north, and Bond Head's militia fled south. That was the most memorable battle of the Upper Canada Rebellion. When news arrived in the USA, it caused peals of laughter—those Canadians don't even know how to organize a decent revolution!

Two days after the battle of Yonge Street, Bond Head's men went north and took the rebels' tavern and burned it to the ground. That was what you did with enemy edifices in those days. The militiamen could not find Mackenzie, though. The little Scot had skedaddled across the line to New York. Now he would fight the Tories in a series of cross-border raids, after each of which the USAmericans would throw him into jail. The funniest raid took place at Navy Island, situated at the start of the big bend a little above Niagara Falls. The little triangular island was Canadian, but Mackenzie had a lot of US help, including his supply ship, the *Caroline*. Mackenzie took over Navy Island, put his own revolutionary flag up and declared a free republic that would eventually include all of Upper Canada.

The authorities were afraid of Mackenzie's rebels. They would hang some of them and send some of them to Australian convict camps. But they would always defeat them easily and comically. In this case a few of them rowed a boat over to the island and cut the *Caroline* loose. Mackenzie's navy looked wonderful as it sailed over the lip of the falls. During the skirmishing and bombarding that took place, one of the USAmericans was killed. This meant that hotheads on the US Senate floor would start demanding another invasion of Canada.

Whenever the USAmericans want to prepare their people for a war, they ask them to remember something. Once it was a little mud mission called the Alamo. But usually, you remember, it is a ship of some sort. When they wanted to go to war against the Spanish and grab up property around the world they said, "Remember the *Maine*," a US ship that may have been sabotaged in Havana harbour. In the first year of the twenty-first century, the people were being roused against the mysterious enemy who had blasted a big hole in the side of a US warship in the Middle East. In 1838 they were supposed to rally around the memory of the funny little *Caroline*.

But miraculously, the US did not invade Canada this time. They would leave that work to the Fenians, groups of Irish and Irish Americans who would periodically cross the border with guns and torches.

There had, though, been as many USAmericans as there were Canadians in Mackenzie's army. Some of them were imprisoned, and seventy of them were sent to Australia, which action must have had lawyers scurrying. Mackenzie's uprising looks feckless from our vantage, but he was a most serious revolutionary, and there were a lot of people afraid of him. Another miracle occurred, however, when he was allowed back into Upper Canada, where he was yet again elected to the Assembly, serving until 1857. During that time he always lived in penury, which one cannot say of many successful politicians.

As the years went by Mackenzie's radical demands would become government policy, and his US daughter would give birth to a boy named William Lyon Mackenzie King and tell him every day about the heroism of his grandfather. She told him this even after her death, even after her son had become the most successful politician in Upper Canadian history.

More gentlemanly reform

Certain phrases used to remain in Canadians' minds long after they had forgotten the Canadian history they had kind of heard in school. One is "the Plains of Abraham." Another is "the Riel Rebellion." The most peaceful one is "the Durham Report."

It is hard to imagine anything more Canadian than the Durham Report. It calls for radical changes within the context of conservative expectations. It is one of those things, like universal medicare, that USAmericans don't understand. The report is named after a man called "Radical Jack" Lambton, 1st Earl of Durham. When the British government got nervous because of the uprisings in the Canadas, it decided to create a commission to figure out why they had happened and what should be done to forestall another revolution in the colonies. Durham was given the job as high commissioner and the position of governor general for British North America. In Quebec they knew that they were seeing something new when the governor general arrived with an entire orchestra and trunks full of books.

He had credentials as a radical reformer. In Britain he had been calling for such things as a secret ballot and the vote for all taxpaying men. The government was glad to get him out of England for a while. When he arrived in the New World in May 1838 he found the Canadian jails full of disappointed rebels. Most of them would be set loose and pardoned. A few would be shipped, the governor general thought, to Bermuda. There had been a few hangings before he arrived, but he put an end to that solution.

Even before crossing the Atlantic he had done a lot of homework, and had thought of a radical rearrangement that would keep the colonies safely inside the British sphere while giving them what seemed like a measure of independence. Why not make a confederation of the Canadas and the Maritimes? First he would listen to what all the delegations had to say.

He was a little taken aback. The Maritimers said that of all the possibilities available, joining up with the riotous Canadians would be on the very bottom of their list. The English merchants of Montreal told him that they deeply desired a union of the two Canadas but wanted nothing to do with the Bluenoses. The representatives of Upper Canada said that they would do all right by themselves, thank you very much. Everyone was afraid that if there was a federation, too much power would be given to some other part of it. Boy, thought Radical Jack, if anyone ever manages to make a country out of these BNA provinces, it will be an amalgamation of regions held together by their opposition to one another.

Lord Durham spent most of his time in Quebec, but he did visit Toronto for a little over a week. There he talked matters over with William Baldwin and Robert Baldwin. William Baldwin had sent a

letter to the Duke of Wellington in 1828, calling for responsible government in his colony. His son Robert was a second-generation reformer.
They proposed a step that even the stuck-up Nova Scotians could not
abjure. Why not have the governor of a province choose his Executive
Council, or cabinet, from the party that holds a majority in the elected
Assembly? Then in matters that are clearly domestic the governor would
act according to the advice that this group gives him. Here was a way to
empower the locals without forcing them to seek independence.

I like it, said Lord Durham.

He thought that it would work everywhere but in Lower Canada.
Lower Canada had had its constitution suspended and was being run by
martial law before he showed up. Lord Durham was a little disappointed
in Quebec. It appeared to him that the French Canadians, influenced by
their Church and not fond of the French elite who played footsie with
the English, could not get the hang of Britain's progressive civilization.
Giving self-government to these people, he thought, could be disastrous.

In the fall of 1838 he got word from his government that he could not
exile those dangerous rebels to Bermuda. He was the governor general
of British North America, and Bermuda was not in British North
America. He might think of sending those traitors to Newfoundland,
but he had no jurisdiction in Bermuda. Radical Jack knew bureaucratic
jiggery when he saw it. He figured that London would interfere with
anything unusual that he might do. He decided to quit the job. Besides,
it was November in Quebec.

When Lord Durham went back home, Lower Canada reverted to
martial law. So much for the English promises of reform, said the
Patriote leaders, and two days after Lord Durham left Quebec, the rebellion was on again. This time the new governor general, Sir John
Colborne, 1st Baron Seaton, and his army came down hard. The rebellion was very short, and when it was over a dozen rebels were hanged
and sixty were exiled to Australia. Australia was a lot farther away than
was Bermuda. But then Colborne was not as radical as Lambton.

Two months after his arrival in London, England's most liberal peer
had a report ready for the Crown's perusal. Durham states that much of

his concern is for British people who might want to go to North America; he suggests that the large land reserves for the Church and Crown be cut severely and that the colonies quit the policy of assigning huge land grants to developers. A lot of the report proposed the ideas of the Baldwins in Toronto. The mother country should have the say in four major matters: constitution, intercolonial trade, foreign relations and public lands. All domestic questions should be in the hands of the governor's Executive Council, but that Council should be chosen from the majority party in the Assembly. Each member of that Council should be a minister responsible for some department, such as transportation or education.

Another major proposal was the reuniting of the Canadas. Durham was interested in progressive civilization, and he believed that the people most likely to advance it were the British. The French Canadians would require education to be brought up to snuff. Durham had been surprised to find that the normal French Canadian did not have a strong desire to celebrate his great luck and embrace English ideas. Durham had found "two nations warring in the bosom of a single state." If the habitant could not be moved by logic and example, he would have to be assimilated.

Durham proposed a legislative union of the Canadas: "If the population of Upper Canada is rightly estimated at 400,000, the English inhabitants of Lower Canada at 150,000, and the French at 450,000, the union of the two provinces would not only give a clear English majority, but one which would be increased every year by the influence of English emigration; and I have little doubt that the French, when once placed, by the legitimate course of events and the working of natural causes, in a minority, would abandon their vain hopes of nationality."

In Upper Canada the Family Compact were not too crazy about responsible government, but they liked the idea of union. In London they thought that the idea of colonialists becoming cabinet ministers was ridiculous, but they did see the logic of provincial union and re-education of the French speakers.

GETTING TOGETHER

10

John A. Macdonald
(NATIONAL ARCHIVES OF CANADA/C-21604)

Until 1829, US presidents had been situated by the eastern states and their establishment built on the ruins of the old British establishment. Andrew Jackson represented life on the frontier. He was the anti-Congress president, and he was not afraid to use his veto. He replaced the regular authorities with a kitchen cabinet, and went after the big Northeastern banks.

Andy Jackson did not like complications, and the Indians were complicating US life. As an army officer in 1817 he had chased Indians across the border to kill them in Spanish Florida. Now in the 1830s he oversaw the efforts to move bothersome tribes from the east side of the

Mississippi over to the west side. The English were no longer around to help the Indians, and for a while the US policy would be to shove them westward. Who knew anything about traditional methods of securing a livelihood? The Indians were all the same, and a lower form of life anyway. The whites had to have room to plant cotton and the like, and room to set up shacks for the black people they were moving westward across the ocean.

President Monroe had issued the Monroe Doctrine in 1823, announcing that any future colonization of the Americas would be done by the US rather than any Europeans. In 1845 a grandiloquent magazine editor with the splendid name John L. O'Sullivan coined the phrase "Manifest Destiny," to name and justify the US belief that there was a Divine plan that it should annex Texas, California, New Mexico and Oregon, and then get Alaska and Hawaii and the Philippines, etc., etc. Anyone with any experience of the USAmericans knew that their aspirations did not lean only westward but also northward and southward.

Sam Slick back in Halifax could have told you that the Yankees were a lot quicker when it came to imagining empires and making deals, and that you would really have to be on your toes to keep up with them in this westering business. The only Brits that seemed all that interested in the West were the directors of the Hudson's Bay Company. But pretty soon the various Christian Churches would head out west with the traders, and there were always speculators who eyed river country.

In 1840 the old Selkirk Settlement was in the hands of the HBC, and the price for acreage was kept nice and low. But no one bought any. The majority population was made up of Métis people who figured that the land was just naturally theirs anyway. Farther west the Native people were living a good balance between their happy pre-history and a mutually beneficial trading relationship with the fur people.

By 1840 James Douglas, a huge man with some Creole blood, had been a chief accountant at Fort Vancouver in the Columbia River country for ten years. He had a mixed-blood wife and a lot of children and very good connections in the HBC. He did not like Indians all that much, and he could not stand the Yankees. Fort Vancouver was turning more and more into an agricultural place as well as a trading centre. The Oregon country was starting to fill up with Yankees, and if you lifted your ear a little you could hear a US politician's view on the proper border between the Hudson's Bay Company and the USA. "Fifty-four-forty or Fight!" suggested this voice. Fort Vancouver was at forty-five-sixty.

The Province of Canada

In 1840 the British government finished reading Lord Durham's report. "This is ridiculous," said Lord John Russell, who had just been ensconced in the Colonial Office. "How could we send out a governor responsible to us, and then have him turn around and be responsible to an elected assembly? Now, this idea of joining the provinces, hmm . . ."

The British government passed the Act of Union. It would incorporate Lord Durham's solution to the French-Canadian problem, but ignore his views on local democracy. The aim was to have a unified province in which power would remain in the hands of English speakers.

All right. There would be some elected Canadians, and these men would form a lower house of government called a Legislative Assembly. There would be eighty-four men, but here was the catch. It was decided that though Canada would be a unified province, it would be a union of two noticeable halves, renamed Canada East and Canada West. There would be forty-two assemblymen elected in either half. See the genius of the plan? As long as at least one English-speaking assemblyman was elected in Canada East, the English would have a majority, because no French-speaking guy would ever be elected in Canada West.

There would be an upper house, Legislative Council, and these fellows would be appointed by the governor to lifetime posts. There would also be a cabinet, called the Executive Council, and they would be chosen or dechosen by the governor.

The governor, of course, was appointed by the Colonial Office in London.

In June 1841 in Kingston, the House would meet for the first time.

Thus began the process of confederation among the British North American colonies. During the next quarter of a century the Canadian union grew, while the union to the south looked as if it would break to pieces. The British, of course, rather enjoyed watching as the US slipped on the economic banana peel and fell into a secessionary war that lasted until the bloody federal victory of 1864. That victory, in fact, did a lot to bring about the victory of the confederation forces in Canada.

The war of southern secession in the US was brought about by a fundamental difference in attitudes toward black people. In the South the slaves were deemed necessary to southern agriculture. In the North it was generally believed that the blacks should not be slaves but rather an underclass with no hope of equality with whites.

Britain had made the slave trade illegal in 1807 and abolished slavery all through the empire (including captive South Africa) in 1833. Slavery had been abolished in the French colonies in 1794, and was reimposed by Napoleon in 1801. Chile banned slavery in 1823. In 1824 it was banned through Central America. Mexico banned it in 1829, Bolivia in 1831. Also in 1831 Brazil banned the importation of slaves, and then over the next half century passed progressively liberal laws about slavery. The Second French Republic freed the slaves again in 1848. Colombia banned slavery in 1851, and Venezuela followed suit in 1854. The Dutch Colonies did away with it in 1863. Now slavery existed in Puerto Rico, Cuba and a little in Brazil. And in the United States. It would not be the last time that the USA stood out as a champion of an earlier social idea, let us say.

Abraham Lincoln's senate passed the Emancipation Act in 1863. It was ignored in the Confederate States of America. In 1865, with the end of the war, it could not be ignored, but for political reasons it was not much observed. The great national poet Walt Whitman theorized that the war had been a great injury to the nation but that now having survived it, the nation was stronger. The robber barons who built great railroads and other systems to bring victory over the South and get fabulously rich while doing so, now looked westward (and northward, and southward). If Canada wanted to escape liberation it had better get busy dealing with its own factions.

A more immediate prompting was the latest method of invasion from the South. These were the pesky Fenian raids. Just as Irish USAmericans and others in our time send money to the IRA terrorists, so in 1857 the Fenian Brotherhood was organized to fight for Irish freedom from Britain. Their way of doing this was to invade Canada and New Brunswick. A lot of the Fenian Brothers were veterans of the Civil War. Their first northward push was in New Brunswick in April 1866. A lot of people in New Brunswick were at the time of this inter-ruption arguing the merits of confederation with the Canadas. This external annoyance pushed sentiments over toward confederation.

In June another batch crossed the border at Fort Erie and walked halfway to Port Colborne, engaging some resistance at a burg called Ridgeway. There the Irish-Americans had themselves a little victory. Then they went home for the weekend. Another group walked across the border into Canada East and shouted patriotic slogans for two days before walking back into New York State.

The Fenians were not just helpful jokes. They would bring to mind the threat of the republic, and in 1868 they would bring US-style poli-tics to Canada, with the assassination of D'Arcy McGee.

There were a few Fenians in Canada West, too, and the Tory news-papers of the time liked to stir up fears of an Irish (read Catholic) upris-ing joined by invading ruffians. And it was not as if all citizens were united in congratulating themselves for not being part of the USA. In the late forties the English merchants of Montreal were less than exul-tant about the growing powers of the French Canadians, and saw the US as a good example of a market economy unfettered by social spending. In 1849, some 325 businessmen signed an Annexation Manifesto, calling for annexation by the US. Among these Annexationists were John Abbott, a future Canadian prime minister, Alexander Galt, a future Father of Confederation, and Antoine-Aimé Dorion, eventual leader of the radical Parti Rouge and soul of the Liberal Party when it gathered around Alexander Mackenzie, the second post-Confederation PM.

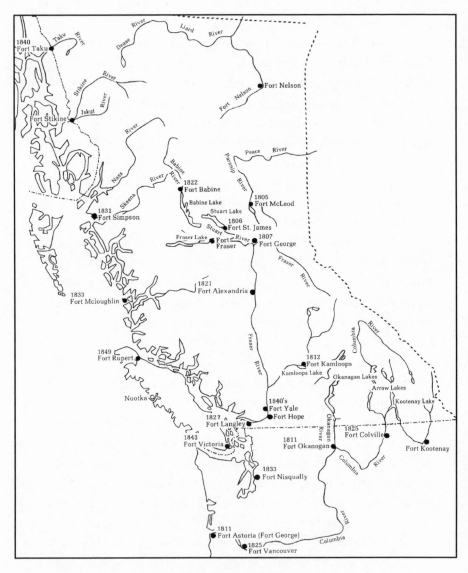

Forts of the British Columbia Area
(*BRITISH COLUMBIA RECALLED: A PICTURE HISTORY 1741–1871,*
BY DEREK PETCHICK AND SUSAN IM BAUMGARTEN,
HANCOCK HOUSE PUBLISHERS LTD., COPYRIGHT 1974, P. 43)

There were Annexationists on the West Coast, too. Vancouver's Island was made a Crown colony in 1849, where the HBC had just chosen to make six-year-old Fort Victoria its Western capital. That year of 1849 was ominous, but not just because of Montreal Annexationists and Crown colonies. There was a terrific gold rush in California, and down there everyone was trying to get in on the action. When the California gold was no longer panning out, bearded guys with wild eyes filled the valleys of Idaho. Then someone found something and talked too loud way up the Fraser River.

By early summer of 1858 there were thirty thousand gold-rush guys coming north into New Caledonia, bringing guns and whisky. Some of them just walked across the so-called border from worn-out mines in Idaho. Twenty thousand of them landed at little Victoria's harbour, outfitted themselves as best they could and found their way across the water to the mainland. The HBC and the dainty little town of three hundred Brit souls were overwhelmed. Every time you woke up and looked out from between your curtains you saw two new hotels standing between you and the Pacific Ocean. The place was suddenly full of USAmericans, including a few dozen black people who had fled the new anti-Negro laws in California. Soon the USAmericans were taking over the outfitting business on the south end of the colony, and the Hudson's Bay Company store could not keep up with the competition. There were instant bars, newspapers and boot stores, with Yanks selling to Yanks, and not quietly.

So when it came to discussions about the political future, there were quite a few locals who figured that this nice island was going to be part of the States, lucky island!

Well, land prices went through the roof, and the HBC got into the habit of turning a great profit on real estate. James Douglas was an edgy man. As governor of the colony and head of the HBC he had to understand that immigration meant good times, while he knew from his reading that where US businessmen went, the US flag was sure to follow. The USAmericans had marched into Mexico eleven years before. Oregon was going to become a US state in 1859.

On the first day of 1858 Douglas passed a law making all gold mines along the Fraser River system Crown property. Miners had to get licences to dig or pan. When US boats started running up the Fraser, Douglas, the vice admiral of the island colony, told them that these were British waters and HBC trade country. The Yanks kept pouring in. Tons of gold dust scampered south across the border. Miners wore pistols and hired Native people at rock-bottom wages. Douglas kept sending news of all this danger back to London, but England was busy in China and India, taking care of business. Finally they sent out a bad novelist and new colonial secretary named Sir Edward Bulwer-Lytton to check things out. Bulwer-Lytton did not like the HBC much. He explained to Douglas that his company had a charter for furs, not gold and not land. American miners were good for business, he said. But Douglas held back his big fists and renamed Fort Dallas, calling it Lytton after the secretary.

On August 2, Queen Victoria named her new colony British Columbia. The name was a reminder to the goldwalkers and their politicians back home. It would stretch from the US border to the Simpson River and from the Rocky Mountains to the coast, and include the islands the Brits called the Queen Charlottes. James Douglas would be the governor of this colony as well as the island, but now he would have to step down as HBC director. He had managed somehow to amass a fortune while directing, so his big family would not be destitute. On November 19 he trudged through the mud at Fort Langley to observe the lowering of the Company flag and the raising of the British Jack in the relentless rain.

Still, it was a long way to the Red River Colony. When supplies from the Red River Colony came into British Columbia or Vancouver Island, they came by way of the USA. The new governor knew a threat when he saw one. In the USA land was getting scarcer. There was talk that the USAmericans were conferring with the Russians about taking Alaska off their hands. If British Columbia were to have the United States to the south and the United States to the north, the colony might imagine itself a berry in a raven's mouth.

The Hudson's Bay Company's monopoly was going to expire in 1859. All that prairie land would technically not belong to anyone. It was vaguely British, but who was going to be able to protect it if thousands and thousands of USAmericans moved up and then demanded protection by the US army? That's the way they operated. It was a long way out there, some Canadians said. We have enough problems here in Canada. We do not need any more provinces that speak English, said Lower Canadians who saw confederation coming up. But those damned Yankees are building railroads like crazy, said a lot of Reform Liberals. We don't even have rail links between Toronto and Halifax.

The US war with the Confederacy complicated matters, to say the least. A lot of Canadians joined the Blue Coats to fight against the slave economy. But the British, still smarting from bad experiences with their former colonies, built warships that wound up in Grey Coat hands. These ships made a great nuisance of themselves in the Union shipping lanes, and when the war was all but over, President Lincoln started talking about reprisals, especially the receiving-huge-acreage kind of reprisals. Luckily this sort of talk tapered off after Lincoln's assassination, and the work was left to the feckless Fenians. In 1871 the case was closed when Britain agreed that it should pay some monetary compensation.

But the big new republic was a place in which business and the military were learning to butter each other's buttocks. If military annexation was not going to look all that good, there were always economic means. In 1854 the US and British North America had signed a Reciprocity Treaty, which had proven quite handy for the businessmen on both sides, and during their big war, the US had been happy to get fish, food, minerals and wood without paying tariffs on them. But when the war was over, the US Senate began to listen to the complaints of businessmen whose business was fish, coal and lumber. Listen, said these businessmen, we need protection from these foreign traders. Don't you remember that we just recently fought a couple of wars with them? Don't you realize that if we put up tariffs they will eventually beg for annexation so they can make a living? The US withdrew from the Reciprocity Treaty in 1866.

This was the kind of thing that made Canadian schoolchildren decide that history was kind of boring. US schoolchildren, of course, never heard about it. But over the years there have been a lot of apoplectic fits, suicides and desertions caused by the tariffs that keep showing up at the US border.

The uncles of Confederation

With the USAmericans filling their half of the continent, and thrusting railroads into the West, and with the British involved with the Crimean War and later colonial adventures, the Canadians and other colonials had to fight for their own survival. Strong differences of opinion arose about the way to do this. Party politics became very important and sometimes very peculiar.

In Canada East there were the reformers called the *rouges* and the status-quo people called the *bleus*. They are commemorated today by the neckties worn in parliamentary photographs, the Conservatives in blue and the Liberals in red. In Canada West there was a wide range of Tories, but the most effective party was a group that their leader John A. Macdonald called the Liberal-Conservatives. Their foes were the Reform Party, an unstable coalition of farmers and republicans and idealists.

All right. The *bleus* formed ties with the Tories, and the *rouges* lined up with the Reformers. But there was another way of bisecting the pie. Canada was still made up of two halves, and East is East. Remember those Upper Canadians who used to be outpopulated and figured that they could protect themselves from having French rammed down their throats by having just as many representatives as the Lower Canadians? Well, now they could not help noticing that they had a much higher population than did Canada East, and yet only the same number of representatives. That was manifestly unfair. They now wanted more than responsible government; they wanted "Representation by Population." That became a rallying cry of the Reformers.

John A. Macdonald was a Tory. "A British subject I was born and a British subject I shall die," he was famous for saying. He shared the usual English prejudices about the French, but he always supported their rights. He thought that they would eventually be assimilated, and he was a progressive conservative. His arch foe was George Brown, publisher of *The Globe* in Toronto. Brown never bragged about being a British subject, and he saw no reason to mollycoddle the French in Canada East. Though born in Scotland, he had been a boy in the USA. He called his demand for rep by pop a democratic demand, but he knew that his followers would know code language when they heard it.

There are certain relationships that last through the political ages long after the individuals in them have gone to politician heaven. In the march to Confederation John A. Macdonald and George-Étienne Cartier, leader of the *bleus*, would form a political friendship so iconic that it would have a major highway named after it, the freeway from Windsor to Quebec, also known in Ontario as the 401.

There had been a lot of coalitions through the 1850s, but they were made between people who didn't trust each other. If you are a fan of internecine political struggle and betrayal, you will really enjoy reading somewhere about the governments of Canada from 1849 to 1867. But I am in a hurry to get to 1867. It is a number that has fitted nicely in my head since I was a boy. The BNA Act. What a satisfying phrase to say! Notice what you do with your lips, then your tongue and teeth, and then your open throat as you say those first three letters, and then the closure when you finish the act.

While the USAmericans were settling their problems with blood and vengeance, the British subjects were getting bogged down in an unwieldy system. For example, whenever there was a really important measure to settle, it had to be passed by a majority in the Assemblies of both Canadas. By 1864 the only group that could form a government were the Macdonald-Cartier people. But George Brown and his Reformers could gather enough factions to stymie any move the blues might make.

What to do? It was a bad idea to have a deadlock while the Northern USA was creating the most mechanized war machine of all time. George Brown, bless his democratic soul, sent a message to the

Tories, suggesting a grand coalition. At the same time he suggested that a long-time solution would have to include reforming the constitution along the lines of rep by pop. And making a union of British colonies, said Macdonald. That too, replied Brown. Macdonald was a garrulous fellow who liked to make political deals in taverns. He was also a genius at raising money and votes. He knew how to compromise and when to shout in your face. He would make a deal with George Brown, share a London cab with him and join him in petitioning the home government, but he would never like him one bit. George Brown's newspaper kept running cartoons picturing John A. Macdonald in fancy checked trousers with a bottle of spirits jammed into a back pocket. Macdonald was thinking of these caricatures when he wrote his mother: "I am carrying on a war with that scoundrel George Brown and I will teach him a lesson that he never learnt before. I shall prove him a most dishonest, dishonorable fellow & in doing so I will only pay him a debt I owe him for abusing me for months together in his newspaper."

So in the middle sixties Macdonald's Tories, Cartier's *bleus* and Brown's various Reformers were looking for a better union. In the Maritimes there were Tories and Reformers feinting and thrusting about a possible union (or re-union) there, or maybe even with the bumpkins to their west. But all this edging toward federation left out one group that would be heard from later. This was the Parti Rouge. The forces of radicalism had fallen into confusion since the Rebellion. Nationalism was taken over by the Church. The English authorities did not object much when the sense of a French-American nation became identified with the most conservative organization on the ground.

The Native people were not invited to negotiations about a unified BNA. Apparently their great experience in creating confederations was of no use to the settlers.

Charlottetown, Quebec, London

Those Maritimers, encouraged by the British government, decided to have a conference of their premiers in Charlottetown in September

1864 to discuss confederation of their region. Gen. William T. Sherman
would spend that month turning the state of Georgia into a nightmare.
President Mitre had settled in to lead the new confederation of the
Argentine provinces.

The boys from the Canadas decided to drop by. Now, John A. was
not really hot about confederation, but he did have good reasons for
going along with it, as long as it did not lead to some kind of independence from Britain. He could not stand the whole nest of republicans and Fenians and salesmen to the south, and he hated the very
thought of their getting their hands on Rupert's Land and the prairies.
John A. did not give a fig for the prairies personally, but he knew what
would happen to his land if the Yanks got their eager fingers on the
country between Canada and British Columbia.

So Macdonald and Brown and Cartier showed up at Province House
in Charlottetown with a wagonful of champagne and brandy and
schmoozed the eastern politicos. The Maritimers didn't get to make
their proposals; they had to listen to speeches by the Canadians as the
waiters topped up their glasses. They heard about the danger from the
South, they heard about how the relationship with Britain was getting
to be sentimental rather than necessary and they heard about a dream
of creating a country. After the seven Canadians had got through
talking, everyone went for a little socializing in Halifax and agreed to
have a conference in Quebec in October. This time the Maritimers
would get a chance to speak.

On October 10, a month after the start of the Charlottetown ameni-
ties, thirty-three delegates from five governments, including
Newfoundland, started talking. No one from British Columbia could
make it. The rest were in historic Quebec, where Champlain had sat and
made up a government two and a half centuries before. The Atlantic
people talked about their long experience as civilized societies. The
Canadians had come prepared with a list of suggestions, most of them
having been in the hands of Mr. Macdonald, the wisecracking lawyer in
the fancy trousers. Without too much exaggeration, you might say that
Mr. Macdonald was an author and Canada was his book, just as Thomas

Jefferson had written the USA ninety years before. But Mr. Macdonald was determined to write an English book.

The delegates sat in a big room that did not look much like the high-windowed place depicted in the famous painting of the Fathers of Confederation. Famous historical paintings set in Quebec City are always fanciful, whether of General Wolfe lying down or lawyer Macdonald standing up. The delegates argued the famous Seventy-Two Resolutions, hammering out sentences, being careful with commas. They were doing the work of constitution, and look what was happening—the Charlottetown meeting had inspired a dream; now for the first time the colonials were working out a plan for constitutional government, and when they were finished, they were going to present it to the British Parliament.

That made Macdonald a little nervous. But he figured that he could write a country that was still British because it did not want to be USAmerican. What he really wanted was a system like Britain's, in which there was just a unitary national state, with regional representatives but no provincial bodies. What he dreaded was a system such as the US one in which the provinces or states had strong rights and met in a federation that became useful in case of war or maritime trade. What he would settle for would be something in between, a confederation with a Parliament based on the British one.

The first resolution would pretty well sum up the Canadian innovation: "The best interests and present and future prosperity of British North America will be promoted by a Federal Union under the Crown of Great Britain, provided such a union can be effected on principles just to the several Provinces."

Pretty Canadian, eh?

There was a profound national dream sharing the space with spirits of a more worldly source. But there were some differences. There were those, for example, who feared rep by pop because it might lead to extreme freedom and thus chaos. That problem was handled by providing for an appointed upper house that would take care of the establishment's interests. The Canadas would have twenty-four senators each, the three Maritime provinces would have twenty-four, and Newfoundland and the West would get four each. With details such as this to get into writing, the conference went on for two weeks, and as it did it became clear that this Kingston lawyer Macdonald was the biggest talker. He also produced the best-drawn doodles in the margins of his copy of the resolutions.

His finance minister, Alexander T. Galt, was the father who made the economic arguments. One can understand the old boy Toryism of the group by noting that Galt was a director of the British North American Land Company, and a big railway promoter. He had been going to England to try to get the Brits to help him build an intercolonial railway. Now he studied replacing of the British authorities with a powerful centralized authority within easier reach. He said that the new federal government should assume the public debts of the provinces that entered the union. Also this new federal government should finance the railways that would be required to make the union workable. In order to raise the money needed for such an enterprise, the federal government should be given the power to collect taxes and customs. Then the federal government should send 80 cents a head to the provincial governments to pay for schools and roads and the like.

People such as John A. Macdonald and Alexander T. Galt envisioned themselves as figures in the federal government rather than the government of Canada West.

Would they buy it?

Now the well-oiled conventioneers had to take their proposals home to their provinces. If these proposals got by the naysayers in Halifax and Charlottetown, etc., they would have to be taken to London. One could be sure that there would be enemies in every capital.

Early 1865 saw debate over the union proposals in all the provincial legislatures and all the provincial newspapers. In Canada West there was not all that much of a fuss, because it looked obvious that the province had more than any other to gain. George Brown mumbled about the expensive railway, but he liked the appearance of rep by pop. In Canada East the *rouge* leader, Dorion, complained that the union was really just a bigger legislature that made the French minority even smaller. Cartier said don't worry, we will be able to use our own legal system and language.

Nova Scotia was home to the most famous anti-confederationist of them all. Joseph Howe was a Reform champion, a journalist who had fought for responsible government and a recent premier of the province. Now he was an imperial fishery authority, and in his spare time he wrote speeches against confederation, calling it the "Botheration Scheme." The current premier, Charles Tupper, had a terrible time with Howe's followers. In New Brunswick the voters punished Premier Leonard Tilley and his cabinet, throwing them out of office in 1865. The legislature of Prince Edward Island looked at the comparative size of their province and Canada West and begged off. Newfoundland, whose delegates had been more observers than idea guys, did not bother paying attention to the plans of these johnny-come-lately colonies.

The Native and Métis people along the Red River had their own ideas of home rule.

It did not look as if the coastal provinces were going to be gathered into this new country very soon. But fired with hope and whisky, John A. Macdonald gathered his friends and enemies and sailed for London, where he and George Brown and Cartier and Galt presented the Canadian case to the overdressed officials there. The British gave them a warm welcome. When Joseph Howe and a gaggle of anti-confederation Maritimers showed up, the Brits told them to go home. The Brits were in favour of a BNA confederation. They figured that with a kind of democratic country to its north, the US might not be so eager to keep invading.

But there were four colonies that seemed to want to stay out. The Brits gave up on Newfoundland. You would have to go to war with the Newfoundlanders to persuade them to change the colour of their socks. But the Colonial Office did some meddling in Nova Scotia and New Brunswick, and the governments of these two provinces changed overnight. In addition, the English announced that they would finance the railways between provinces.

Then when the Fenians did their invading, and the US reneged on
reciprocity, confederation looked like a good bet. I'll drink to that, said
John A. Macdonald.

In the meetings that went on over the fall and winter of 1866, John
A. Macdonald's main concern was that they not manufacture another
United States. The system of government should be based on the British
parliamentary system, though there would have to be adjustments made
regarding provincial entities. He did not, however, want these latter to
wield the power that the US states did. There would be no war between
the provinces in his country. But there was French Canada. Well, French
Canada would have its own legal code, its language and its school
system. That ought to take care of any problems there. Oh, and Quebec
would always have a minimum of sixty-five seats in the House of
Commons, even if, like the Indians, they were bound to disappear as a
people.

Good, we will call it the Kingdom of Canada, said Mr. Macdonald.

Uh, well, no, said the Colonial Office. The USAmericans had
rejected a proposal to make George Washington a king, and it might be
a good idea to cool the king business.

Leonard Tilley, who was back as premier of New Brunswick, had an
idea. He had been reading the King James Bible and had come across a
passage in the Seventy-second Psalm, a prayer by David, son of Jesse,
asking God to see that his king be wise and powerful: "He shall have
dominion also from sea to sea, and from the river unto the ends of the
earth."

Well, that last part could refer to the mighty St. Lawrence, and the
last few words might make people think that the new nation resembled
its southern neighbour a little overmuch. But the founders of
Confederation liked "from sea to sea," and made that the official motto
of the new country. And they would name it the Dominion of Canada.

On July 1, 1867, the British North America Act was proclaimed. The
United Canadas joined Nova Scotia and New Brunswick in a union of
overseas British subjects.

11

GET RIEL

Louis Riel, 1865
(NATIONAL ARCHIVES OF CANADA/C-006688D)

Years passed.

Look, if they can say that in nineteenth-century novels, why can't I say it about nineteenth-century history? Henry James said that novels were based on history.

The years after the BNA Act legislation were years of nation building. If you like history, you will find a lot to enjoy in the last third of the nineteenth century. If you are the kind of person who thinks that ice hockey is exciting, you might wake up for a while during the Riel Rebellions.

Keep moving

Any prime minister would have to ride a big wave in the last third of the nineteenth century. In the 1800s the population of Europe increased more than it had in the previous *ten* centuries. It would have been even more dramatic if people had stayed home, but between 1870 and 1910 twenty-five million Europeans took off for the Americas. During the same period, machines were being invented every day, and there were mass migrations from countryside to cities to tend the new gadgets. Charles Darwin began to posit the principles of biological change. Karl Marx began to instruct workers that they could take responsibility for social change. Psychologists and other social scientists got in on the act. It would not be long until some bright soul invented the idea of "political science."

So in 1867 John A. Macdonald had to figure out how to go about constructing a new country along conservative lines in a dramatically changing era. He had always been wary of the rambunctious folks to the south, and now he was really worried: the US had bought Alaska from the Russians, and now they were busy with lawyers defining the Alaska border, creating a big southward-reaching panhandle of land on the coast.

Macdonald had been a shoo-in for prime minister in the September 1867 election, but he did not have an overwhelming mandate. George Brown had been defeated. All his Nova Scotians except Charles Tupper had been defeated. The Fathers of Confederation were feeling like deserted dads. When the Nova Scotia legislature sat in 1868 all they wanted to talk about was separation.

What could the Nova Scotia people do? Their argument had always been that they were British, not Canadian. But now the British were telling them that Confederation was their route. Oh no, thought the politicians, we are not happy with philosophical conundrums. What do you want, republicanism? they were asked. Heavens, no! Civil war? Unthinkable. Even Joseph Howe got the message. He stopped thumping for repeal and started demanding a better financial deal for his ex-colony.

The US and Nova Scotia were not Macdonald's only problems. He had to form a cabinet that would include men from lots of places and organizations that did not trust one another. Well, actually, the governor general had asked him to start working on his cabinet before July 1, assuming that the man who wrote most of the BNA Act would be its most logical developer. He chose seven Conservative ministers and six Reformers. Five ministers came from the province now called Ontario. Four came from Quebec. Two came from New Brunswick and two from Nova Scotia. Macdonald had to balance French speakers and English, Catholics and Protestants. Until he heard about a peculiar so-called government in Red River country, he thought he had the machine oiled. Time to take the rest of the day off and have a drink.

So Macdonald had to take care of two major problems. He had to keep the factions within the new country from bickering overmuch, and he had to do something about the West. With Alaska in its hands, the US was going to do everything it could to manifest its destiny. We already know that its radical poet Walt Whitman was expecting Canada to leap gratefully into US arms. Its most famous conservative poet knew which way the republican wind was blowing. At the end of the Civil War, James Russell Lowell wrote: "America lay asleep, like the princess of the fairy tale, enchanted by prosperity, but at the first fiery kiss of war the spell is broken, the blood tingles along her veins again, and she awakes conscious of her beauty and her sovereignty." If there was one thing Canada's prime minister was afraid of, it was blood tingling along the veins of this creature they were having the audacity to call "America." It was time to get some pink ink onto the map of the West.

For a decade and a half businessmen had been trying to organize some kind of communication between the Great Lakes and the West Coast. Roads, railways, telegraph systems, mail services, all came to naught as the men in bush outfits could not get financial backing from the men in banker's trousers. Meanwhile, the USAmericans were running mail through St. Paul, and the men who had become millionaire railroaders during the Civil War were now laying track across the West.

Canada said to Britain, would you please buy the West from the Hudson's Bay Company and help us keep on confederating? Not interested, said Britain, too expensive. We could see about making a bargain, said the HBC. Then the Colonial Office told everyone to shut up and announced the terms of the deal. They would not buy the West and hand it over to the Dominion, but they would lend the Dominion the money to buy it. The price would be 300,000 pounds, and the HBC would be able to hang on to a lot of very nice land around its posts and in the most arable countryside it hadn't bothered with yet. In April 1869 the British had possession of the enormous Rupert's Land to go along with the seemingly endless North West Territories. When all this was passed over to the new country, it would quadruple Canada's size.

Mixed reactions/réactions Métis

Gone were the days when the European countries could sail to the "New World" and fight for acreage. Now these North American countries would be vying for space. To some inhabitants of the West, that did not seem to be much of a difference.

The new situation was pretty confusing for local HBC storekeepers and horse wranglers and law keepers. If they had to call a cop, how far away was this cop? Who was going to stop the Yankees from selling their whisky to the Indians and mixed bloods?

The Natives and Métis were less confused. Around the old Red River Settlement, the Métis had been a recognizable distinct people for longer than anyone could remember. The ethnogenesis of the Métis is complex and shaky. Mixed-blood communities in the fur business formed the beginnings of some important cities—Sault Ste. Marie, Detroit, Chicago, Milwaukee, Winnipeg. When New France, after a century of tolerance, began to frown at the idea of European-American families, a lot of mixed-blood men went west into the interior of the continent. Called *bois-brûlé* or *chicot* in the Northwest, they began to worry when the people arriving from the Canadas starting talking about settlement—in English. Early in the nineteenth century HBC governors and English developers wrote letters home, describing this separate "tribe" of people who talked about their own country with their own flag. A lot of white racists could not be bothered noticing a difference between Indians and Métis. No wonder Louis Riel did not have much trouble making an alliance with Big Bear.

When the white racists, or to call them by their preferred name, the Ontarians, paid any attention at all to the Métis, they saw a mixture of Indian and French, two creatures that were going to be caught under an avalanche of white Protestants coming from the east or from across the Atlantic to fill the Prairies with farmers.

While the BNA Act was being haggled over, Louis David Riel was just a student. He was born in the Red River Settlement, but by 1865 he was in Montreal, being schooled as a priest and studying Napoleonic law. He was working in the USA when the act was passed, and a year later he was back in St. Boniface.

He had been educated in Lower Canada. He knew how the powerful English business people and Protestants felt about the country and who owned it. He knew that the Prairies were designated to be Old Macdonald's Farm. Macdonald must have heard that there was a people out there on the edge of the world who considered themselves to be in the centre. But Macdonald was an Ontarian. It was very hard for him to imagine a Canada that was not simply a much bigger Ontario. Riel knew this, too. His people spoke French and danced to fiddle music and followed the ancient bison. They were not French and they were not Cree. They were not a little problem inside a confederated Canada. They were the Palestinians of their valley.

When some white Protestant surveyors from Ontario showed up and said could you stand somewhere else, please, because we have some geography to do here, someone in moccasins stood on the chain. The people of the Red River valley were used to slender pieces of land that reached back from the river's bank. These foreigners from somewhere back East were trying to make squares in the dirt. Worse, as far as these strangers from back East were concerned, this dirt was unoccupied country.

Then John A. Macdonald sent Wandering Willy out to run things. This was William McDougall, who got his nickname because of his habit of jumping from one political faction to another. For the moment he was a Liberal member of Macdonald's cabinet. The prime minister sent him out to take over as lieutenant-governor of Rupert's Land, an enormous territory whose boundaries and physical features could only be imagined. Ironically, given Macdonald's feelings about the USA, he had to send Willy by way of St. Paul, and he heard of Wandering Willy's feckless adventures via USAmerican telegraph.

McDougall hung out in a luxurious St. Paul hotel until his sixty wagons of supplies were assembled for the ride north. Now it was snowing in the wind during the day and well below freezing at night. When the lieutenant-governor's party arrived at the forty-ninth parallel they were prevented from crossing by a small group of Métis men on horses. These gents figured that if the strangers from back East did not get to stand on Red River dirt and make some kind of highfalutin proclamation, it would still be Métis and Indian land.

Wandering Willy decided to spend the next little while in a log cabin in Pembina, North Dakota. All this Canadian nation building was of interest to the USAmericans, of course, and there were plenty of reporters hanging around in Pembina, sending comical dispatches back to Eastern US newspapers. Someone brought the papers to Macdonald, who was seen to slap his forehead with an open hand, then have a medicinal draught.

Then Wandering Willy performed one of the great heroic acts of Western Canada. One night there was a terrible blizzard, and thinking that a border is hard to defend in a blizzard, McDougall loaded up one of his carts with bottled spirits and British flags and loyal attendants, to drive his way north, somewhere across the international boundary, probably. There he got out and stood on the snow that was on the Rupert's Land soil, probably, and read the proclamation he had spent the past two days writing. It was all about the British queen and her generous plans for this new land. The wind was so loud that his attendants could not hear his words. They could hardly hold on to the snapping flags, and there was no question of standing at attention.

Then Wandering Willy headed back to Pembina. His men had a few celebratory drinks and wondered whether they had a chance of surviving their attachment to this noble fellow.

The real rebellion

It would appear, thought the leader of the Métis brotherhood, that these English did not learn anything at Seven Oaks. Riel was now secretary of a National Committee. On November 2, they took the HBC's Fort Garry and invited delegates from the Red River community to come there and create a nation that could stand up to the Eastern invaders. The official date for transfer of the huge HBC land to the Crown was supposed to be December 1. This was not going to happen. Riel drew up a list of rights and declared a provisional government. The Canadians would eventually be strong enough to fight their way into the country, but maybe two governments could sit down and talk about a more peaceful way of coming to terms.

Macdonald called Wandering Willy back to Canada and postponed the transfer. Things had got scary when a group of Canadians tried to start an armed rebellion against the Committee. Riel's men captured these guys and then let them go when things got quieter. John A. Macdonald sent a priest and Donald A. Smith, a big HBC honcho, to talk to Riel's people.

Smith persuaded Riel to hold a convention of Red River citizens and got him to arrange that half the forty delegates be English speaking. In late January 1870, this group okayed Riel's provisional government and set about arranging for ambassadors to go to Ottawa and negotiate Confederation. Macdonald's government was going to enter its third year as a peacemaker. The people of Red River received hints that they would be able to keep their land.

Then some heavy-drinking racists got into the act. A few of the former Fort Garry prisoners and some added riff-raff met in Portage la Prairie, waving guns and trying to arouse Protestant anger against the dark-skinned pretenders. One of the rabble was a surveyor from Ontario named Thomas Scott. Scott figured that he was doing Canada's work and was therefore a sign of the future. But Riel's constables grabbed the rowdy conspirators before they could start a firefight.

The provisional government of Assiniboia held courts martial, more to legitimize its rule than anything else. No one would have been executed for treason if Thomas Scott could have held his temper. According to police reports and later legend, the Orangeman was so incensed at being detained by people of an inferior race, loser's language and idolatrous religion that he screamed racist invective at the secretary and rushed at his throat.

He was executed by a firing squad on March 4.

So when the Red River delegates arrived in Ottawa, the Ontario police threw them into jail. John A. Macdonald, Father of Confederation, got them sprung and held some meetings with them. He was biding his time till his soldiers could make it to the Red River, after the snow had turned to mud and the mud had turned to dust. Riel knew which way the wind was blowing; he retired from history for a while.

So in the summer of 1870 Canada and Britain passed the Manitoba Act, making a little province out of the former Métis nation. Although the Ontario Orangemen fumed, Manitoba was to be a province in which both French and English would be legal languages, kids could go to Catholic schools and the Métis people would be guaranteed some land at least.

Getting from sea to sea

There must have been times when Prime Minister Macdonald wondered what in hell he had got himself into. No one even knew how wide this theoretical country was, or how far north it extended or whether anyone could point out Baffin Island on the map.

Macdonald had reason to look on the petitioners from British Columbia benignly. There was not much of a white population out there yet, and a lot of the whites were USAmericans who had arrived during the gold rush. The situation was pretty volatile. In 1859 there had been a little war fought over an English pig that got into a Yank garden on an HBC island. It was all a bit funny, but James Douglas was not laughing. He knew that there were many people, some of them newspaper people, who favoured morphing the colony into US Columbia. There were others who liked the idea of an independent country.

In 1870 some delegates from Victoria travelled east on a US train and went to see Father Macdonald. When they came back they had this news: Canada would assume the heavy BC debt, build docks and hospitals, invite six members of Parliament and three senators, and construct a $100 million railway between Ontario and the West Coast. In 1871 British Columbia became Canada's sixth province.

Macdonald walked among the winter snowbanks and the summer mosquitoes in Ottawa, and looked east and west, at all he had to hold together. He knew that it would not be easy, but he knew that it could be seen as simple. The West would be an immense farmland, the East would be a mighty industrial engine, and railways would join them, bringing wheat to the East and farm implements to the West. The Dominion Lands Act of 1872 said that any settler in the territories would be guaranteed a quarter section of land and a chance to acquire another quarter section cheaply after three years of homesteading.

But first the country had to stabilize the West. There was no telling how many Riels and Yankees were out there. Macdonald did not much like the US model of westward expansion, in which the army set up forts and rode out of them to kill Indians. He favoured a civilian force that could keep the Yankee whisky smugglers south of the line, and organize meetings between the Indians and the settlers. They should wear bright red coats that would stand out against the earth colours of the West. In 1873 the North West Mounted Police arrived on the plains. It is hard to imagine now, but the first three hundred were chosen for their breeding and social literacy. They may not have had as much education as Louis Riel had, but constables had bookshelves in those forts on the prairies.

Getting a police force across the country was a lot easier than following it with a railway. Macdonald and his tracks had a vociferous and stubborn opposition in the House. The new country, put together with so much labour and love, would collapse if the Tories put the taxpayers' dollars into a strip of steel leading to nowhere. Oh, the insults that crossed the august hall would have made a boilermaker blush—but not a company lawyer.

There have been ten thousand books written about Macdonald and the Canadian Pacific Railway and the Pacific Scandal. During the election campaign of 1872 there was a lot of shady money being passed from pocket to pocket. Macdonald had always been a genius at buying votes, but he did not know how to earn or save a dollar. It happened that there were a couple of big businessmen vying for a contract to build the long railway, and they paid every politician they could find.

Macdonald's Tories won a second term in 1872. Then allegations of bribes started flying out of newspapers and across the floor. My hands are clean, announced the man they called Old Tomorrow. Washed in alcohol, opined some of his foes. The Liberals (the new name for the Reformers) heard from a fellow who worked in a certain lawyer's office, this chap being the lawyer for a certain tycoon and would-be railroad nabob. It turned out that this fellow who worked for this lawyer had removed some papers from his boss's safe and had sold them to the Liberals for $5000. It was a bargain: among the papers was a telegram sent by John A. Macdonald to the would-be railway nabob a few days before the election. "I must have another ten thousand. Will be the last time calling. Do not fail me. Answer today."

One day Old Tomorrow read those very words as quoted in a story that appeared in the Montreal *Herald*. You will not be surprised to know that the *Herald* was a Grit newspaper.

During the fall session of 1873 he looked through a haze made up of equal parts pain and alcohol and watched his old friends drift away. The only encouragement for Confederation's dad that year was the entry of PEI into the club. That made seven. At the end of the year he offered his resignation to the governor general, Frederick Temple Blackwood, 1st Marquess of Dufferin and Ava. Lord Dufferin held his nose and offered the prime minister's job to the Liberal leader, Sandy Mackenzie, a Puritan and democrat and stonemason. The real power of the Liberals was held by the Ontario premier, Edward Blake, and George Brown. It looked as if the transcontinental railway was doomed.

Mackenzie called an election for 1874, and when the Tories could not face the idea of running anyone but Macdonald as leader, the Liberals just about cleaned the House.

The Liberals came to power just as Canada was feeling the effects of a worldwide depression. It would not be the last time this would happen. Obviously this was no time to be trying to finance mega-projects. Instead, Mackenzie sent his people to Washington to preach reciprocity. But the USAmericans did not see that reciprocity would give them an advantage, so they rejected the idea.

Liberalizing the country

Sandy Mackenzie, the self-made businessman, was a poster boy for Liberalism. He believed in laissez-faire economics and egalitarian politics. Like Macdonald, he was born in Scotland, but unlike his predecessor he was not enamoured of the British class system. He was the only Canadian prime minister before the 1920s to refuse a "Sir" in front of his name. He believed that history was a march toward democracy, and that a politician should act out of principle rather than opportunity. Obviously, if he was going to act on such beliefs he would soon wear out his welcome with the voters.

Mackenzie's government started passing a series of acts that would alter the relationship between government and the individual, with the intent of offering hope to the latter. Its first act was to provide the secret ballot for the next federal election. Only a coward would want to sneak away and hide his beliefs from his fellow man, sputtered Macdonald. Mackenzie followed up with the introduction of Hansard, as used in Britain, so that voters could keep track of what their honourable members were saying on the hill.

Then the Liberals introduced their bill to create a Supreme Court. Macdonald had twice introduced such a bill and had been turned down twice. Now he had to jump up and trash Mackenzie's Supreme Court idea. Of course he rather liked it, because it promoted the concept of federal rule over the provinces. His opponents liked it because it tended to promote Canada's independence from Britain. In one of the most confusing acts in Canadian history, Canada's Supreme Court was named the last-chance arena—except for the exceptions. The exceptions would still go to Britain.

While Macdonald quietly enjoyed British Columbia's threats to secede because they were not getting their railway, Mackenzie did what he thought he could afford—he encouraged small railway enterprises east or west, and he had the surveys done in case times got better and Canada could actually lay tracks across the prairies and over the mountains.

But the depression went on and on, and it is hard to be a prime minister during a depression. Sandy the Baptist stonemason decided that the best thing he could do was tell the truth to his countrymen and hope for the best. That did not cut any ice with the politicos in British Columbia, who were fighting, they said, for a railway or secession. All right: the economy, the Tories, the Westerners, the US and the railway nabobs were against him. At least he had the support of his own party. Nope. Now Edward Blake came after him. First Blake offered to take over the PM's job, saying that he would let Sandy have the public works ministry, the least popular position in the country. Then he went around Ontario waving his arms and frothing at the mouth and saying that Canada would be better off without British Columbia and the prime minister. When Macdonald heard about these rants, he rubbed his hands and smiled, looking forward to the next election.

Make that a double

John A. quit waiting for the fruit to drop into his lap and started shaking the tree. Remembering his triple vision of a few years back, he created something called the National Policy. What a clever phrase! It suggested two things: that unlike the incumbents, the Conservatives had a policy, and that unlike the incumbents, they were a national party with a view of a wide nation. Macdonald had seen the unification of Germany and the unification of Italy in the past decade, and he had never taken his eye off the Yanks. Blake's colourful insults of British Columbia ("a worthless sea of mountains") would suggest that the Ontario Liberals were regionalists. So the National Policy called for tariffs that would protect Eastern business, big immigration that would develop the West and a federally backed railway that would hook them together.

The parliamentary sessions of 1877 and 1878 could have been scripted by a demented satirist who had had too much vanilla to drink. Honourable members hurled insults and books across the room at each other. Legislators lay asleep on their desks and the floor. Dressed-up gents hooked arms and did ribald dances while others bellowed rude songs. Once in a while John A. Macdonald had to be restrained from hurtling across the room and throwing his bony body upon a Liberal loudmouth. Sandy Mackenzie, the honest, polite Baptist, looked like a man who should have been in bed. Still, he felt that he had served the electorate better and more honestly than his predecessor had, and when he lost the election of 1878, he could hardly believe that Canadians would rather have a colourful old scoundrel than an even-handed and thrifty democrat lead them into the eighties.

Now that Canada's natural government was back in power, Macdonald asked England to let Governor General Dufferin stay awhile, even though he was apparently angling for a step up to India. Dufferin was a railway man and, more important, a British-and-Canadian railway man. The Liberals would keep on saying that Canada wouldn't go broke if we just let little lines in the West hook up with the new Great Northern Railroad just below the line. A British subject I was born, Macdonald would start. Yes, we know, his opponents would interpose.

Macdonald listened to the Grand Trunk Railway bid. This was a Toronto outfit, but their idea was to pass through the big hub of Chicago and along the south shore of Lake Superior. Charles Tupper countered that the line should start by heading to Hudson Bay. There is not a square foot of usable land between Ottawa and Hudson Bay, bellowed Edward Blake. Macdonald decided to listen to the bid of the Canadian Pacific Railway Company, a syndicate representing some very rich and very powerful Canadian capitalists, including James J. Hill, a Canadian who had been building railroads in the US, George Stephen, who ran the Bank of Montreal, and Donald Smith, who ran the Hudson's Bay Company. Isn't it funny the way the same names keep popping up when there is a dollar to be looked over?

We remember that two hundred years earlier the Hudson's Bay Company had been given carte blanche over a significant percentage of the globe's surface. Now another private company was going to get a wondrous deal, this time from the Canadian government. In February 1881, the Tories dodged the missiles hurled across the House and passed the CPR Act. There were already about 750 miles of track laid under Mackenzie's system, and the CPR took possession. They also got $25 million (this was late in the nineteenth century, when a dollar could buy a day's work in some places). For the sake of symmetry, perhaps, they also got twenty-five million acres of good farmland on the prairies, and they would not have to pay taxes on it for twenty years. (Lord Jesus, what about us? asked a few families living in sod huts and trying to make wheat grow.) And while taxes and tariffs were going up for most companies, the CPR would pay neither on their equipment and supplies. The government also prohibited any railway building between the CPR and the forty-ninth parallel.

In exchange the CPR would reach the West Coast by 1891.

The first year went pretty slowly. But in 1882 the company hired a new man to run things. This was a flamboyant fellow named William Cornelius Van Horne, who was a rail veteran, though just thirty-nine years old. The only problem was that he was a USAmerican. Macdonald had a drink and said, all right, as long as he knows about the National Policy. By 1888 Van Horne would be president of the company. By 1894 he was Sir William Cornelius Van Horne, and he lived in a magnificent stone mansion on stone mansion row in Montreal. The Château Clique was still around, though the source of the money and power had shifted.

The steel was going down fast, but the money was running out faster. The story of the CPR financing is scary and tiresome. The depression was taking another dip, shares were just not selling and the Liberals were talking about long lines of rust on the Western plains. Worst of all, the British did not care a fig about Macdonald's dream. They were not interested in promoting emigration, and they had no money for a railway to nowhere. Macdonald had to lay the future of his party and his country on the line. He put another $5 million into the pot, but got a mortgage just in case.

If you can afford to ride the train from Vancouver to Montreal, you will be deeply impressed by the country you pass through, the Fraser Canyon, the Rockies, the never-ending forest of short trees in Northern Ontario. Over and over you will say, "How the hell did they do it?" You will look down at a distant river at the bottom of a frightening gorge and think for a few seconds about the underpaid homesick Chinese immigrants who fell down there, holding a satchel of dynamite.

Hon. Donald A. Smith driving the last spike to complete
the Canadian Pacific Railway, Nov. 7, 1885
(NATIONAL ARCHIVES OF CANADA/C-003693)

You cannot see any of those people in the most famous photograph in Canadian history. It was taken November 7, 1885, at an unpopulated spot named Craigellachie after some high rock in Scotland, where Donald Smith (soon to be Lord Strathcona) had been a boy. Smith and other top-hatted CPR officials had taken a train from Montreal to be here in Eagle Pass, west of the continental divide, to drive the last spike, a tradition that had started on the US railroads west. In the picture Smith holds a big gandy dancer's hammer as if he knew what it was, while other bearded white men look on, well-dressed toffs in the foreground, railway workers way in the back. No one made any speeches or played any trumpets. The Montrealers got on the train and continued to Port Moody on the coast. With the camera folded and taken away, the Chinese workers were allowed back to tidy up. A few Shuswap people looked on from their trapline. They were never going to show up on Sherbrooke Street.

GUNS ON THE PRAIRIES

Gabriel Dumont, Red River
(GLENBOW ARCHIVES/NA 1063-1)

It was lucky for the prime minister that the CPR was up and running by 1885. The second Riel Rebellion had started in 1884. Many people call this one the North West Rebellion, to point out that Riel was just one of the players, that this was a Native resistance, not strictly a Métis one. Riel and his great Métis strategist, Gabriel Dumont, were allies of the legendary Indian chiefs Poundmaker and Big Bear and Piapot.

During the seventies Louis Riel would just not go away. Macdonald sincerely wished that there were no such person. The main problem was that Riel had become a major hero in Quebec. He was the champion of French-Canadian rights on the Prairies. In Ontario, just to show that

Quebec troublemakers were right, the Orangemen were calling for the hanging of the murderer of Thomas Scott. It did not matter that Scott had been a bigoted, foul-mouthed drunken lout; he had been assassinated by a ragtag bunch that resulted from the sexual congress of two inferior races.

Macdonald was feeling the fires that would threaten to scorch every prime minister from now on—the heat provided by friction between Quebec French and Ontario English.

Maybe the Orangemen would be mollified if the actual shooter of Scott were punished. Ambroise Lépine was arrested and tried and sentenced to death. Now the Quebec press and intellectuals had to be mollified. Lépine's sentence was reduced to two years.

Now if Riel would just cool it. But oh, no: he had to bring his cause right into Macdonald's house. In 1873 his friends persuaded him to run in a federal by-election. In the 1874 election he was, of course, returned. Imagine how the Central Canadians felt when their disruption in the West, Canada's most wanted outlaw, was sent by his people to Parliament! He went to Ottawa and signed the registry as the member from Provencher, but he never sat in the Commons. The leader of the Orangemen, Mackenzie Bowell from Belleville, introduced a bill to have the Western Father of Confederation prevented from representing his constituency.

Now what could Macdonald do? In Quebec they were saying that his party had subverted the parliamentary rules of democracy and decency. Macdonald thought that he would offer a great deal. He would give utter amnesty to both Riel and Lépine if they would stay out of the country for five years.

But before the PM could do so, Louis Riel became Louis La Rochelle, a patient at a mental hospital in Beauport, just outside Quebec City. From now on friends of Louis David Riel would find a new rebel. His campaign had turned religious. He would write a large prophecy that does not get studied in Canadian universities the way that Walt Whitman's prophecy gets studied in US universities. Riel saw North America, especially the Canadian half of it, as the ground for an entirely new kind of land, one in which all religions, European, Asian and North American, would be explicitly enfranchised, where there would be land grants for all minority communities. Crazy, they said. When he left the asylum, he went to the USA, first to New York State, then to the West, becoming a schoolteacher in Montana. During his time there he married Marguerite Monet and became a US citizen.

In those days it was common for families to move back and forth across the border. Most people on the Prairies had family members in both countries. In 1884 the Riels moved north.

Batoche

When the province of Manitoba was created out of the former Métis homeland, a lot of the people moved west to join the Métis who already lived along the Saskatchewan River. All during the seventies the Canadian government had been signing treaties with the Native people, which meant that the Natives would give up their traditional hunting grounds and learn to be farmers. There were also white pioneers living dirt poor in the territory. The bison were getting pretty scarce because they were being massacred before they could wander north to Canada. Once in a while women had to make soup out of thistles.

But there were sixty thousand people in the territory, more than there were in the province of Manitoba or the province of British Columbia. Poundmaker knew that in the fur trade white people tried to turn his Blackfeet against the Cree and Sioux, and he spent a lot of time at meetings that would keep peace. He suffered greatly when he saw starving children in his camp. Gabriel Dumont, the Métis leader, was also a fine treaty maker. He had his people at peace with the Indian people and acted as liaison between Indian and white settlers. He was well qualified for the task, speaking English and French and all the Native languages in the region. In 1875 he had become leader and spokesman of a Métis commune that was trying to learn how to survive as farmers now that the bison were lying on the ground, robbed of their skins. He lived in Batoche, a Métis village on the South Saskatchewan, near Prince Albert. In 1884 a new church went up at Batoche, St-Antoine de Padoue. The Church in Quebec did not like Riel, but in Batoche the church was a Métis church.

Dumont would be a powerful organizer and spokesman for the Métis. William Henry Jackson, a young University of Toronto grad, lived in Prince Albert, where he acted as secretary for the Settlers' Union, the white people who were also protesting conditions in the territory. He insisted that a province be created west of Manitoba. He said that the Easterners would try to drive a wedge between the white settlers and the Métis, just as their forerunners had tried to make the Indian nations distrustful of one another.

Dumont and Jackson wrote to Louis Riel in Montana and invited him to the territory. Riel came north with his family, and said that he would be pleased to help the so-called North-West Agitators, but that he would also have to include the disaffected Indians. In July 1884 Riel met with Big Bear at Jackson's house. One is tempted to call it the most important meeting in the history of Western Canada. On arriving in Canada in the spring, Riel had made sure that he had the support of the Scotch Métis as well as the French Métis. He would now be the charismatic spokesman for nearly all the people who occupied the Saskatchewan valley.

Riel set up headquarters at Batoche, and during the second half of 1884 he travelled the country, making speeches, gathering complaints and preparing a petition to send to Ottawa. In December John A. Tory read the petition, and began to get the notion that Westerners were unhappy with the way they were treated and would like to have a province so that they could resist the federal government.

Macdonald was worried that Louis Riel would become a rebellious hero across the country. Ottawa was already getting threats of secession from the farmers' union in Manitoba and depression-influenced petitions from the Maritimes. With the Church taking an ultra-conservative position in Quebec, unhappy habitants were talking about Riel as their national leader. If the Conservative Party were to lose Quebec, it could not be sustained by the Orangemen of Ontario.

Prairie crops failed again in 1884. Farmers cut the young wheat and fed it to their starving animals. Conditions were worse in the Prince Albert–Batoche region than they were anywhere.

Never before had so many diverse peoples come together to address a Canadian government. The petition contained Riel's history of federal mistreatment of the Métis fifteen years earlier. Then it went on to demand more enlightened treatment of the Indians, monetary assistance for the Métis, provincial government and representation in the federal government, a northern railway and tariff relief for the whites.

The federal government acknowledged receipt of the petition and forwarded a copy to the Colonial Office. Things promised to go slowly, but the people of the Saskatchewan valley began to entertain hope that their political and economic conditions might strike the hearts of the shiny-shoed men back East.

It was not that Riel was universally adored by the white people of the West. Some hated him because he spoke French; some looked down on him because he had Indian blood; some opposed his leadership because he was a USAmerican; some maintained that he was insane. His chief enemies were the priests. The Church was afraid that its adherents, especially the Métis people, were going to look to the "Prophet of the New World" as their leader rather than kowtowing to the pope's emissaries. The clergy joined the Tory newspapers and the lieutenant-governor in trying to have Riel hustled back across the border.

Riel put it to the people. He held meetings with French Métis, Scotch Métis, Indians and some white settlers. He suggested that having helped create a petition, he was now desirous of going back south. All the groups pleaded with him to stay. He stayed. He waited for the helping hand of Ottawa. Finally he decided that he could get provincehood for Saskatchewan as he had got it for Manitoba. On March 19, at the church in Batoche, Riel declared a provisional government.

There were some major differences, however, between the Saskatchewan River in 1885 and the Red River in 1869. Riel himself was now seeing religious visions as well as political ones. He was conducting a crusade, trying to create a new Eden to be populated by Protestants,

Catholics and Jews. When he asked his Blackfoot allies to assault Fort Battleford, he ended his dispatch, "Whatever you do, do for the love of God. Under the protection of Jesus Christ, the Blessed Virgin, St. Joseph and St. John the Baptist, and be certain that faith works wonders." His theatre of war was different as well. In 1869 he had declared a provisional government on land that was not yet part of Canada, that was almost unreachable from Canada and that had no army or police patrolling it. Now he was acting inside a territory belonging to Macdonald's country. The North West Mounted Police had been in the vicinity for two years. And there was a brand new railroad that could bring troops to the Prairies *tout de suite*.

The NWMP were thin on the ground, of course, and they had unhappy Indians to face as well as citizens of this new breakaway nation. Poundmaker, the magnificent Stoney who had become a Blackfoot leader, rode into Battleford and ransacked the Hudson's Bay store. Then for a month the white soldiers barricaded themselves in their barracks while the Indians enjoyed their new town. Meanwhile, there was Indian trouble at Frog Lake, a little village near Fort Pitt. Big Bear's starving people had shivered through a Saskatchewan winter in torn clothing. There

Big Bear, Cree chief
(NATIONAL ARCHIVES
OF CANADA/C-1873)

was no wild game about. The territorial agents told them that they would get groceries for hard labour. Big Bear's Cree people spent some of their grocery money on hunting ammunition. Now some of the radicals slipped out of their chief's control and massacred nine people at Frog Lake. Big Bear pleaded for an end to killing. At Battleford,

Poundmaker instructed his soldiers not to shoot the enemy troops when they escaped the barracks.

When the whole thing was over, Poundmaker and Big Bear were thrown into jail for treason.

Like Big Bear and Poundmaker, Louis Riel tried to tell his defence corps to go easy on the invaders. For Riel and Dumont the most famous encounter took place at Duck Lake, a little town on the river. On March 26, 1885, a group of Mounties under L. N. F. Crozier, the most famous Mountie in the territory, were chased away by Dumont and his snipers. The Mounties came back with a hundred civilian volunteers, and a fire-fight broke out. Dumont's defenders pinned the enemy down, but Louis David Riel told him to let them retreat.

For the next two months the Westerners won skirmishes here and there, but the National Policy was coming. By May Gen. Frederick Middleton had 800 determined Protestant volunteers on a CPR train that was headed for the Saskatchewan territory. By the time these troops had marched to Batoche, there were 175 defenders waiting for them, and by the time the siege had wound down, they were firing nails and stones at the Easterners. Dumont's white rebels had left him before this. The battle was clearly between white men from Ontario and mixed-blood people who lived here.

In the final confusion, Gabriel Dumont escaped to the United States, but the prophet David Riel, holding a wooden cross in his hand, prayed while the Canadian boys pushed him toward his fate.

Regina

On July 6 the man who was not permitted to take his seat in the House of Commons was charged with treason. On July 20 the trial began in Regina, where the federal government conducted its territorial business. Gabriel Dumont wanted to ride north with a squadron of Métis commandos and rescue his government's leader, but in the city named for a white queen, there were hundreds of guards waiting for a chance to shoot at someone darker than themselves. Riel's lawyer wanted to plead insanity, but Riel did not want his visions thus characterized.

Meanwhile, General Middleton was riding around the Northwest, jailing the Indians he was most afraid of, and sealing the others inside their reserves. There is nothing to eat on this land, they told him. Try harder, he replied.

In Regina the trial of Louis Riel was conducted in English, of course. Riel gave two strong speeches in that language, in which he stated his hope and belief that in the future he would be regarded as "more than the leader of the half-breeds." The jury found him guilty of treason but asked for clemency. Riel was a symbolic figure now, and he filled the doorway to whatever future this country would see—a country with French and English speakers, an East and a West, Protestants and Catholics, white people and non-white people. The white Protestants owned an awful lot of Canada's newspapers. In May the Toronto *News* had offered an editorial that encapsulated the intellectual and ethical argument of the time: "Strangle Riel with the French flag! That is the only use that rag can have in this country."

Riel's condemnation was appealed twice, to no avail. But his execution was postponed while some doctors from Ontario tested his sanity. Two said that he was sane. The comments made by the third doctor disappeared from the official report. Well, if you check the trial of Louis Riel in detail you will find a great number of snags that would have stopped the procedure had it happened in a calmer time. Even the prime minister was excitable. When asked whether he might spare his rival's life to keep peace in the fragile nation, Macdonald reasoned, "He shall hang though every dog in Quebec bark in his favour."

When the prime minister was not referring to French Canadians as animals, he said that their sanctification of Riel would fade as they took up a new cause, such flighty creatures were the French Catholics. The Métis out West, too. When it was suggested that he might solve his problems there with munificence rather than munitions, he said that if you gave anything to the mixed bloods they would "drink it or waste it."

This from a man who had consumed a great lake of alcohol and had to have his financial condition rescued by party faithful.

On November 16, 1885, Louis Riel was hanged. Sixteen of his Métis companions received jail sentences. Big Bear and Poundmaker, tired of being peacekeepers, were sent to jail. Eleven Indian men were sentenced to death, and eight of them were hanged. Remember W. H. Jackson, the white rebel settler? He was tried for complicity with Riel's uprising but was discharged.

The Métis people were pretty well crushed. From now on the Canadian government did not have to worry about them, as waves of immigrants and land speculators travelled westward on the iron horse.

Louis Riel's body was buried in the cold winter ground in front of the cathedral in St. Boniface. His name would be kept alive for at least another century, as the nationalists in Quebec treated him as a martyred saint, and the writers and composers and painters of the whole country seized upon his life, rebellion and trial for artistic material.

The country itself would be reshaped, as the Conservatives, who had until the 1880s depended on Quebec for a base of power, lost that province. The Liberal Party had a young leader there, a man named Wilfrid Laurier, who said that if he had been brought up beside the Saskatchewan River he would have defended his home against Middleton's army.

Spiked

The last spike had been fumbled into the high ground of Eastern British Columbia nine days before the latest Father of Confederation was dropped through the trap door in Regina. The National Policy had triumphed, and now everyone was jumping on board the bandwagon and the train. Financiers in England finally saw the promise of a great dominion stretching from sea to sea. Parliament no longer clawed at Macdonald's dream. In the summer of 1886 the seventy-year-old prime minister and his wife took a two-month trip by train to the West Coast. Through the Rockies and down the Fraser canyon they rode up front on the cowcatcher. In Victoria, the prime minister visited for the first time the riding he had represented after being defeated in Kingston in 1878.

For years and years John A. Macdonald had been on his deathbed. Every once in a while he would disappear, sometimes to the US, to recover from a plethora of nineteenth-century disorders. At most of his fundraising meetings someone would rise up in the back of the room and bellow, "You'll never die, John A.!" And by golly, that appeared to be true. Furthermore, by the time that he came to wage his last campaign he was in many places identified with his party and his party was identified with his country. The cause of Confederation had arisen from the Upper Canada Conservatives, and over a quarter of a century Macdonald gathered the great expansive figures to his cause, leaving the Liberals to run the provinces and try to hold back progress. But he would never get a Quebec lieutenant to equal George-Étienne Cartier, who had died in 1873.

The party was supported by big business in Ontario and the conservative Church in Quebec. The biggest threat to these pillars had been thwarted in the defeat of the upstarts in Saskatchewan. But when Old Macdonald offered up his final ee-aye-ee-aye-oh in the 1891 election, he knew that he would not be around at the next one, and he was worried that his party would not, either. His opponent was Wilfrid Laurier, a man born the year that the Canadas were united. Laurier had been going around preaching "commercial union" with the US. When Macdonald heard that phrase he knew that it meant becoming a supplier to the US user. For the last five years of his life, all Macdonald's speeches were about saving Canadian sovereignty. In his seventh campaign since Confederation, he did not have much in the way of particulars to offer his wide nation. He attired himself in the Union Jack and told the crowds that the Liberals were going to sell the country out from under them.

He won by the slimmest majority he had ever experienced. Wilfrid Laurier was a handsome Opposition leader. His speech tinkled like silver on glass. He would be prime minister one day—everyone knew that. But in the 1891 campaign the Tory banners proclaimed, "The Old Man, the Old Flag, and the Old Policy." This was before all politicians thought that you had to be in support of New something.

On March 5, Macdonald won his election. On June 6, he died.

On his deathbed he whispered to his best young cabinet minister, John Thompson, of the justice department, "Do everything within your power to prevent Abbott's becoming prime minister."

Hello, goodbye

John J. C. Abbott, a prominent lawyer from Quebec, succeeded Macdonald as prime minister. In the 1890s Canada had six prime ministers. If you go around asking your friends who those six prime ministers were, I'll bet that you won't find anyone who can tell you. Tell them they don't have to be in the right order.

In 1891 the Tories were having a hell of a time finding someone who wanted to take over the top job. Anyone who did it would look like small droppings after the Old Man. And who wanted to be captain of a ship that was sailing toward a waterfall? So the party went to the Senate and persuaded Abbott to handle the job till they could find a leader. Abbott hated politics and had been a politician all his long life. Now he was seventy years old. The trouble was that so was everyone else. The most logical choice was Father of Confederation Charles Tupper, but Tupper was high commissioner in London, the top ambassadorial job going, and he liked the life of ease in that great city.

So Abbott snoozed in the Senate while the justice minister, young John Thompson from Nova Scotia, did the dirty work in the Lower House.

Then rose the constitutional hassle that would be avoided as much as possible by the PMs of the nineties. In 1870 the Manitoba Act had said that there would always be Catholic schools in the province and that no one could pass a law against them, ever. Now two decades later the Protestants in Manitoba were trying to do just that. In 1890 a transplanted Irish Protestant from Ontario, Clifford Sifton, led the battle against French and Catholicism on the Prairies. He was the anti-Riel.

He was also the attorney general of a Liberal government. He passed a provincial law against French and Catholicism. The bishops in Manitoba and Quebec got angry, of course, and Macdonald spent the rest of his life trying to support his legislation. He was not a French speaker, and he thought that people who were were lesser folk in some ways, but he was more liberal than most Protestant liberals in 1891.

The Privy Council of Britain ruled in favour of Manitoba but said that the Canadian government could reinstall separate schools if it wanted to go through the legislative process. Edward Blake smiled serenely. Wilfrid Laurier smiled too, making sure that this smile was not seen in Quebec. Clifford Sifton rode around on his show horse, announcing that provincial rights had been upheld.

Prime Minister Abbott said that now he had had enough. The party had to come up with a successor. This time they chose John Sparrow Thompson, the attorney general, who was aghast at the racist laws of those Westerners. All he wanted to be was a judge, but he knew that if he did not take the party's top job some old goat with a tired brain was going to sit in the PM's chair and let the Liberals take apart all Macdonald's hard work. He was too nice a person to be in federal politics at all, but in November of 1892 his wife, Annie, talked him into saving the country.

Now the Manitoba schools question belonged to Johnny Thompson, the first Catholic prime minister. He had grown up in a family of Protestants who supported Joseph Howe, and converted to Catholicism and federalism. He knew the hearts on both sides. He found himself in the middle, between the feds and the provincials, between the Quebeckers and the Orangemen, between Westerners and Easterners, and between Canadian autonomy and imperial policy. Whatever he did about the Manitoba schools question would have him in deep trouble with at least half the country.

He decided to postpone the Manitoba schools question.

The USAmericans came along with something to divert everyone's attention. Having bought Alaska at rock-bottom prices, they decided that every seal in the North Atlantic belonged to them. The British and Canadians countered that international waters started three miles off the

Alaska coast. Now, it so happened that US fishermen were hauling in codfish well within three miles of the Nova Scotia coast, so what did they care about any three-mile limit? The fact is, they suggested, that the whole shebang was going to be part of the USA pretty soon. So as early as 1886 they had started seizing Canadian and British ships in the open Pacific and jailing their crews. The Brits sent a note from time to time. The USA said, in effect, wanna fight?

Fortunately, in the spring of 1893, the US had been induced to put the case before some foreigners, and meetings were held in Paris. To their disbelief, the USAmericans were told that the foreigners—Italians, Swedes, French, Norwegians—did not agree that the US owned the ocean the pope once granted to Spain.

One of the Canadian delegates at Quai d'Orsay was the Canadian prime minister. There were two things that John Thompson really liked: Europe and food. He worked really hard at the negotiations, but he also had to consume eight-course French meals. When the US delegate presented some old documents showing that the British had ceded the Pacific seal trade to the Russians, and it was proven that the documents were forgeries manufactured in the USA, every vote at the meeting except the two US ones went against the US position. The US would have to stop grabbing British and Canadian ships.

Five-foot-seven Thompson was packing on the pounds. The British brought him and his wife over to smoky London to offer their thanks. The prime minister really liked the chops and sausages glistening in the grill rooms. He had his clothes taken out at the seams when he got back to Canada, where his popularity seemed to be high, perhaps because the people did not know him. He travelled Ontario, making speeches, getting himself ready for the election he would call in 1895 or 1896. Whenever anyone asked him about the Manitoba schools question he would say that he could not discuss it because it was before the courts. It had been before the courts for four years. Thompson hoped that he could keep it there for another two or three.

He would be fifty-one years old during the election campaign. Maybe politics was not such a bad life. He owed it to the country to give it a try, and he began to feel that maybe the Conservatives could hang on till the new century, after all. They sure liked him in England; he became only the fourth colonial to be named to the Privy Council. In late 1894 he decided to visit Europe again. The ostensible reason was the ceremony to induct him into the Privy Council. But he also wanted a few more of those French dinners and English chops. At Windsor Castle, while the queen was talking her imperial dinner talk, the Canadian prime minister died at his plate.

Bring them on

Okay, maybe now Charles Tupper would come home and lead the party. No, the old man had never enjoyed anything as much as he enjoyed being Canada's ambassador to England. The soft chairs, the good sherry, the dressing up every night.

So the caretaker's job now went to the man who was appointed deputy prime minister while Thompson was away. For some strange reason this was the enigmatic Orangeman Mackenzie Bowell. Bowell was a skinny little guy who had been getting elected in Belleville since 1867. John Thompson had sent him to the Senate and made him the first ever minister of trade and commerce, but Bowell's main job was to bring in the right-wing Orangeman vote to balance any sign that the Tories were soft on Quebec.

Bowell was a bad-tempered little egotist with fewer brains than he thought he had. No wonder he had been able to hold on to his seat since Confederation. Still, it was a surprise to just about everyone when the governor general made him the prime minister of Canada in December 1894. He was just in time to handle the Privy Council's decision that the federal government *could* overturn the Manitoba law that denied funding for French schools. He could have followed the lead of his predecessors and pretended that he was about to do something. But just as he fooled everyone by becoming PM, he fooled everyone by demanding that Manitoba reinstall the French Catholic schools. People stood around with their mouths open—the first federal politician to side with the Catholics in Manitoba was the famous Orangeman from Belleville!

The skinny little guy sat in the Senate while the House of Commons became a loony bin once again. But now his party was staging its own internal gang war. Quebec representatives were threatening to bolt the party if the legislation was not implemented. Rednecks in Ontario seats threatened to bolt if it was. Laurier was having a similar problem over in the Liberal Party, but at least he was just in Opposition. His strategy was to keep quiet and, if pressed, come out in favour of both Dominion and provincial rights.

Now the Manitobans decided to make it extra hot for the PM. Why was it always Manitoba that had to be making trouble for the feds? The Manitoba Liberals held a snap election and won it on a promise to fight Ottawa on French schools. This really got the little PM's back up. He took his bill to cabinet for polishing. Half his cabinet stood up and said they were out of there if he persisted. But the party's father, Macdonald, had always insisted on federal power. Too bad—without a cabinet the senator was not going to win anything in the Commons. His party offered him a deal: he could stay on as figurehead PM while Tupper ran the show in the House. Then when the election was called in the spring, he would step down and Tupper would lead the party to glory.

"Nest of traitors!" he said about his cabinet and went back to the Senate, where he repeated that phrase over and over till he died ten years later.

Okay, now Charles Tupper, the bullheaded old enemy of Joseph Howe, finally came home from his cushy digs in London, at the request of the dissident ministers. All his life the old country doctor had been the most faithful of party men. But it was not likely that he would rescue the Tories from the brink. Rather, he would make a noble figurehead on a ship that was going to sink ass-first into the worldwide depression.

He could have snoozed and posed for photographs, this bullheaded grand old man. He could have let the Manitoba schools question ride until after the election. But he had pushed Confederation down the gullets of recalcitrant Maritimers. He forced a second reading of the bill that would reintroduce Catholic school funding in Manitoba. Now the Liberal leader had to rise up in opposition. So the old Baptist who could not manage a real French sentence championed the French Catholics, and the bilingual Quebecker stood up against the ultramontane clerics and the Rielistes. Laurier did not think that his stance would lose him the coming election—he figured that the French Canadians would vote him in just to see a French-Canadian prime minister.

Tupper kept the House open long and late, and told old Tories with weak bladders to hold it, while the Liberals argued for provincial rights. But time ran out on him. He had to call the 1896 election with the Manitoba schools question unanswered. He would just have to surprise everyone and win the election and save those little Manitoba kids.

But though he won his own down East seat in 1896, and though he took most of the seats in Manitoba, he lost Quebec and Ontario to the Liberals. The Conservatives had made a country, but they were not ready for the twentieth century. Charles Tupper was the last Canadian prime minister to have been born in England. He was the most famous and respected old man in the country. But the Liberals were back, and a lot of them were speaking French.

A CENTURY GOING WEST

13

Pioneers of the Qu'Appelle Valley, 1885
(ARCHIVES OF SASKATCHEWAN/NA-2145)

Locomotives made their appearance in more and more mill towns and metropolises. Soon there would be men in balloons over Toronto. In England there was talk that working men would be voting for Members of Parliament, and they might even get their own political party. The streets of Ottawa were being paved. As a new century approached there was a general fascination with the new. The artists and poets of Canada, however, still loved canoes and paddles and Indian princesses.

There is a poet that professors of Canadian literature like to force on their students, especially in older universities around Ontario, one Isabella Valancy Crawford, who self-published her only book of poems in 1884, just before the Liberals took over the country. The book contains the poem that those professors call her masterwork, "Malcolm's Katie." It is full of wigwams and wampum and moccasins. Its language is made of poetic strivings that feature the excesses of the worst poetry of a hundred years earlier. A tree is "the mossy king of all the woody tribes," and soon it is to fall to the rapacious blades of unstoppable immigration, "the quick rush of panting, human waves."

Wagons westward

At the end of the nineteenth century there was indeed a rush of immigration to Canada, and especially the West. The USA was pretty well filled up, and now the only available land was on the Canadian plains. In the fifteen years of Laurier's government, the population of the West would grow exponentially. Luckily for Laurier, the world economy picked up nicely just as he arrived. Being a subtle politician, he took credit. At the same time, he refashioned the Liberal Party. It had traditionally been made up of reformers and continentalists, but now it came to resemble the Tories, as Laurier continued the policies of Old Tomorrow. Young Today raised tariffs and built railways.

He did remain different in one sense. Macdonald and his party had from the beginning envisioned a strong federal government with some bothersome responsibilities left to the member provinces. Laurier and the Liberals leaned more toward provincial rights and the notion of the federal government as a convenience for the united provinces. One could point out that Laurier was not a designer of the BNA Act, and therefore did not have the reverence for it that Macdonald and Tupper had. For example, Article 93: Education. Article 93 is very hard to read. I think that a lawyer might even find it hard to read. Try it sometime. It starts by saying that the provincial legislatures "may exclusively make Laws in relation to Education," subject to four provisions. Mainly the provisions protect denominational schools at the time of Union. When Manitoba came into the Union, there were separate schools because there was a large French-speaking population. Now there was a small

French-speaking minority, and some of the non-French wanted to make it even smaller.

The fourth provision of Article 93 says that the governor general can cause remedial legislation if the province passes an anti-minority law.

Wilfrid Laurier was in a dilemma. He knew that his party favoured the Manitoba law. He also knew that his fellow French-speaking Catholics favoured the denominational schools. Further, he knew in his conscience that the BNA Act at least *allowed* protection of the French schools. For the rest of his life he would describe his fear that Canada's politics would be fought on sectarian lines. But in the matter of the Manitoba Schools Act, he contributed to the process. He effected what he called a compromise, but that pretty well added up to a victory for the people who wanted to make sure that Canada did not become a bicultural country all the way across. This was a "compromise" that would turn out to be one of the most important national decisions ever made in this country.

Laurier got the federal and provincial governments to discuss the matter, and what they came up with essentially restricted denominational schools to Quebec and New Brunswick. In a classic tactic made to appear liberal and democratic, it was decided that any religion could be taught—in short periods after the end of the school day, and that in predominantly French-speaking parts of Manitoba there could be teachers who spoke French as long as they could speak English as well.

Then, his government having ensured that the West would be English speaking, Interior Minister Clifford Sifton started herding immigrants onto the prairies. He sent advertisements to Europe and the United States, looking especially for the right kind of immigrants, Northern and Western Europeans and white Protestant USAmericans. Over the nineteenth century a lot of Canadians had moved south, and now they were urged to come back and pick up a good deal in the West. Canadian agents went overseas and gave expense-paid trips to Western Canada to foreign journalists. The Canadian government would do a similar service to the Canadian arts a century later, paying foreign students to do their post-graduate work on Margaret Laurence or Glenn Gould.

Collective immigration had been going on since the 1870s, depositing pockets of non-English society on the prairies. Sifton did not mind as long as they were not French speakers. First seventy-five hundred Mennonites, persecuted in Russia, came and employed their Siberian skills. Then the Icelanders came and set up farming and fishing communities around the big lakes of Manitoba. They were followed shortly by Swedish and Finnish and Norwegian communities. Jewish refugees from Russia settled in Manitoba and Saskatchewan. Canada offered free homestead land, and then the CPR started selling its land cheaply. My orphaned immigrant grandfather, Jabez Harry Bowering, put a down payment on a quarter section of CPR land in 1892, though he was making only $50 a year.

But as an English boy he was an exception. Clifford Sifton knew that the British Isles were getting to be out of emigrant material, and though they had been sturdy enough to populate the Maritimes and Ontario, it might take a tougher kind to handle the hard life on the Prairies. So he looked to the Slavs and other subject peoples of the Russian and Hapsburg empires. By the time that the Tories got back into power in 1911, Canada's ethnic makeup had changed greatly: in addition to the products of the British Isles and France, the future bread basket would be home to the languages and foods and newspapers of Ukrainians, Slovaks, Serbs, Hungarians, Poles, Czechs, Croats and Romanians.

In the late 1890s two more railways, the Canadian Northern and the Grand Trunk, worked their way across the West, the hard labour done by Eastern Europeans who also bent their backs on homesteads that would not produce good crops for a few years. The farther these plots of land were from the railway, the farther these families had to trudge over prairie grass or snow to develop a speck of chopped soil hundreds of miles from the nearest school or hospital.

In 1896 another kind of immigration occurred farther west and north. One late summer day a Canadian prospector found a big chunk of gold in a creek that ran into the Klondike River in Yukon. Don't tell anyone, he urged his friends, and things went quite well for them all the rest of that year. But early in 1897 they were in Seattle, and anyone could see that they had gold dust in their hair. Before summer, there were thousands of galoots with shovels over their shoulders hiking to the Klondike. Businessmen in Victoria, a great number of them USAmerican, said that this was a great boost for the economy. Vancouver, too, became a staging ground for the miners and the women in the entertainment business who were on their way north.

And at last the West had caught up to the East in the literary race. Around the world a lot more people knew "The Cremation of Sam McGee" by Robert Service than Isabella Valancy Crawford's "Malcolm's Katie."

Business was going kind of bad in the Maritimes. For a century East Coast entrepreneurs had seen Britain and Europe as their primary market, partly because the US kept tariffs up. The method by which they reached this market was the wooden sailing ship. Unfortunately, in the last third of the century the wooden sailing ship was being replaced by newer technology, and the old shipbuilding companies were on their way to colourful heritage. A lot of workers were looking for jobs in central Canada or the US. It would have been smart of the entrepreneurs to invest in the shipbuilding business, to modernize it; but they had always thought of ships as tools, not part of their wealth making.

What did they do instead? They bought into the National Policy. Rather than selling their stuff in England, they would sell it in Ontario. At first that seemed to work, and the trains were full of Maritimes fabrics and steel, but eventually East Coast businesses were up against it. The entrepreneurs blamed the high freight rates. Maybe they did not notice that entrepreneurs in Ontario and Quebec were making the same things that they were making. In any case, it was not long till the Ontario and Quebec businessmen started buying up the faltering plants in the Maritimes. Nova Scotia businesses would become branches of Montreal businesses, and soon the Nova Scotia plant would be closed, and people in Halifax would be customers of the central provinces while their own province was de-industrialized.

So Halifax a hundred years later would be a beautiful city, but it would never have the population base to acquire a Canadian Football League franchise.

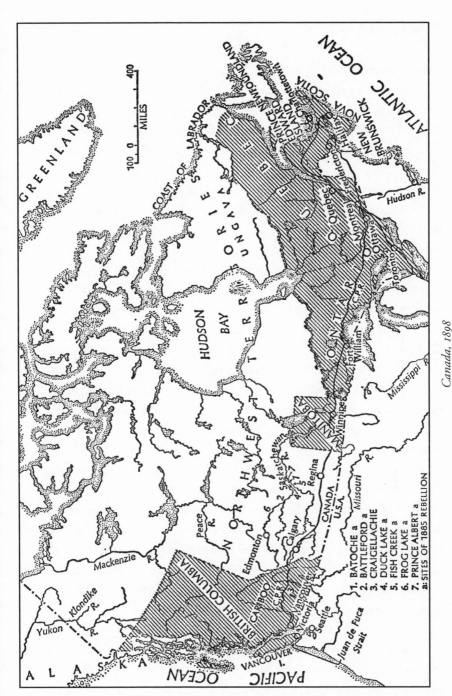

Canada, 1898

(*THE PENGUIN HISTORY OF CANADA,* BY KENNETH MCNAUGHT, PENGUIN UK, 1991)

1. BATOCHE a
2. BATTLEFORD a
3. CRAIGELLACHIE
4. DUCK LAKE a
5. FISH CREEK a
6. FROG LAKE a
7. PRINCE ALBERT a
a: SITES OF 1885 REBELLION

Whose dog is this?

All the railway building and prairie filling got Canadians thinking of themselves as a nation. That resulted, of course, in turn-of-the-century racism. One could find "No British Need Apply" on job postings, but also quiet and not-so-quiet opposition to all kinds of people, Ruthenians from Europe or Celestials from Asia. An awful lot of people wanted the country to appear as much like England as possible. But others, from the prime minister on across, wanted London to know that we were not just the tail wagging on their dog. Canada's place in the empire was negotiable. Brits such as Joseph Chamberlain, the colonial secretary, could not conceive of that possibility.

The British cabinet just assumed that when they wanted to go on an adventure in Africa, for example, their imperial children would hop onto the war wagon. In 1882 the cabinet had shelled Alexandria and sent Scottish troops in to take over the running of Egypt and the canal. The canal, of course, had to be safe from the locals because that was how England went to India to keep things in order there. Then Gen. "Chinese" Gordon went on his goofy expedition to pacify the Sudan. In 1885 the British asked various offspring around the world whether they would send troops to march up the Nile. Not a chance, said John A. Macdonald.

In 1898 the British finally subdued the Sudan, and India was safe for the moment. But then India was imperilled again by the Boers in South Africa. The strongest fellow in the Cape Colony was its former prime minister and diamond king, Cecil Rhodes. Rhodes thought that the British should rule an unbroken line of nations that stretched from the Cape to Cairo. That way India would really be safe. So the Brits invaded the little Boer states that stood in the way of that corridor, and by 1899 Britain's biggest war since the US sedition was on.

Now what was Wilfrid Laurier's Canada going to do? In London they really liked the handsome young Gallic prime minister. He was over there for Queen Victoria's Silver Jubilee in 1897, and when the Brits put on the biggest parade in their history, the Canadian prime minister's coach was right behind the golden carriage of the royal family. They made him a member of the Privy Council, Sir Wilfrid Laurier. The queen wanted to see what he looked like in those tight trousers and all those feathers. Britain was now the largest world power. When Laurier was picked from among the others for special patronizing, it could have turned his head.

Well, he liked the pomp. He liked the archaic clothing and horses and loud trumpet fanfares. But he was not going to say yes to Joseph Chamberlain, and the Imperial Conference was his show. Chamberlain was looking forward to more adventures in Africa, and he saw Laurier as his lieutenant. But Laurier would not say yes. Chamberlain liked to give little talks on the innate superiority and the destiny of the British "race," as they said back then. He said that it was "infallibly destined to be the predominating force in the future history and civilization of the world." He had forgotten that his favourite prime minister, though his name had come from a British romance, was French Canadian.

He did not know, perhaps, that Laurier believed in provincial rights in his own Dominion. He was not likely to welcome Chamberlain's idea for a confederation of the colonies. According to Chamberlain, all the colonies would join in a military force led from London. No, said Laurier, we do not think so. The colonial secretary then laid out Britain's plan for an economic union with headquarters in the British capital. We disagree, said Sir Wilfrid. Five years later the British would offer the same proposal. No, said Ottawa. Five years after that, the same thing. Same answer, too.

But in 1899 Chamberlain went to war against the farmers of the Transvaal, and in Canada there were still a lot of people who had been fed all their lives with the idea that Britons were the chosen people. Young men were eager to go and die romantically for Queen Victoria and the empire. Older men in the Anglo parts of Canada urged the government to join the Mother Country's adventure. Quebeckers, though, said that this was just one more of the Britishers' expansionist attacks on some weaker people, and none of Canada's business.

Oh no! Would every issue that came up split the country between

Quebec and Ontario? Prime Minister Laurier wished it were one hundred years later, when French and English would have grown up together and were no longer squabbling. For now he would have to work out another of his famous compromises. Canadians could go as volunteers in the British forces but not as organized military cadres from Canada. Laurier passed an Order-in-Council (i.e., a law that does not have to pass through Parliament) stating that Canada would pay for the gear and transport of a thousand men who wished to cross the Atlantic and the equator to go and kill Dutch-African farmers.

But it would not stop there. Other groups of avid warriors would follow. Union Jacks filled the streets. Somehow the British propaganda machine made it appear that these filthy Boers were a major threat to our noble old queen and the greatest ruling people the world had ever seen. Donald Smith, the old CPR man, organized a cavalry outfit named after him, Lord Strathcona's Horse. In all, seven thousand Canadians fought in Lord Kitchener's shameful war. They formed a small part of a British force of a half million troops fighting eighty thousand farmers who did not even have uniforms. The job usually consisted of burning farms and keeping women and children in concentration camps. The Boers were not wonderful people—they treated the Africans like dirt. The Brits would prove a little more subtle.

It is difficult now to imagine the patriotic fervour of the Brit Canadians. Some historians believe that the Canadian effort in South Africa did a lot to promote Canadian pride and independence from Britain. The same is usually said about World War I and World War II, and a hockey game against the Russians sometime in the early 1970s. But yes, we were gung-ho—so much so that we made a hero out of a goof named Sam Hughes. The Boer War was as far from funny as one can get, but it did produce Sam Hughes, a bombastic nit who, despite being dismissed for military indiscipline in South Africa, ended up minister of the militia in the Borden Cabinet in 1911.

He was a Tory Member of Parliament for Victoria North (later Victoria-Haliburton) starting in 1892. He ran a newspaper, as so many politicians in Ontario used to do, called the Lindsay *Warder*. Here is what it proclaimed on its masthead:

A union of hearts, a union of hands,
A union no man can sever,
A union of tongues, a union of lands,
And the flag—British union forever.

For years, Sam Hughes had been trying to organize a volunteer militia, and opining in the Commons that every young Canadian lad should have to learn to shoot a rifle.

No one has ever been able to explain how it was that patriotic young men would rally to Sam Hughes's jingoistic proclamations. But he became a kind of icon of Brit-Canadian patriotism in 1899, and made it to the front as a supply officer. There he promoted himself to general, had a lovely uniform designed and went about, as he reported in his newspaper, winning the war for the empire. The horrified Brits made him remove the uniform and asked the Canadian prime minister to bring him home. After the war, Sam spent a lot of time writing to important politicians to see whether his Victoria Cross had been lost in the mail.

A more serious career, too, was given a boost by the Boer War. Henri Bourassa was a descendant of the scampering rebel Louis-Joseph Papineau. Laurier had persuaded the youngster to run in Labelle, and now Bourassa would become the noisy little brother that Laurier wished he could keep quiet. Looked at a hundred years later, Bourassa's nationalism seems ordinary, but in 1899 the Tories and other Anglophiles saw him as a scary monster of sedition. When Laurier enacted his Order-in-Council, Bourassa walked into his chief's office and resigned, the only MP to oppose the war effort with more than a murmur. Have you asked Quebeckers their opinion on the colonial war? he inquired of his PM. Quebeckers, replied Laurier, do not have opinions—they have sentiments. From that point on, it would be harder and harder to promote Canada's wars in the province of Quebec.

Bourassa was re-elected by acclamation, and was soon the focus and spokesman for Quebec anti-imperialism. He was a Liberal but he was a Parti Rouge man. When the Boer War came to a miserable end in 1902, he urged a resolution in the Commons, to call for Britain to give independence to the conquered states. Laurier said that the British flag would guarantee the conquered Boers the best life any people could desire. Bourassa began to look around at the Union Jacks in Quebec.

Saving the West

At the turn of the century the USA was gathering up islands in the Caribbean and the South Pacific. They had managed to yank away an enormous North American acreage from the Spanish, but what they really wanted was to control the Pacific Coast from Baja California to Alaska. Most US politicians and businessmen still dreamed of a greater USA stretching north to the Arctic Sea, but while waiting for destiny to become manifest, they would try a pincer movement on the Canadians. For the bellicose US president Teddy Roosevelt this meant a big thick Alaska panhandle. Speak softly and carry a big pan, he would say.

When the US bought Alaska from the Russians in 1867, their purchase included some coastal fur-trading posts that stood a lot farther south than the northern border of British Columbia. But for nearly thirty years no one had bothered making a survey. In 1896 the Klondike gold rush started, and in 1898 the territory of Yukon was created to protect the Klondike from private armies, such as the one Teddy Roosevelt would lead into Cuba. Still, the US was interested, and after another president was shot and Teddy Roosevelt was elevated into the job in 1901, people started paying attention to the panhandle. The Russo-American bill of sale was not accurate, mentioning the height of land. The US contended that this height of land was way to hell and gone in the interior. The Canadians said that it was the arête of the mountain chain nearest the ocean. The latter would have meant that Canadians could sail up fjords into Yukon.

To show that his nation was really really interested in negotiations, Roosevelt amassed troops along the Alaska-Yukon border. He did mean business. His government would often push their way into little Latin-American countries and tell their governments what to do.

The issue would be settled by a panel of three US judges, two Canadians and one Brit. Roosevelt said that if the results were not to his liking he would settle the matter in other ways "without further regard to the attitude of England and Canada." The jurists were supposed to be impartial. Canada sent two impartial jurists. Roosevelt sent three men who had been loudly supporting the US view. The Brits sent Lord Alverstone, who handed the thicker panhandle to the Yanks. This was about the hundredth time that the Brits had screwed the Canadians in international dealings involving the USA. Prime Minister Laurier began to think that maybe Canada could do with its own department of foreign affairs.

What about the other coast? It was hard not to notice that rich and influential USAmericans liked to spend their holiday time in Newfoundland. Noting the Yankee predilection for picking up islands, Laurier encouraged the governor general, Albert Henry George Grey, 1st Earl Grey, to make a few friendly visits to Newfoundland, perhaps to discuss matters such as fishing and Confederation. Teddy Roosevelt had built a huge navy that was already patrolling Latin America, enforcing the Roosevelt codicil to the Monroe Doctrine. Laurier wished that he had his own navy.

But the real action was out West. Sifton's immigration policy was working fine. Trainloads of Galicians and Prussians were headed for the prairie grass. The world was enjoying economic good times. Everyone liked the handsome prime minister, even while they pressed him culturally. He had won re-election in 1900 and 1904. It was time to convert the southern half of the North West Territory into provinces. In 1905 Alberta and Saskatchewan became the eighth and ninth provinces, making the romantic prime minister proud and providing more trouble. One of his hands was in a vise operated by Clifford Sifton, the other in hot water boiled by Henri Bourassa.

Again grown men were going to start shouting at each other over the language spoken in schools. Laurier thought that the Manitoba Act of 1875 would be fine for the two new provinces. Sifton said that Bourassa was in the arms of the evil bishops of Quebec and that Westerners should not have French shoved down their throats. My followers are thinking that Canada might not be such a good deal, said Bourassa. The French-speaking kids are a minority out there, said Laurier, the idealist—aren't we Liberals supposed to be protecting minorities? Can we be for provincial rights against an iron Ottawa and turn around and force English on Métis children?

I won't have my grandchildren reading French, declared Sifton, and resigned his job as minister of the interior. There was a hullabaloo, and eventually Laurier settled for the usual compromise. The students in the new provinces would study in English and maybe a half-hour of French after school. Freedom from another language was secured across the Western plains.

The prairie mossbacks were not the only Westerners urging racism on the federal government. In 1900 the premier of British Columbia was James Dunsmuir, one of two brothers who had got immensely rich by exploiting underpaid miners and winning land concessions from the government. In an official letter from Victoria to Ottawa he buddied up to Laurier and said that Britain's liberal views about race and immigration were due to ignorance and distance: "If the people against whom we desire a measure of protection were in their standard of living on par with our own the competition of Japanese and Chinese would be a legitimate one, but I need not point out to you what has been contended so often and with so much force against an indiscriminate and unrestricted immigration of Mongolians, that, without lowering the general standard of living necessary to meet the decrease in wages, it is not possible for white labour to exist in the face of a system that has grown up under conditions entirely foreign to Anglo-Saxon communities."

A century later local white people would be complaining about the influx of Chinese millionaires from Hong Kong, who were driving up prices.

On April 19, 1907, a twenty-one-year-old man named Tom Longboat won the eighth running of the Boston Marathon, passing all his competitors and 100,000 spectators. He sprinted the last mile, uphill, in a snowstorm. There were no other runners in sight until another five minutes had passed. Tom Longboat became the most famous athlete in the world. He was an Onondagan lad who had sprinted away from his residential school and just kept running. Sportswriters called him the Racing Redskin.

Yeah? You and whose navy?

One day Sir Wilfrid Laurier, having won a fourth general election in 1908, looked at the map of his newly renovated Canada and noticed that it was met on three of its four sides by oceans, and that a good part of the fourth side was made of great lakes. Shouldn't a country surrounded by water have a navy? Little England had a big navy. Roosevelt's USA now had a big navy. Germany had been building a big navy for the last little while. In fact, the Brits were building a bigger navy because of the German navy. Peru had a bigger navy than Canada's.

At the Imperial Conference of 1909 Britain went back doggedly to its usual position vis-à-vis the rest of the empire. This time the Brits said that they were in favour of one big sea force, to be called the Royal Navy. It would be commanded in London and supplied by colonial money and sailors. Again. Laurier smiled politely, praised the British defence command and suggested that Canada might build its own navy. The Australians, usually more amenable to London's desires, had decided to build their own navy. It was, after all, surrounded on all sides by ocean.

Don't worry, said Laurier. We will send our ships to help the RN in any legitimate action. It is just that the twentieth century is supposed to belong to Canada, and it is about time that we had our own military forces to see that no one tries to take it away from us.

The main narrative in the story of Canada is its growing independence from Britain and then its growing subservience to the United States. The Tories always said that the best way to protect Canada from the US was to retain the royal connection. The Grits always said Canada was no nation at all as long as it acted like a little bit of England. Wilfrid Laurier enjoyed the fuss that was made over him in London, but he wanted to go down in history as the man who led his country toward sovereignty.

In January 1910, Laurier's government introduced the Naval Service Bill. It called for the building of five cruisers and six destroyers to start with. Canada is going to be so proud, thought the PM with the shining white hair. But oh no, here we go again. The folks in the Maritimes liked the idea because at last it looked as if something might be done about hard times. The folks out on the Prairies said what do we care about oceans? How about these crippling freight rates we have to pay? How about chopping the damned tariffs so we can buy tractors in Minnesota? The Tory leader, Maritimer Robert Borden, agreed with Laurier about the navy, but Ontario walruses in the Conservative Party snorted about treason, demanding that Canada contribute directly to an imperial navy. The Quebeckers, led by Laurier's ex-protégé, Bourassa, protested that this navy would be followed by conscription, and sweet Catholics from the French-speaking farms would be slaughtered in England's Asian or African wars.

The Naval bill passed, but the prime minister was nearly seventy years old. He was not going to see a lot of Canada's century, so he wanted to do whatever he could do to be identified with it. As both Canada and the US filled up the West and replaced the original people there, they looked quite similar doing so. As usual, there were a lot more gunshots on the US side, accompanied by a lot more flags. But western Canadian cities grew up looking a lot like western US cities. In Europe the cities grew out of hamlets and towns, so that there was a big church in the middle, with streets leading from the outskirts to the centre. In the Eastern states and provinces you might find something like that. But out West the cities grew along railways and wagon roads, so that you could stand at one end of town and look right through it to the other end.

If you wanted to know about international news you relied on the US news services. You read US books. And so did your schoolchildren. You read US popular magazines. Later you listened to US radio stations and watched US movies and television. Your family had likely moved back and forth across the forty-ninth parallel a few times. If you were going to go to a university it might be in Montreal and it might be in Chicago. Certainly the Yanks who came to Calgary or Winnipeg for work or to the Klondike for gold did not always acknowledge the fact that they were in a foreign country. For this reason a lot of people were glad that the picture of the king was on display in the post office.

Canada would need more than a little navy to protect its sovereignty.

Maybe Laurier was too fond of his success in the West. The Westerners were agitating, as always, for free trade and reciprocity. It would be a hell of a lot cheaper and quicker to buy a plow in Montana than to wait for one to come from Toronto. But the businessmen in Ontario wanted to sell things out West. They liked tariffs just fine, thank you. Laurier should have counted the votes in Ontario.

Twenty years earlier, in 1891, he had lost his first election as leader because he had tried reciprocity against the National Policy. Then in four elections he ran on the Tory platform and saw that the country would indeed follow his white plume, as he had requested. His mother had named him after a character in *Ivanhoe*, after all. Now in 1911, Laurier looked around and decided to go back to old Liberal free trade. How could such a clever old dude be so dumb all of a sudden?

He should not have listened to that 350-pound US president. In 1909 Henry Ford had started driving automobiles off the end of an assembly plant in Michigan, and the North American world was changed forever. Now US president William Howard Taft whispered in Laurier's old ear, Psst—tell you what; let's have free trade, and we will no longer complain about the preferential trade you carry on with Britain. He didn't tell the Canadian PM about the letter he had once written to Teddy Roosevelt about North American free trade: it would make Canada, he wrote, "an adjunct of the United States."

Who would have known?

Champ Clark, who was speaker of the House of Representatives in Washington, made a speech in which he stated the normal US governmental hope that the US flag would soon fly from the Rio Grande to the North Pole.

What a surprise!

Laurier could not get his reciprocity bill through Parliament and had to go into the 1912 election with it. Now he was being opposed by just about everybody. His great stalking horse Clifford Sifton had rallied sixteen prominent Liberals and gone to talk to the Conservative leader. Sifton was a friend of a lot of Toronto and Montreal entrepreneurs. He liked tariffs a lot. Henri Bourassa had a new Quebec nationalist party, and he talked endlessly about Laurier's navy. He dressed people up as sailors and sent them around to farm folks' doors, asking about eligible draftees. Laurier promised that his navy would be made up of volunteers. Quebec mothers listened to Bourassa. Tupper and the other bluff Tories stood in front of Union Jacks by the dozens and claimed that Laurier was selling the country to the US. Bourassa shouted that Laurier was selling Quebec to the British Empire.

Laurier said that all he was was a good Canadian. That was not going to work in 1912. He would work as the country's all-time favourite leader of the Opposition until his death in 1919.

14

OLD KIT BAG

Sir Wilfrid Laurier
(NATIONAL ARCHIVES OF CANADA/C-3930)

Even with all the nationalism that characterized the country in the early part of the century, Canada was never going to be able to defeat the US one on one. The US population and taste for violence was just too much to overcome. So Canada, armed not with manifest destiny but only a prime minister's claim on the century, did a little modest imperializing itself. Laurier and Borden both kept mentioning the round number ten to Newfoundland. From time to time Ottawa would say that St. Pierre and Miquelon really should be part of the country, and even made a little gesture toward Greenland. But while the politicians were mounting their phantasms, the Toronto and Montreal businessmen, led by the bankers, were taking over the best intersections in the cities of the British West Indies. If Canada was still a branch plant of Britain in some ways, maybe Trinidad could be a branch plant of a branch plant. Or a future province?

Meanwhile, US businesses were in Quebec, buying up the forests and forest towns for pulpwood to haul away to make US newspapers, buying the electric power industry, the textile industry and so on. Buying the provincial government.

Ships? I'll show you ships

Every year in school we all had to write an essay about the causes of World War I. Only an innocent simp would say the war was caused by that Princip guy shooting the dressed-up Austrian. There were two main sources of tension leading to World War I: (1) the Serbian rulers did not want to get pushed around by the Austrian leaders, while the Russian leaders said that they would take care of their fellow Slavs, and (2) the Germans passed a law saying that they could build a giant navy, and the British got nervous about whether they indeed did rule the waves and the colonies on the other side of the waves.

Starting in 1909 the Germans and Brits held talks aimed at putting an end to the naval arms race, while each country set about building dreadnoughts that could throw shells twelve kilometres from their many cannon. Things were brought to a savagely comic crisis in 1911 at Agadir, Morocco. The Moroccan sultan was afraid of a rebellion by his subjects and called for French help. The French, being European colonists, got set to start a protectorate, which was a fancy word for a colony. The Germans, who were always ready to mix it up with the French, decided to send in the fleet to protect German citizens in Agadir. Unfortunately, there were no German citizens in Agadir, so they found a German citizen in Mogador, and told him to get his ass down to Agadir to be protected. It worked: while France got to make a protectorate of Morocco, Germany got a thick slice of French Congo in return.

Well, no, it didn't really work: in both Germany and France, severe disappointment in the deal led to the resignations of all sorts of cabinet ministers and the fall of the French government. Now the British told the French that they could rely on their help in any war against Germany, and then the Brits told the Germans that they would rather go to war than have anyone think that their navy was afraid of anyone. Yeah? said the Germans. Yeah! said the Brits. Yeah? said the Germans. And so on.

So the German and British governments passed some more naval laws, and it got really noisy in shipyards in both countries.

This is when Robert Borden, the new prime minister of Canada, a Tory but not a fawning Anglophile, went to England to check out the navy. He met with the British PM, H. H. Asquith, and he met the strutting naval chief, Winston Churchill, and he went and visited the noisy shipbuilders. Then he came home and faced the second great Canadian naval blockade. He had already scrapped Laurier's tinpot navy. The Conservatives' bill called for Canada to send $35 million to Britain, not for the Royal Navy but to build three mighty warships for imperial defence. The government suggested that Canada would someday get those ships back and that they would be manned by Canadian sailors.

Opposition leader Sir Wilfrid Laurier said that there was no great imminent crisis and that Canada would be smarter to build its own navy. Bourassa and his *nationalistes* said that Canada should not send money to support British imperialist adventures. The Canadian Parliament was turned into the first circle of some outlandish hell. The great filibuster was on. Liberals and *nationalistes* stayed awake all night reading irrelevant texts in both languages to honourable members who snored on their desks.

Borden turned to a slick young Conservative lawyer from Manitoba, Arthur Meighen, who suddenly dropped in a motion for closure before the Grits could get their suspenders over their shoulders. Laurier's men fought closure tooth and nostril. Eventually the government's navy passed. But Laurier had been PM for fifteen years. He had the Senate in the crook of his arm, and the Senate killed the prime minister's navy. Laurier, worried about posterity, had made himself Quebec's man and turned Bourassa into a supporting character. Australia and the other colonies sent their money to the bellicose mother country while Canada formed its reputation for peacefulness.

Our first naval engagement

Canada's first naval engagement was to take place not in the Atlantic but in Burrard Inlet, a stone's throw from the dock in Vancouver. The winter of 1913–14 was bad for money people in Vancouver, bad for investors and bad for employers. So it was bad for the employed and worse for the unemployed. It was time to look around for some Asians to blame. This time they saw a boatload of Sikhs, whom they first called Hindus, and then ordered to go home.

In 1910 the Laurier government, responding to the BC government's complaints, passed an Order-in-Council to restrict Indian immigration to Canada. Hey, said some of the indigenous people called Indians by the whites, why didn't we think of that? Then the Appeal Court of British Columbia found Laurier's ban invalid. Then the Borden government passed an Order-in-Council in 1913, which applied only to British Columbia. The rule stated that immigrants could come only on ships that sailed directly from an Indian port to one in BC. There were no such ships.

In May 1914 a Japanese ship called the *Komagata Maru* arrived in Burrard Inlet. It had been hired by some Punjabi activists, and it contained 376 British subjects who desired to join their families and friends in the lumber business in the forested province. Many of these British subjects were wearing turbans on their heads because they were Sikhs, and all of them had skin darker than your average Anglo-Saxon. There had been Sikhs in the BC lumber trade for a while, but the Asiatic Exclusion League had been spending most of its attention on Chinese and Japanese immigrants. Now they went down to the harbour to shout racial epithets at the *Komagata Maru*.

A handful of Sikhs managed to get ashore in May, but for the rest the harbour door was shut, and the ship remained moored for two months while lawyers scuttled back and forth. The newspapers were filled with stories of the threats to safety caused by illegal Hindus and somehow connected with the looming war in Europe. As summer got warmer and supplies and sanitation ran out on the ship, the crowds at the dockside grew. Once in a while police and customs agents would try to get aboard, but Sikhs are not reluctant to throw chunks of coal in such situations.

Another ship, the *Empress of India*, was prepared to take the visitors home. The federal government won its case on July 18 and ordered the unsuccessful immigrants to get out of town, but 175 policemen could not fight their way on board. The crowds on the seawall raised a mighty cheer when they saw the HMCS *Rainbow* steam around the corner of Stanley Park. It was the Canadian navy to the rescue. The *Rainbow*, whose normal duty it was to protect Victoria harbour, came to a stop and trained its guns on the Japanese vessel filled with hungry and ailing British subjects. The *Komagata Maru* sailed from the inlet, followed by the Canadian navy and the thankful bellowing of the white Canadian citizens on shore.

It was the Canadian navy's first victory.

How did Canada have this ship the *Rainbow* when all the bickering was going on in Ottawa about whether we would build our own navy? Well, in 1910 the Brits sold two surplus cruisers to Canada to use as training vessels if they could get a naval college going. The HMCS *Niobe* in Halifax and the *Rainbow* in Esquimalt constituted the Royal Canadian Navy in early 1914.

Well, except for the two submarines.

When the British Empire declared war on Germany in August 1914, British Columbia mobilized quickly, though in a good British way— that is, the Victoria Cricket Association did not cancel any matches. The HMCS *Rainbow* was sent out to protect grain carriers from German warships, leaving Victoria defended only by some shore batteries. Thank goodness for the subs.

A shipyard in Seattle was just putting the finishing touches to two submarines to sell to the Chilean navy, which news a company director told some Brits who had been meeting in Victoria. The Brits decided to ask the British Admiralty for permission to suggest to the Yanks, before their neutrality laws came into effect, that perhaps the empire might get first dibs on the submarines, just inquiring, you understand. Fed up with all this English dithering, BC premier Richard McBride bought the subs and had them delivered the night of August 4, hours after Britain's declaration of war against Germany. When they appeared at Victoria on the morning of the fifth, advice got to the shore batteries just in time to stop them from firing on BC's new navy. Two days later the federal government took over the subs and put them at the disposal of the imperial armed forces.

Pack up your troubles

When Britain declared war against the Central Powers, Canada was automatically signed up. This made people who saw the world through the economy happy, because the usual depression had hit when the Conservatives took over government, and now unemployment was going to go down and prices for wheat were going to go up. A peculiar unity wafted across the land, with Quebeckers and Anglos joined to hate the Hun. Even Bourassa said that Canada should ride to the defence of Britain and France. There had been a lot of little short wars in Europe in the past few years; that's what everyone thought was going to happen this time. The boys will be home in time for Christmas, everyone said. Oh *Tannenbaum*!

Well, at least the squabbles between French Canadians and regular Canadians were put behind us while we got together to put down the kaiser. Prime Minister Borden pledged "every sacrifice." The leader of the Opposition, Laurier, would often repeat his motto, "Ready, aye, ready." No one knew that they were going to funnel boys into the bloodiest war in history. Canada was going to have sixty-five thousand of its young people killed. The US, with ten times Canada's population, would have fifty-three thousand killed. The worst years transpired before the Yanks entered the war. In the years after the war, the Canadian people would consider their dreadful contribution to be a payment toward international respect and identity.

The end of summer 1914 was a great time for portly Sam Hughes. He was still waiting for his Victoria Cross, but now he was Robert Borden's minister of national defence. He got dressed up in khaki and started recruiting Canadians to wrest poor little neutral Belgium back out of the filthy hands of the Boche. By the end of September he had amassed thirty thousand volunteers at Valcartier, the biggest military presence ever seen in Quebec. There they received some rudimentary training, consisting largely of marching and learning to make up a cot.

Then Sam Hughes started outfitting his recruits for the mud of Northwest Europe. He knew some manufacturers on a personal basis, and even his own secretary got in on the act, with a patent on the personal shovel these troops would later try to shove. Sam got them boots that unfurled from feet in the trenches. But his least successful gift was the infamous Ross rifle. Shortly after the Boer War the Canadian government had tried to get Britain's Lee-Enfield people to manufacture their excellent rifle in Canada, but the Brits said no deal—if you want Lee-Enfields, buy them from us. Sir Sam turned to his Scottish-Canadian friend Charles Ross, maker of a dandy target rifle. Sam Hughes loved target shooting, and the Ross rifle, long and light, was excellent on the range.

The only trouble was that World War I was going to be fought in the mud, not on the range. If a Ross rifle got anywhere near mud it would jam. It would jam if you tried to use it for rapid fire, too. The back sights had a habit of falling off. Canadian soldiers died in the mud, attacking their own weapons. Whenever a Canadian infantryman encountered a dead British soldier, he would help himself to the youth's Lee-Enfield rifle and ammunition.

For four years young men crouched in fetid trenches and hurled metal at one another in the names of their respective monarchs and nations. The logical end of late-nineteenth-century imperialism had arrived, and it brought with it the logical end of the Industrial Revolution. Airplanes flew overhead, dispensing machine-gun bullets and bombs. Huge guns flung shells for miles and broke eardrums nearby. Once-beautiful Flanders was now made of mud and shattered trees and barbed wire and huge holes. Very fat rats gobbled unburied horses and men. Ypres was a Flemish town near which the Allies had a salient. This salient was attacked by the Germans in force, and for the first time massive clouds of poison gas rolled cross the battlefield. The Algerian troops upped and ran, and the Canadians took their places, pissing in their hankies and holding them to their faces. Their Ross rifles jammed. They fell in the poisoned mud. The Germans came within an inch of victory, if you can call anything in WWI a victory. Six thousand more Canadians died.

The prime minister said that we needed a lot more recruits.

Over there, over here

Canada was full of recent immigrants from Central and Eastern Europe, but 1915 was not a good time to have a German name in Canada. The BNA Act had said that in times of emergency the cabinet could act quicker than Parliament to ensure "the security, defence, peace, order and welfare of Canada." Borden's government, pointing at that catalogue, had passed a War Measures Act in 1914. This meant that if you were a recent immigrant who had come from any part of the German or Austro-Hungarian empires, you could be stuck in a work camp. More than eight thousand of these "enemy aliens" were rounded up in Canada. Later, when an election became unavoidable, the Tories passed an act that took the vote away from recent immigrants from countries with which Canada was at war.

There were Union Jacks flying from every pole in Canada. The newspapers were at war, urging young men to enlist. The businessmen were at war, selling stuff to the armed forces, and sinking profits into more patriotic production. The young men in Quebec tended to stay in the fields rather than swarming to the Union Jacks. Sam Hughes was sending English-speaking recruiters into the Quebec towns, and he did not see anything wrong with that. Wilfrid Laurier made a thousand speeches calling for unity against the Hun, but Sam Hughes and Henri Bourassa kept the young habitants behind the barn. The Anglo Canadians demanded that something be done to get more French Canadians into the meat grinder. Here we are, they said, sacrificing our boys on the sad soil of France while you ingrates from New France are hiding from Sam's recruiters.

Sam Hughes called them terrible names. He railed against civilians in general and even called the prime minister a girl. Robert Borden looked for a way to lose Sam Hughes and still get his recruits. The news, after the terrible year of 1915, began to trickle down that it could be a long war. The civilian planners and generals on the Allied side knew that a long war favoured them. The Allies still ruled the sea approaches, and as time went by countless ships could converge on the coasts of Europe. The Central Powers had hoped for a quick win, and now that they were bogged down, they hoped to prevail by virtue of their new weapons and control of the continent's transportation lines. People back home in Melbourne and Halifax would now get used to the phrase "war of attrition." The numbers of casualties were numbing: the Allies lost 600,000 men in the summer of 1916 along the Somme River in northern France.

In the US there were some people who wanted the Allies to win. There were others who were pulling for the Germans and Austrians. Most wanted the US to stay out of the war, probably because it did not offer the prospect of new US territories. Later, when it looked as if a German victory would make things tricky for US trade, the US government began to favour the Allies a lot more.

There was, according to the BNA Act, supposed to be an election in 1916. By common usage, there should have been one in 1915. The War Measures Act might have been sufficient to counter the elections law, but no one wanted to start a fight that would lead to the Supreme Court and maybe beyond. Borden and Laurier were friends. They had agreed that there could not be an election in 1915, and they had made a deal that there would not be one in 1916. The Liberals, though, were not going to let the Tories sit on Parliament forever, so it looked as if 1917 could not run out before there was a wartime election. Nineteen-seventeen was a hell of a year.

On Easter Monday, Canadian troops took Vimy Ridge, the first great Allied victory and the campaign that made Canadians sure that they were a separate and honourable country. The ridge was six kilometres long and overlooked the British positions. The Germans had trench after trench built, machine-gun nests, artillery and tunnels through which vehicles could supply the dug-in gunners. The Canadians built a model Vimy Ridge and practised assaulting it. They looked at gun flashes and located every enemy cannon. At five-thirty in the morning the biggest artillery attack of all time turned the sky over the ridge to dust. The Canadians ran a hundred metres and hugged the quaking ground as another enormous artillery barrage screamed overhead. Then they ran uphill again. By seven-thirty the Canadians had taken the ridge and supplied one of the prettiest graveyards in Europe.

20th Bty., C.F.A., taking up ammunition on pack horses
to forward guns during Battle of Vimy Ridge, Apr. 1917
(NATIONAL ARCHIVES OF CANADA/PA-1231)

The prime minister went across the ocean and tried to visit every Canadian lad in British hospitals and continental trenches. He was deeply moved by what he saw and saddened by the fact that so many youths at home found it more urgent to work on the farm than to put on a uniform. Those dying soldiers needed help, and though he knew that he was dooming his political career and probably damning his party forever in Quebec, he decided for conscription. After the announcement in May, Bourassa jumped all over Borden, saying that there was no reason for Quebec lads to fight Prussians on behalf of the British. He did not mention France. First a lot of the Quebec lads started riots, smashing newspaper windows and so on, then they headed for the trees and spent the rest of the war as coureurs de bois.

The government, under the eye of the solicitor general, Arthur Meighen, passed the Wartime Elections Act, a complicated manoeuvre whereby the vote was given to overseas soldiers, along with lists of Tory candidates. The vote was given to female relatives of soldiers, and it was taken away from anyone who was a conscientious objector or had taken the oath of allegiance after 1902 and had come from any of the Triple Alliance countries. There were 300,000 Canadians in Europe. The election was pretty well cooked. But why not? After all, the Liberals, if they were to get in, could not be expected to carry on the war successfully.

While they were at it, the Tories decided to conscript money, too, imposing a tax on business and a tax on income for citizens. Both taxes were described as temporary wartime measures.

Still, suggested Meighen, just in case, I have another little plan. Let's appeal to everyone's patriotism and suggest a coalition government, one in which politicians can put aside their party differences and work shoulder to shoulder for a final victory over the Hun. Borden kind of hoped that his friend Wilfrid Laurier would join the Union government, but Laurier was getting a lot of flak from Bourassa, and he was worried about his immortal reputation in his home province. Some important English-speaking Liberals joined up, but it was hard to get any to join the cabinet. The Quebec Liberals, still kind of led by Laurier, said that they would not support any government that liked the Red Coats.

So Borden was in no great danger of losing the 1917 election. But the early winter of 1917 was not going to be gentle, whether in Belgium or Canada. On December 6, eleven days before the election, Borden was campaigning in Prince Edward Island. At 8:45 a.m. some people in his entourage said that they had heard a bang somewhere in the distance. In Halifax, where everyone's day was shaped by the war, a French munitions ship had a little collision with another foreign vessel, and the spark thus created set off the largest man-made explosion in history. The north end of Halifax and Dartmouth were flattened. It looked like a Belgian town; more than 1900 people were killed, and many more blinded by glass and mutilated by wood and steel. Half the city was left homeless in the furious blizzard that ensued. The prime minister who had visited muddy trenches in France now made his way to Halifax, guided around the remains of the city by a youth whose family had been reduced from eleven to two.

An exhausted Borden, bedevilled by carbuncles on his neck, too weary to write speeches, came back to Ontario and told people what he had seen in France and Nova Scotia. He won the election so handily that Laurier got only two seats in the West. This made Laurier and Borden both sad—there were now two Canadas again, and how was the twentieth century going to belong to either of them?

Peace, in a manner of speaking

During the first three years of the war, eight thousand millionaires were created in the USA. They made part of their money from trade with the Central Powers and part of it from loans to the Allies. In 1917 the Germans launched a lot of very big submarines and roamed the Atlantic. If the Germans were to win the war, the Allies would never be able to pay their US loans. The US entered the war late in 1917. There were English amputees being sent out to man the trenches. If the US troops had not arrived in Europe, the Allies would have been conscripting corpses.

In the fall of 1917 the Bolsheviks took over the mighty Russian Empire and signed a ceasefire with the Germans, freeing them for action against the West. It was a very good thing that the USAmericans had finally come to help the Allies. Still, back in Canada, recruitment was slower with conscription than it had been without it. In Quebec a new theatre of the war commenced. With no French Canadians in the federal cabinet, and English-speaking recruitment offices in the province, a lot of younger Québécois felt as if they were an occupied nation. In March a gang of Patriotes torched a recruitment office and a police station in Quebec City. Canada declared martial law and sent in troops. When this campaign was over there was one wounded soldier and four dead rebels. Laurier wept in his office. Borden chewed his moustache.

In 1918 Canadian soldiers did Vimy Ridge one better. Adopting a method that would be developed fully in the next war, they combined artillery, air support, tank rushes and rapid infantry movement to crash through the German lines at Amiens and send the enemy sprinting. They chased them all the way to the German border. The Germans, unable to imagine enemy troops on their ground, decided to sue for peace.

When the feds passed the Conscription Act they also passed some serious anti-union legislation. Strikes were declared illegal for the course of the war. So were unions considered to be affiliated with serious social-ist movements. In British Columbia, the workers, led by the miners of the Kootenays and the Island, saw another government lining up with the mine owners to screw working people. Ginger Goodwin, a pepper-pot coal miner from Yorkshire, became the most exciting orator on the workers' behalf in the Pacific province. Between his invigorating sentences he had to stop and cough. The draft board made him exempt owing to his bad health, but when it looked as if he might make a politi-cal difference in the province, the draft board reclassified him.

Ginger did what a lot of dissenters did—he headed for the woods outside Cumberland, on the Island. His friends knew where to find him so that they could bring him food and news. The cops had a harder time, and there were lots of cops, including some US Pinkertons. Eventually a local cop named Campbell, a guy with a bad reputation but sympathy for the businessmen, got lucky and shot Ginger Goodwin dead in an ambush. You should have a look at the photographs of the funeral parade for Ginger Goodwin on the main street of Cumberland. That day, August 2, 1918, there was a general strike through all the mining regions of BC and in Vancouver. Businessmen hired goons to attack the long-shoremen's hall and to club streetcar drivers back into their cars. The police stood by and enjoyed the order. In places such as Winnipeg, there were folks who looked on the BC general strike with interest.

Eighty years later there was a little strip of highway approaching Cumberland that was named after Ginger Goodwin. In 2001 the signs came down and it was revealed that the mayor of Cumberland hated unions and liked the new business-friendly Gordon Campbell government of BC. The main street of Cumberland is still named after a big mine owner.

Tom Longboat spent 1916 to 1919 in Europe, running against athletes among the Allies. He saw the great battlefields, and for some mysterious reason was reported killed. After the war he found out that his role as a professional long-distance runner had disappeared, as people looked elsewhere for their entertainment. While hunting for a job in Edmonton, he pawned his collection of gold medals. The sportswriters who had lauded him as a kind of freak in 1907 now liked to draw portraits of an "Injun" with a thirst for hootch.

Death keeps coming

When it came time to settle the peace treaty in Paris, the USA tried to screw Canada, and the British, as usual, decided to go along with that idea. The Brits and USAmericans and French (even after 100,000 deser-tions) wanted to shape the post-war world without any interference from the lesser countries. Borden dug in his heels and stiffened his carbuncular neck. He wanted representatives from all the nations that had served. The USA, having been at war for a year, refused to see Canada as anything but a part of Britain. Canada, having lost 65,000 lives, sassed back at the Yanks, who had lost fewer. Finally the US president allowed that he could tolerate a token representation from Canada, South Africa, Australia and New Zealand, but none from Newfoundland.

Canada lost another fifty thousand people in the Spanish flu epidemic that stormed around the world in 1918 and 1919. It was brought back to Canada by returning soldiers, yet Labrador and Quebec suffered the highest death rates. Villages were left with only old people alive. Like the war, the flu killed the young and able-bodied. How was the country supposed to progress with so many young men and women gone?

During and after the war it would be common practice to use Canada's trained military to fight the socialist threat. During the Ginger Goodwin one-day strike the Seaforth Highlanders used their machine guns to keep things quiet on the Island. In the summer of 1918, four thousand Canadian troops and Mounties were sent to Siberia to protect Murmansk and Vladivostok from the Germans and then from the Bolsheviks.

Through 1919 back in Canada, returned soldiers staged a number of riots, attacked people with European accents and pounded on anyone belonging to a leftist organization. Maybe some of them acted on their personal initiative. They trashed the property of employers who hired foreigners or socialists. In Drumheller, Alberta, for example, mobs of veterans broke into the homes of striking miners and chased their families into the Badlands.

Now that Borden's wartime ban on strikes and lockouts was presumably over, the workers of Western Canada became very active. The One Big Union movement was scaring the trousers off businessmen and their hirelings in various governments. These people could not help noticing that a lot of the unionists were Germans and Ukrainians and Poles and Russians. It was not all that hard in 1919 to plant fears that the Russian Revolution could be exported—the Communists always used the word "international." Troublemakers were saying that class affiliation was more important than nationality.

Then one day in May 1919, the skilled tradesmen of Winnipeg, Canada's third-largest city and the hub of its railway system, laid down their tools. Then the short dark unskilled workmen walked away from their crummy jobs. Then Protestant Church ministers started offering sermons in favour of working-class families, the way that Jesus of Nazareth might have done. Then municipal, provincial and federal public servants walked, and this Winnipeg General Strike could no longer be kept a secret from the folks back East.

Oh no, not Winnipeg again! There are just too many non-Brits out there! First there was the Pemmican War. Then the Riel Rebellion. Then the Manitoba schools question. Two years ago Manitoba gave the vote to women! Now the Winnipeg General Strike. The Red River nourishes a lot of agitators with foreign accents.

Thirty thousand workers were in the streets instead of at their lathes. Loyal citizens wrote letters to Ottawa, saying that they could not understand the language being spoken by the strike organizers. The country's railway hub was in the hands of the Anarchists. Finally, Ottawa acted. First all the post-office workers were fired. Then a law was passed making it illegal for foreigners to suggest changing the political system—such outlaws could be shipped out of the country without getting a glimpse of a judge. The mayor of Winnipeg made outdoor assembly illegal. The police started raiding union offices and arresting people whose names were known and peculiar. Now for the first time, a lot of war veterans joined the Protestant preachers in supporting the workers. This was really scary for the businessmen and their hirelings in government. So police on horseback rode against walking placard-carriers. There was a lot of yelling and people trying not to get maimed. The police opened fire, and one citizen was killed. The mayor of Winnipeg read the Riot Act.

The Winnipeg General Strike petered out, but it had lasted for nearly two months, and it sent a message to workers and plutocrats across the country.

A third party heard from

That message was that if workers and farmers wanted to make any headway, they would have to do it by getting into the country's political system. In Britain the unionists had learned that lesson and created the Labour Party. In Canada, particularly in the West, there would be a lot of new movements. The first important one was the Progressive Party.

After Laurier died the Liberal Party was headed by a civil servant named William Lyon Mackenzie King. He liked to remind people that his mother's father was a rebellious man of the people. In 1920 Robert Borden retired to write and golf, and left the party to Arthur Meighen, an Anglophone Conservative who had invented the War Measures Act and applied it in the capital city of his province.

These two met in the election of 1921, but they also met the Progressives, a group made up of old-fashioned anti-tariff farmers, Christian socialists and left-wing Liberals. The regular Liberals won 117 seats. The Conservatives won 50, none in Quebec or the Prairies. The Progressives won 65. Prime Minister King talked Progressive leader Thomas Crerar out of acting as Official Opposition, and poor Meighen had to take on the job. King and Meighen hated each other like crazy.

MACKENZIE KINK

William L. Mackenzie King
(NATIONAL ARCHIVES OF CANADA/C-027647)

So Canada entered the twenties with three major political parties representing three regions and three language groups, if we can suggest that a lot of the Progressive farmers and farm workers had Eastern European names.

The Progressives were not the only Western response to the perceived non-concern of the Grits and Tories. In Manitoba there was every variety of radical left. Saskatchewan would remain for a while the only base for Liberals in the West, because the Liberals had always been sure to get onside with the farmers, but there was still a strong grainmen's resistance there. Alberta set the tone for its continued response, defying Ontario

and Quebec by welcoming US money and ownership. The 1914 discovery of natural gas at the Turner Valley field launched Alberta's energy
industry. Canadian investors failed to recognize the opportunity, but the
USAmericans were more astute, and almost half the oil workers were
from across the line. In British Columbia there was a sharp cleavage
between robber baron financiers and red-flag workers and fishermen.

The world price for wheat fell to just above zero in 1931, and the soil
of Saskatchewan and eastern Alberta turned to dust. A big percentage of
the farmers that had responded to Canada's welcome a decade or two
earlier were in severe danger of losing their farms.

Meanwhile, the Maritime economy was continuing its skid, and
while the West was being developed, the Atlantic region was seeing its
percentage of seats in Parliament descend. As the Western farmers called
for free trade, Easterners demanded higher protectionism. Their own
Prime Minister Borden had put an end to preferential railway freight
rates for the Maritimes, and now their rails were turning cold.

Things were not hunky-dory for the feds in Quebec, either. In 1918
J. N. Francouer introduced this motion in the Quebec Legislature: "The
Province of Quebec would be disposed to accept the breaking of the
Confederation Pact of 1867 if, in the other provinces, it is believed that
she is an obstacle to the union, progress and development of Canada."

What could Ottawa expect? Here was a large province that had had
to get by during the war with no representatives in the prime minister's
cabinet. Here was the province invaded by Sam Hughes's Anglo soldiers.
More and more thinkers in the province were thinking about a
Francophone Catholic island in "an immense Anglo-Saxon ocean," as
the Abbé Lionel-Adolphe Groulx put it. Groulx took over from
Bourassa as the focus of Quebec nationalism in the twenties. He was a
country bumpkin who became a schoolteacher, priest, expatriate student
in France and eventually history professor at the Université de Montréal.
In 1917 he had founded an anti-conscription movement called the Ligue
des droits de Français, as well as a monthly journal called *L'Action
française*. Like most movements and journals called "Action something"
in the twentieth century, it tended toward right-wing racism.

Abbé Groulx was interested in racial purity and ethnic determinism. He saw a "French type" formed by history and geography, having "ethnical and psychological hereditary traits" that should be preserved and continued. He urged Quebeckers to memorize their history as a brave people fighting against massive oppression, against materialism and secularism. He took as his example Dollard des Ormeaux and tried to make of him a national symbol. Dollard's heroic stand against the Iroquois who were bent on attacking Montreal in 1660 would be the model for habitants three centuries later. The Iroquois, who did not have the "living germ" of Groulx's people, are nowhere in his writing considered to be defenders of their land against violent outsiders.

Groulx's most enduring text is his novel *L'Appel de la race* (1922). It is an attack on Ontario's 1912 regulation that limited French instruction in Francophone schools to an hour a day. Public discussion of the regulation was characterized by vituperative racism on both sides. The novel takes place in Ottawa, long before public signs there would be bilingual. Its hero is a French-Canadian lawyer who has drifted toward the Anglos, being educated at McGill and having married a Brit and fathering four "biracial" children. In the course of a lot of stereotyping and allegorizing, the family splits in two, and the lawyer returns to his pure-wool heritage, hoping to see the end of the marriage called Parliament.

As good times edged back into Canada and Quebec in the later twenties, Groulx would no longer be speaking to huge crowds of torch-carrying Patriotes. He would be in his classroom at the Université de Montréal arguing for his heroic Quebec, while across town at McGill Stephen Leacock would be lecturing in favour of the marvellous world created by the British Empire.

Remember Chanak?

There were still a lot of pip-pip immigrants from Blighty who doted on the British Empire and its white man's burden. But a lot of Canadians were learning to distance themselves from the white man's burden just as much as they did from the US's manifest destiny. The militarists found it hard, though, to let go. The militarists in London did, too.

Chanak was a little Turkish port in the Dardanelles, where the Turks had won a rare battle against the Allies in the Great War. There were English sailors and soldiers hanging out there now, doing the usual postwar occupation bit. The Ottoman Empire and the Hapsburg Empire were both told to break it up at the Treaty of Versailles, but now the Young Turks had their own firepower and had chased the Greeks out of their country. The Brits at Chanak were getting very nervous. Under the treaty they were supposed to keep the Dardanelles demilitarized. Now the forces of Mustafa Kemal were bristling their moustaches and rifles, and London cabled the dominions, asking when they might expect to see some Canadian and Australian troops in the Balkans.

William Lyon Mackenzie King wrote in his diary that night about his anger at the arrogance of the Brits. He sent a message to their PM, David Lloyd George, stating that the days when Britain could announce that Canada was at war were over. The Canadian Parliament, he said, would from now on decide whether Canada would go to war. This was, of course, back in the days when the House of Commons was bigger than the Prime Minister's Office.

Of course the Tories yelled to high heaven that we ought to click our heels and say, "Aye, ready!" But really, a hassle within the borders of Turkey would have been a hard sell to young warriors so soon after the enormous war in Europe. You can just imagine what Henri Bourassa and Lionel Groulx had to say. Luckily a conference settled the matter before an imperial crisis could develop.

So Mackenzie King sent his message to the Brits and to the Canadian Brits. There would be other steps toward independence during the twenties. After half a century of having London sell the Canadians down the drain in fish talks with the US, Canada did its own deal in the 1923 Pacific halibut treaty. In a few years we would start to appoint our own ambassadors. Some people, even some Liberals, began to suspect that the century would not belong to the Canadians, but there was a growing feeling that Canada would.

Popularly, the twenties are remembered as the Roaring Twenties, a time when flappers jumped out of fancy automobiles and into public fountains. The truth is that there were a lot of poor people in the twenties. Their lives were limited by inflation and poor working conditions. But by the middle of the decade economic conditions, as they say, improved. Wheat prices went up, and there was a steady market in a Europe trying to recover from war. Canada did not exactly inundate the world with manufactured products, but won a reputation as a resource country. Two-thirds of the world's pulp and paper came from Canada. So important was the industry that major US newspaper owners would decide to buy whole pulp and paper towns, such as Baie-Comeau, Quebec, where little Brian Mulroney grew up, singing Irish songs for an Irish-American tycoon. Vast expansions of hydroelectric facilities led to expansion in mining and milling. By the end of the twenties more than two-thirds of Canadian homes had electricity in them. That might seem pretty rudimentary in Boston or Toronto, but it was a big deal in Moose Jaw.

One of the most spectacular successes in the export game was hootch. In 1919 the United States had passed an amendment to their Constitution whereby it became illegal to sell or buy drinking alcohol except for medical purposes. Now, it would be awfully hard to sustain a roaring decade in the F. Scott Fitzgerald sense without a lot of booze, so if you lived next door to the US and could afford to manufacture and deliver Canadian rye whisky and Scotch, you stood a good chance of making a fortune and founding a highly respectable Canadian family.

High-speed boats and trucks of derring-do braved the international boundary and risked the coastal waters. The US Coast Guard seized ships and the US announced loudly that they were disappointed in their northern neighbours. Unfortunately, as with all prohibited commodities, the US firewater trade was taken over by organized crime. The romantic Al Capone, on being asked about his connections up North, replied that he did not know where Canada was, thus putting himself in a pretty big group of USAmericans. But he had an island in the middle of Lake Erie and an elegant tunnel, they say, under the streets of Moose Jaw.

The future's so bright

Mackenzie King was quite satisfied with himself. He had brought good times back to his country. He had lowered taxes and balanced the budget. He had persuaded some of his Liberals to come on back from the Progressive Party. Now in 1925 he wanted a majority government so that he could transform his nation into a world leader. He called an election for October and relished his final triumph over that Pecksniff Meighen.

He should have asked more questions of all the spirits he consulted at table rappings and in the candlelit gloom of his bachelor's digs in Laurier's old house. When the results were in, the Liberals had fallen to 101 seats. The rump Progressives had 24. Meighen had 116. King had lost his own seat in North York.

Hoorah, I am prime minister again, said Arthur Meighen.

But King sidled up to Julian Hedworth George Byng, 1st Viscount Byng of Vimy, the feckless governor general, and suggested that his Liberal-Progressive coalition could run things for a while, and it would not be long till he found himself a constituency to represent. Good show, said Lord Byng, pip pip, give it a go.

This was the first half of the famous King-Byng affair.

Now King fixed it so that he would represent Prince Albert, Saskatchewan, in the Commons, and in the meantime he instruc-ted his Quebec lieutenant, Ernest Lapointe, to give speeches about

Lt.-Gen. Sir Julian Byng, G.O.G. Canadians, May 1917
(NATIONAL ARCHIVES OF CANADA/PA-1356)

punctuation in the House. In those days, before you had to be a Quebecker to be prime minister, the prime minister always had a Quebec lieutenant.

Phew! That was close. King told himself that he could govern with a minority. He would have drunk a toast to that, but he was a teetotaller. He might converse at night with a painting of his mother. He might sleep with dogs and prowl the streets, looking for stray women to buy soup for, but he did not fog his mind with alcohol. Nevertheless, now alcohol reached out and tipped him out of his chair. With the change of government King had got rid of his minister of customs and duties because there were rumours that this boyo was profiting personally from US thirst. Unfortunately, the new minister of customs and duties and hard liquor did not understand his boss's preference for the high road. The Conservatives were really happy to discover a scandal in Liberal management for a change. Arthur Meighen was jumping up and down in his seat as if he really had to go. The Liberal-Progressive government set up an investigation and were just shocked by the findings. King pretended to be alarmed by all this, but said heh heh where only his dog and his mother's spirit could hear. He was going to get Meighen again.

King walked on his short legs to the governor general's place and said that he would like to dissolve Parliament and hold another election. Byng put on what he hoped was an intelligent face, and said no, he thought that Meighen the Tory ought to get a chance, what with his 116 seats and all. King put up a big show of defiance, but the king's representative stood firm, and poor Arthur Meighen became the second man ever to be remade PM after a hiatus. Heh heh heh. This was the second half of the famous King-Byng affair.

All across the country the voters and others were utterly confused about what was happening in Ottawa.

The new leader of the Opposition had been reading a lot of law books in his mock-struggle with the governor general. One of the arcane little bits of legal folderol said that if the governor general appointed anyone prime minister, that person had to resign his seat and run in a by-election. If he wanted to name any cabinet ministers, these gents, too, had to resign and run again. What was poor Meighen to do? If he and all his potential cabinet guys were to resign, his Tories would never survive a vote of confidence, and he could be sure that that chubby little balding miscreant would demand a vote of confidence. Meighen thought he saw a way out: he would wait for his own election campaign in a safe riding, but his men would be an "acting cabinet" and not paid more than any backbencher.

For a couple of days King just took a few potshots. Meighen, sitting behind a curtain so that he could hear what was going on, thought that his manoeuvre had worked. He did not know that the superstitious King was waiting for the right day and the right hour to make his move. On the last day of June 1926, he sprang his Catch-26. He stood up in the House, his face as innocent as a child's, the morning's breakfast drying on his waistcoat. He said that he just wanted to have a little question clarified for him: had the government's cabinet members taken their oaths? He had been reading a lot of governmental law books, you see, and it appeared to him that the cabinet was illegal if its members had not sworn their oaths. Of course, if they *had* been sworn in they were illegal because they had not resigned and run in by-elections.

Behind his curtain Arthur Meighen was whispering words he didn't know he knew. Mackenzie King got wound up and began denouncing a group of snakes that were flouting hundreds of years of British parliamentary democracy. He painted himself as the empire's defender against the malfeasant enemies of democracy. He, more than any politician in the land, had worked hard for Canadian independence, suggesting that he was heir to his grandfather's rebellion. Now he wrapped himself in the Union Jack. Arthur Meighen was chewing on his curtain.

Next day was July 1, Canada's fifty-ninth birthday. The House sat, and on the third day of the session Mackenzie King's people brought down the Conservatives in a vote of non-confidence. The motion succeeded by one vote. It was the first time a Canadian government had fallen that way.

Now, thought King, Byng will do what he did before—he will call on the leader of the Opposition to try to run the country. But Byng told Meighen that he could dissolve the House and call an election for

September. Mackenzie King pretended that he was enraged. But now he had a wonderful campaign theme: he would rail against Britain's manipulation of Canada's sovereign electoral process. The fact that he had just recently taken the opposite stand would probably not be noticed by the electorate. King would be all maple leaves and beavers for this campaign, and sweep out of his Saskatchewan seat into Ottawa as the champion of Canadian pride.

Tom Longboat found a steady job that would take him through the thirties and last for nineteen years—working for the street-cleaning department of the City of Toronto. It involved collecting garbage and scooping up leaves and horse manure. Lou Marsh, the most famous sportswriter in Toronto, had been calling Tom Longboat racial and animal names for a couple of decades. He really enjoyed the image of the ex–world champion with a shovel.

Persons and others

In September 1926 Mackenzie King and his Liberals surprised a lot of people and won their first majority, however slight. Now, with a growing economy and a hard-won self-confidence, Canada could be moved forward in two regards: social reform and international independence. King had once published a book about making a better society, *Industry and Humanity*, in which he argued that government and industry should be partners in the raising of the populace's standard of living. He saw Canada, you might say, as one big company union.

So King passed the first old-age pension bill, whereby a person who reached the age of seventy and really needed some help could get $20 a month from the government. Tory financiers screamed that the country would crumble into dust. Meanwhile, King balanced the budget, dropped freight rates in the Maritimes and lowered taxes across the board.

Overseas the reinstated prime minister checked out the London soothsayers and attended the 1926 Imperial Conference, where he talked it up with his fellow first ministers and encouraged an Imperial Committee to come up with something called the Balfour Report, named after a former British cabinet minister. It more or less described a situation that already existed, calling Britain, Canada, the Irish Free State, Australia, New Zealand and South Africa "autonomous communities within the British Empire, equal in status, in no way subordinate one to another."

Meanwhile, on the home front there were strong steps being made in social terms. King, having studied in the slums of Chicago as a student, was interested in leading a party that would introduce programs as well as old-age pensions, like family allowances and workmen's compensation. Although he thoroughly enjoyed the company of single and married women, he did not have a lot to say about women's rights. In the matter of women's rights the provinces would lead the way. You will remember that Manitoba was first to permit women's suffrage in 1916, quickly followed by Saskatchewan and Alberta, and by 1918 women could vote federally. Only Quebec refused votes for women, and would do so until 1940.

The two world wars would give the women's movement great boosts, while their men were dying in Europe. If women could rivet warships together and make steel when there were not enough men to do these jobs, then surely they might be able to do easier jobs such as legislation and jurisdiction. In 1916 the province of Alberta, not yet the bastion of the fanatical right wing, made Emily Murphy the first woman magistrate in Canada. In 1917 Helen Gregory MacGill was sitting as a judge in juvenile court in Vancouver. In 1918 Mary Ellen Smith, daughter of a coal miner and wife of a coal miner, ran as an Independent and won a seat in the BC Legislature. She introduced a female minimum wage bill and got it passed. There were two women sitting in the Alberta Legislature. The first woman to be elected federally was Agnes Macphail, a Progressive from Ontario. Her favourite word was "fight."

Women such as Agnes Macphail and Emily Murphy and Nellie McClung, the dreadful novelist and great politician, scared a lot of harrumphing men. They knew how to use humour, and they knew how to give the sign that they were not going to rest until they got absolute equality. Emily Murphy, for example, led the fight against the homestead laws that said women who wore out their bodies working on a prairie farm could not own it. As soon as Murphy began to preside on the bench, the male lawyers challenged her. Of course these lawyers may have been in favour of women, but they were lawyers, and it was their duty to use every tactic they could to help their clients win. In this case the tactic was the BNA Act.

These lawyers pointed out that in order to preside in court, a judge had to be a "person." According to the arcane wording of the BNA Act, that category did not include people of the distaff persuasion. It was not written by the Mothers of Confederation, after all. Eventually, a lawyer made a big enough stink to get the subject to the Alberta Supreme Court, and there it was decided that yes, indeed, women *are* persons, at least in Alberta.

Then Emily Murphy decided to go further. She wanted to be the first woman senator. The BNA Act, she said, was open for interpretation, and she was a good interpreter. The Act says that a senator had to own $4000 more than "he" owes. She could raise the money. She petitioned Borden, King, Meighen and King the Second to appoint her to the Senate and adjust constitutional thinking for good. Uh, we will get back to you on that, said all the preems. Then Murphy did some more reading in the BNA Act and found that a group of five citizens, persons or not, could petition the Supreme Court of Canada for an interpretation of constitutional rights. She got together with four other witty and accomplished suffragettes and petitioned the court. In April 1928 the Supreme Court overturned Alberta's decision—women were not persons, not in Canada.

The Famous Five were not quitters. They went over the Supreme Court's head, all the way to the Privy Council. Notwithstanding the fact that the power of the British Privy Council over Canada's Supreme

Court had been for several administrations a disputatious subject, the Privy Council did come down with a decision. England told Canada that Alberta had been right. Women are persons. Women cheered. Anti-imperialists growled. So it goes.

Mackenzie King could not speak a sentence of French, but he knew that Quebec was good for the Liberal Party, and what was good for the Liberal Party was good for Canada. In 1927's diamond jubilee of Confederation he smiled good-naturedly at Quebeckers and showed them the renovations. Postage stamps were made bilingual. You could sing the national anthem in both languages.

Down it comes

Lenin was collectivizing the Russians in a Communist manner. Soon Hitler would be collectivizing the Germans and Mussolini the Italians in Fascist manners. All over the world there would be Communists and Fascists who wished for order. When the Great Depression hit in 1929, the news appeared to be that capitalism and individualism had brought down their own disaster. It would have been a good time to keep a close eye on the European dictators that were popping up all over the place. But when the New York stock market fell and investors started dropping past skyscraper windows, Canadians had a lot of problems to catch their attention at home. Two factors led to trouble for Canada: we made our money by selling resources, and the chief buyer of our resources was the United States. Investors in Toronto would not need the down elevator, either.

But Ontario and Quebec, though they suffered through the dirty thirties, suffered the least of the provinces, because they were providing products for a protected market. In the Prairies housewives with too many skinny children were trying to figure out which clothing could be eaten. It would have been a good time to be a smart lawyer with clients such as the CPR and the HBC and the Royal Bank.

There was such a lawyer. He was R. B. Bennett, and by the summer of 1930 he was contesting a federal election against William Lyon

Mackenzie King the economist. Wiseacres say that King lost the election on purpose because he did not want to take the blame for the coming hard times. Bennett was not all that smart when it came to image: when he became PM he lived in the most expensive hotel in Ottawa and ate a box of chocolates every night. Once in an outdoor speech that anyone could attend he thought he was asking a rhetorical question when he said, Is it my fault? Yes, it is, thundered the crowd.

So Canada might have been poor, but at least it would be independent. At the Commonwealth Conference of 1930 the Balfour Report was hashed over, and in 1931 the British Parliament passed the Statute of Westminster. There have been many bills passed that made Canada a sovereign nation. They have been as numerous as British Columbia centenaries. But when I was a kid I learned that the real deal was the Statute of Westminster.

According to the Statute of Westminster, countries such as Australia and Canada could now pass any legislation they desired, whether the Brits liked it or not. In typical Canadian fashion, one might say, Canada asked that two little strands of dependency be left in place until we were ready to snip them. Certain kinds of legal appeals might be made to the King's Privy Council, and any amendments to the BNA Act should for the nonce be the business of the British Parliament. The next amendment would be the 1940 introduction of unemployment insurance.

There were the usual stuffy celebrations, but what joy could there be in governing a country that might disappear? A half million people disappeared from the Prairies. Life on the Prairies depended on the price of wheat, and no one was buying wheat. Farm folks went to US and Canadian cities and wound up in breadlines there. The only people who appreciated the times were photographers, who made dramatic pictures of empty sand-drifted farmhouses and dirty-faced waifs in Winnipeg soup kitchens.

Down, down

R. B. Bennett was such an easy mark for the satirists. Imagine: during the stone country's time of unimaginable hardship, the prime minister of Canada was a millionaire who just kept finding new ways to make dough. He gathered up real estate and inheritances from grateful friends. People wondered whether he knew what was happening. At any time he was apt to say something like this Thanksgiving Day address: "Canadians should be especially thankful for the manifold blessings that Providence has bestowed upon them."

If you are going to have a Great Depression you are going to get radical troublemakers who tell the poor and unemployed that capitalism does not work and furthermore does not care about folks of the non-rich persuasion. The threat of the One Big Union had been bad enough, but now there were men and women going around talking about social revolution. By 1932 the Conservative government decided that the radicals were a worse threat than hunger. Ottawa had stopped censorship of books and periodicals after the war but now reinstituted it to combat the Red Menace. In British Columbia things got complicated as the Red Menace was joined to the Yellow Peril. Deportation of suspicious foreigners was stepped up, and Communists were hauled into court for preaching "sedition."

The hand of Communism was perceived whenever a group of protesters got together. In 1932 there was a Workers' Economic Conference held in Ottawa, and when the delegates assembled to make speeches in front of the Parliament Building, they were descended on by RCMP clubs and an armoured car and smashed up well. Even the Ottawa *Journal*, about as far as you could get from a socialist rag, opined that this looked like a Fascist government reaction.

The most famous protest was the "On to Ottawa" trek in the summer of 1935. It began when Slim Evans of the Workers' Unity League and twenty thousand other unemployed people left the 20-cents-a-day work camps all over BC and joined in Vancouver's May Day parade. Unemployed men took over several buildings in downtown Vancouver, and were chased through plate-glass windows by policemen on horse-back. Slim Evans thought that it was about time that Ottawa found out about the Depression, so a thousand men jumped onto a train and headed East. By the time the train got to Regina, there were fifteen hundred on board. There they were given assistance by the local poor and the Saskatchewan Liberal government.

But R. B. Bennett did not want an embarrassing show in Ottawa. He leaned on the railway bosses and there was suddenly no train available to the protestors. The trek was at an end. The men decided to hold a big rally on Canada's sixty-eighth birthday and then turn back westward. That is when R. B. Bennett employed his prime minister's prerogative for stupidity. When there were only about three hundred trekkers left in Regina, Bennett sent in the RCMP to arrest Slim Evans and anyone else who wanted to make a holiday speech. Cops chased unemployed men through the streets, and the Red Menace struck back as best they could, aiming sticks at the knees of the horsemen trying to run them down. By the time the remaining trekkers were penned up at the exhibition grounds, there was one dead policeman and a lot of blood on pedestrians' faces. People were reminded of the Winnipeg Strike. Eventually the Saskatchewan government came to the protection of the trekkers and helped them board a westbound train.

One day in the summer of 1932 Tom Longboat visited the Canadian National Exhibition with his family.

The CCFing of Bennett

Bennett and the Tories lost a lot of votes in Regina, but the millionaire prime minister was not going to step back for Slim Evans. He did, however, perceive a threat from the more respectable non-Communist left. In 1932 there had been a meeting in Calgary, Bennett's bailiwick, where farmers and unionists and some progressive MPs and academics discussed the formation of a new national party that would respond to the Depression and drought along radical parliamentary lines. They set up a founding convention for Regina in 1933, where Prof. Frank Underhill from Toronto and the poet Prof. F. R. Scott from Montreal presented a document that would be known as the Regina Manifesto. It said that "economic planning will supersede unregulated private enterprise and competition, and . . . genuine democratic self-government, based on economic equality will be possible."

The party chose a rather boring name, the Co-operative Commonwealth Federation, but the initials, CCF, would be hissed across the land. The enlightened Christian leadership of the Winnipeg Strike would be a crucial element of the movement. Its first leader was J. S. Woodsworth, a Methodist preacher and Member of Parliament for Winnipeg North. The young Baptist minister Tommy Douglas was there, and he would eventually become the first social democrat premier in the country. In the 1935 election the CCF elected seven members to the House of Commons. There were a lot of new parties to emerge from the disaffected West, but the CCF was the only one that caused its enemies to form anti-CCF coalitions.

R. B. Bennett was such a handy cartoon figure, a big round man in a millionaire's suit, a Plushbottom in hard times, munching chocolates in his suite at the Château Laurier. So who could explain his decision to become a reformist in the last years of his Canadian life? In 1931 he had written, "Half a century ago people would work their way out of their difficulties rather than look to a government to take care of them," the kind of Daddy Warbucks talk we would not hear from first ministers until the throwback regimes in Alberta and British Columbia seventy years later. Still, the fat man did become a reformer, though his reforms would work from the top down.

In 1932 he encouraged the Canadian Radio Broadcasting Commission to form a national radio broadcaster to resist the commercial junk coming north from the US. Bennett would become radio man in the next few years, the first politician to talk to Canadians across the country. In 1935 he broadcast five historic reform speeches on thirty-nine stations from coast to coast. He paid for the air time with his own money. Tory nabobs and bank managers fell out of their chairs as their man in Ottawa said things like this: "Free competition and the open marketplace, as they were known in the old days, have lost their place in the system."

In 1934 he had seen to the creation of the Bank of Canada, whose purpose it was to regulate currency and keep the commercial banks in check. He did not go so far as to make it a public institution, but he did insist that it advise the government. He also created a wheat board to regularize marketing of Canada's most famous product. Then in his 1935 Throne Speech he promised a graduated income tax and unemployment insurance. When the PM called an election, Mackenzie King found himself in an odd position—he had to oppose the wheat board, the Bank of Canada, the graduated tax and unemployment insurance. Had Robber Baron Bennett snookered him the way he had snookered Meighen twice?

No danger. What government was going to survive an election in the middle of a Great Depression? In October the Conservatives suffered their greatest defeat ever.

On December 1, Mrs. Pearl Bowering gave birth to a big-headed son in Penticton, BC. "Never again," she said, for the first of many times.

16

TRYING TO STAY ALIVE

Destitute family returning to Saskatoon from the north, June 1934
(GLENBOW ARCHIVES/ND-3-6742)

If you look back over Canadian poetry from the dirty thirties you will not find much about the bad times, unless you decide to look at the poems that have not made it into the anthologies and university reading lists. Most of the poetry from the period is full of frozen lakes and battered pines. An exception among the poets was Dorothy Livesay, a modernist among romantics. Livesay was a love poet who worked diligently for leftist causes. One of her most remarkable accomplishments is a sonnet titled "Comrade." In the octave she recounts the delicacy and sweetness with which her first lover helped her out of her innocence. In the sestet she ends:

I see you now a grey man without dreams,
Without a living, or an overcoat:
But sealed in struggle now, we are more close
Than if our bodies still were sealed in love.

Meanwhile grasshoppers ate the meagre crops that grew in prairie dust. The only things that grew steadily through the thirties were new political movements. In the 1935 election the CCF had elected seven MPs, but something called Social Credit returned seventeen. Social Credit was dreamed up by an English military man and self-described economist named Major C. H. Douglas. He was a lot more sensible than his followers. He disagreed with the Communist formula that based value on hours of work. He said that hours of work on barren soil do not equal hours of work on lush soil. His formula, then, included natural resources, and he said that money was not a natural resource. Money, he said, was coupons. His most sensible point was this: capitalism is based on a self-defeating proposition, that the banks should be able to lend imaginary money to governments and receive payments plus interest in real money.

Unfortunately, the people who flocked to Social Credit in Italy and Canada and Australia tended to be a bit on the fanatical side. The economic theory would disappear inside a movement that attracted racists, Fascists, religious cranks and anti-intellectuals. Ezra Pound was the most famous Social Creditor in the world, but you could travel all over Alberta and never find a Social Creditor who had read *The Cantos*. You would not find that many who had read Major Douglas, either.

They tended not to be readers at all. They got their message from the radio, where "Bible Bill" Aberhart, a Calgary teacher, would invite them to place their innocent hands on their radio sets and receive the blessings thus transmitted from a God who did not demand much in the way of thinking. More revivalism than political campaigning, Aberhart's speeches won over the rural vote, and in 1935 Social Credit became the government of thirty-year-old Alberta. Aberhart and his peculiar group tried to change the financial system, but as similar reformers had found out in Europe, other governments and the banks would get together and make it impossible. The closest that the Alberta government could get was to open a lot of government-backed credit unions.

In 1936 Quebec's version of a right-wing protest party took over the provincial legislature. This was Maurice Duplessis's Union Nationale, a party that promised all kinds of social reform while inveighing against the "foreign" dictatorship of English-speaking business in Quebec. But once in power, Duplessis cuddled up to the Catholic Church and businesses that spoke any language. He kept a cabinet around for official photographs but ruled more and more as if he were Mussolini. He sent his operatives against unions, educators, unusual religions and any groups with progressive ideas. All the while he told Quebec citizens that he was standing up for their rights against Toronto and Ottawa.

Meanwhile, in the Maritimes families remained loyal to either the Conservatives or the Liberals.

First Nations people did not have a lot of time for political parties. As far as the government was concerned, they were either Catholics or Protestants. If they were Protestants, their kids were sent to Protestant residential schools; if they were Catholic, their children were sent to Catholic residential schools. There the kids would be mixed with kids who spoke languages they did not know. It did not matter, though, because all those languages were supposed to disappear and be replaced by one of the two big European languages.

It's the world again

Twenty years before, Canada had sent a lot of youngsters to get killed in Europe, and thus, at least in its own self-regard, had emerged as an independent country on the world stage. Then in the 1930s, the country seemed to join the USA in forgetting about the world and turning eyes inward. Canada, unlike the USA, did belong to the League of Nations, but for the most part it looked forward to being part of the North American emergence that would leave Europeans to shuffle in their ruins. A lot of Canadian businessmen were searching for the best chance to get taken over by US companies.

In 1931 Japan invaded the Chinese province of Manchuria and set up a puppet state called Manchukuo. The League of Nations decided not to provoke the Japanese. In 1935 Italy got ready to bomb and invade Abyssinia. Now some European nations in the League suggested that they should impose sanctions on a European nation that wanted to send its air force against poor herdsmen on parched soil. Let's teach Mussolini a lesson, they said. Perhaps they could forbid their manufacturers of electric toasters and highball glasses to export to Italy.

Mackenzie King was in the Southern US, holidaying with rich friends. His Quebec lieutenant, Ernest Lapointe, was minding the store. In Geneva, Canada was represented only by Dr. Walter Riddell, because R. B. Bennett's ambassador to the League had left for home and was not yet replaced. Dr. Riddell was pretty stupid about Canadian politics and business. He thought that when airplanes were dropping bombs on family tents, there was a moral question involved. He could not get into contact with Ottawa, but he thought that Canada would support him if he tried to talk the European representatives into forbidding delivery of steel, coal and oil, resources any energetic foreign policy needs. Amazingly, the European representatives agreed in principle.

But now at last Lapointe heard about it, and soon Mackenzie King would hear about it. Dr. Riddell's attitude toward Mussolini was so damned naïve. For one thing, when a country goes to war it becomes a good customer. For another thing, the Liberals needed Quebec, and the Church and government in Quebec liked Mussolini a lot, and any sanctions against him would obviously be an attack on a fellow Catholic nation. Camillien Houde, the perennial mayor of Montreal, said that Quebeckers would go to war to support Mussolini.

Ernest Lapointe knew Quebec well. He told King that he would quit and take Quebec with him if Canada supported League sanctions. Lapointe was the head of the Canadian League of Nations society, but he was a Quebecker first. King invoked national unity, and Riddell was repudiated as a quixotic dreamer.

The next crisis was Spain. Quebeckers liked General Francisco Franco as much as they liked Mussolini. The goofy nineteenth-century notion that unregulated capitalism would result in equal opportunity was hard for some people to shake, even in the Depression. But there were more and more people coming to think that government should step in and curb the excesses of monopoly capitalism. The extreme model was, of course, the Soviet regime. To protect the world from Marxist expansion, Western governments put up with a lot of Fascist economies.

In 1936 the leftist Popular Front won the national election in Spain, and General Franco tried to overthrow the new government. Hitler and Mussolini joined up with Franco, and Stalin supported the government. Most Western governments remained officially neutral, but individuals from several democracies volunteered on the government side. In Canada these volunteers were called the Mackenzie-Papineau Battalion, named after the rebels of a century before. The Catholic Church supported Franco, and in Quebec there were a lot of priests and politicians who complained that Ottawa was too soft on Communism.

Mackenzie King was browned off that the anti-Fascists had named themselves after his grandfather, but his government decided to appear even-handed. They passed a law that said that any Canadian found guilty of enlisting on either side in Spain could go to jail for two years. It was also illegal to sell supplies to either side, though this would not stop businessmen from supplying Franco through a third country. When the Fascists succeeded in defeating the government in 1939, the returning veterans were not dumped into Canadian jails, but they were not rewarded with pensions, either.

Mackenzie King really liked visiting world leaders and having his picture taken with them. Toward the end of 1928 he had been travelling around Italy, and managed to get through all the Italian folderol it took to have a meeting with Benito Mussolini. He wrote in his diary that *Il Duce* had a countenance filled with "sadness & tenderness as well as great decision." Now in 1937 he was in Europe again, and this time he wangled a meeting with Adolf Hitler in Berlin.

Mackenzie King's purpose was to tell the German chancellor that in the event of a German attack on Britain or any other part of the Commonwealth that had been formed at Westminster in 1931, Canada would have to make war on Germany. This is what historians of a Liberal bent tell us, anyway. When he got home to Laurier House, King gave a nice long interview to the great historian Bruce Hutchison. Hitler, he said, seemed "a simple sort of peasant" who only wanted Germany to reacquire its pre-war borders. In his diary less than a year later he allowed as to how he admired Hitler for two things, his devotion to his mother and his spiritualism. We do not know whether Hitler wrote the same thing about Mackenzie King.

A year later Hitler's idea of German borders was expressed in his gathering in of Austria and the German-speaking part of Czechoslovakia. British Prime Minister Neville Chamberlain went to Munich and got Hitler to promise in writing that that was that for German expansion. Mackenzie King sent Chamberlain a cable, predicting that the British prime minister would be given "an illustrious and abiding place among the great conciliators."

The Great War redux

In 1939 Japan was all over China, and looking to save the rest of Southeast Asia from Western imperialism. Italy had conquered Abyssinia and was checking around for more underdeveloped countries to invade. Germany signed a non-aggression pact with the Soviets and started complaining about the terrible crimes of the Polish government.

Mackenzie King, who had spent his young adulthood as a negotiator for US millionaires, wrote letters to Berlin and Rome and Warsaw, requesting the maintenance of peace. The requests must have got lost in the mail. The Poles had signed non-aggression pacts with the Germans and the Russians, but nine days after the Soviet-Nazi pact, Germany invaded Poland, and on September 17 the Soviets invaded Poland. By September 27 there was no more Poland. Hitler tried to set up a puppet state, but he could not find a Pole who would head it, so for the umpteenth time Poland was dispersed among its neighbours.

On September 3, Britain and France honoured their alliance with Poland, and declared war on Germany. Mackenzie King had said years earlier that if Canada were to come to the aid of Britain, it would have to be directed to do so by the Canadian Parliament. Now he waited a few days and then called the House in. He announced the government's position—there should be "effective co-operation by Canada on the side of Britain." That wonderful word "effective" is favoured by people and organizations that prize vagueness. But King did promise two things: a defence of Canada would come before any adventures in Europe, and there would be no conscription for overseas duty this time around.

Okay, Mackenzie King was at war with the Axis. He also had to prepare a fight against Quebec, or at least against the usual anti-war fuss in that province. Premier Duplessis jumped up and down and called a provincial election, declaring that Ottawa's war effort was an attack on provincial rights. Here is our chance, said King to Lapointe, and now all the French-speaking cabinet ministers from Quebec threatened to resign if Duplessis defeated the Liberal candidate, Adélard Godbout. That would mean, they warned, that without Quebeckers in the cabinet, the Anglos could pull off another coalition government, and there would be conscription in no time. It worked. Godbout got a comfy majority from the anti-conscription people. Nobody ever said that politics was an exercise in clarity.

Then the weirdo premier of Ontario struck. Mitch Hepburn, the onion farmer, was a Liberal in name but a loony in practice. Now he passed a resolution in the Ontario Legislature that the federal government and Mackenzie King were too chicken to fight the Heinies. King had never been slow to spot an opportunity. He dissolved the House and called a snap election for March 26, 1940, and won a huge majority. Now he had the Canadian people's approval for his prosecution of the war.

When war came round, the garbage collector Tom Longboat joined the Home Guard. He was in his early fifties, and he had an outdoor job. He could also run farther than anyone he knew.

More mud, more blood

So far it had been the infamous "phony war." Canadian soldiers marched around under WWI helmets, but it did not look as if they would be getting onto eastward-bound ships anytime soon. It was called the phony war because British Commonwealth and French troops were not involved. The Russians were invading Finland, and Germany had not yet paid any attention to the western front. London prepared for air raids that should have happened already. There were some skirmishes at sea. Some deluded folks believed that a naval blockade would keep Hitler's attention on Eastern Europe.

Canada did not have a big war machine, but we seemed to have time. The pip pips in London decided that the air war would be the deciding factor in any expansion of the fighting, and that Canada should be the Commonwealth's air force training base. This suited the Canadian government fine, and the expensive process of carving out air training bases was begun. In decades to come some of these bases would be used to train NATO pilots, but for now they would be manned by Australians and New Zealanders.

Two weeks after the Canadian election, Hitler put an end to the phony war and demonstrated the horrifying "effectiveness" of his war machine, introducing a new word to English usage—*Blitzkrieg*. It translates as "lightning war," but in 1940 no one among the Allies needed a translation.

On April 9 German troops overran Denmark and Norway. On May 10 the dreadful machine raced across Belgium and Holland. On June 17 France begged for mercy. A year earlier Britain had stood with France and the Soviets against the Third Reich. Now the Soviets had jumped ship and the French were doing likewise. Britain, along with its little companions in Canada, Australia, New Zealand and South Africa, would try to hold off the Nazi conquest. In the US they were busy making more millionaires.

The US government thought that the fall of France would be followed by the fall of Britain. Churchill was contacted and told that the US would be happy to hold on to the Royal Navy's ships instead of letting them fall into Kraut hands. Screw you, said Churchill, perhaps in more elegant terms. Then Franklin Delano Roosevelt came back with a second offer—he would send fifty archaic destroyers to the Brits in exchange for US military bases in Newfoundland, Bermuda and the eastern part of the West Indies. Churchill was, of course, offended by this typical Yankee salesmanship. Keep your old destroyers, he said, but he did sign the leases for Newfoundland and Bermuda.

Mackenzie King showed that he too could make deals with the USAmericans. He sat in FDR's private rail car in Ogdensburg, New York, across the river from Prescott, Ontario, and signed a handwritten joint defence treaty with the US. The US president got the Canadian prime minister's name wrong, as often happens, but little Willy King always liked it when he got to sit down with presidents and prime ministers. Forgotten for the moment was the prime minister's usual insistence that he would not act without approval from Parliament.

In the first years of the war Canadian fighting men would be seen most often in the skies or on the dangerous North Atlantic convoy run. But there were two major debacles for the ground forces, Hong Kong and Dieppe. In November 1941 two thousand imperfectly prepared Canadians sailed from Vancouver to protect the garrison of Hong Kong from the expansionist Japanese. The Japanese overran the garrison on Christmas Day, and the Canadians began to grow skinny in slave labour camps. Only fourteen hundred of them were alive at liberation and able to come back to Canada and be forgotten.

In the summer of 1942 the Allied command decided to try a raid on Hitler's continent, to see what would happen so that they could plan the invasion that had to come sometime. They noticed that the Canadians had not been chasing the German field marshal Erwin Rommell in Africa, so decided to send five thousand Canuck rookies across the English Channel. All summer the rehearsals kept going wrong, and British officers said pip pip. Won't we need heavy naval bombardment to prepare the way for the Canadian tanks and infantrymen? asked the Canucks. The British admiral said that he was not about to put big ships in such a narrow spot while the Luftwaffe was still patrolling. Well, what about air bombardment? asked the Canucks. The air force was busy elsewhere. So when the tanks and infantrymen hit the beach on August 19, there were a hell of a lot of undamaged Germans waiting for them with artillery and machine guns. Nine hundred Canadians died and two thousand were made POWs in that town from which Acadians had sailed a few centuries before.

Thanks, Canada. Now the High Command had a pretty good idea of what not to do.

Prisoners of war

There were Canadians in prison camps in Asia and Europe. It was time to get some behind wire in North America.

Canada's first WWII internment camps were set up for Europeans, though. Pretty soon there would be German POWs in Alberta and Northern Ontario, plotting escape to the neutral USA. But the first prisoners were not the Germans—they were the victims of the Germans. Britain had decided that it could not afford to keep adult refugees from Germany and Austria because there would be spies among them, so they were shipped to Canada. Canada built twenty-six internment camps. There would be forty thousand people in those camps eventually, some of them enemy soldiers, many of them people who had fallen short of Hitler's racial and cultural ideal.

Camp B/70, for example, built beside the Saint John River a little east of Fredericton, got its first seven hundred internees in the summer of 1940. They were guarded by barbed wire, sentry towers and old soldiers.

Rural New Brunswickers knew that these strangers had come from countries that Canada was at war against. How were they supposed to know the subtle differences between Nazi soldiers and Orthodox Jews?

A year later there was a second camp set up right next door. This one did hold German and Italian servicemen, as well as Germans and Italians who had for some reason stayed in Canada after the outbreak of war. There were also some dangerous Canadian citizens behind wire. Perhaps the most famous of these was that mayor of Montreal, Camillien Houde, who had said those nice things about Mussolini and Marshal Philippe Pétain, head of the collaborationist government in unoccupied Vichy, France. The feds had passed a National Resources Mobilization Act, to register people for internal service. Houde said that it was a plot to introduce conscription and advised Quebeckers to refuse registration. He would stay in detention until 1944, when conscription was begun. At Camp B/70 he was accompanied by Adrien Arcand, the leader of Quebec's Fascist movement.

That mobilization act had been passed because at last it occurred to Canadian leaders that Canada itself was in danger. Britain, the last ally left in Europe, could be bombarded by the Germans, and the Royal Navy could be captured and pointed westward. German U-boats could slip up the St. Lawrence River or into Maritime coves. The Japanese took over a couple of foggy Aleutian Islands, and a Japanese sub actually flung a few shells at a British Columbia lighthouse. Japanese balloons with explosive charges dangling from them occasionally fell into a wet forest. A lot of servicemen hooked up with the US forces and built airstrips in the BC North.

Here was Canada, threatened by two huge and successful enemies, both capable of crossing oceans. There could be spies and double agents and traitors everywhere. So we locked up a lot of people who did not have English last names. We locked up Italians and Germans and Jews with German names, and Ukrainians and Romanians, and so on. On the West Coast we joined our fear of the exotic with BC's traditional anti-Asian activity, and took all the Japanese Canadians away from the coast so that they could not signal to submarines where the choice targets were.

The RCMP infiltrated the Japanese-Canadian community, and eventually made a report that indicated higher levels of patriotism there than in the populace as a whole, including buying bonds, trying to enlist and giving blood to the Red Cross. But there were energetic racists working at all levels of government, and when Pearl Harbor and Hong Kong happened the Japanese Canadians could see the graffiti on the wall. As soon as Canada declared war on Japan, forty Japanese citizens were slapped into jail, all the Japanese Canadian–owned fishing boots were tied up and Japanese language schools and newspapers disappeared.

The JC community tried everything they could to demonstrate their loyalty. Japanese-Canadian soldiers would leave their blood on the ground in Italy. But there were white fishermen and farmers in BC who dreamed of an economic future free of Japanese-Canadian competition. Mackenzie King was slow to give in to the mob, even when it was led by his own MPs. It was not that he didn't keep up his end as a racist. He did not like the fact that Jews were buying property next to his in Quebec. He would be thankful that the atomic bomb was dropped on Asians rather than Europeans. He was not comfortable with the fact that India made it into the Commonwealth. But he dragged his feet when it came to hauling away the Japanese Canadians, because he did not want retaliation against the Canadian POWs at Hong Kong.

At the end of February 1942, twenty thousand people were herded into the Pacific National Exhibition grounds in east Vancouver and then herded to internment camps or deserted mining towns in eastern BC, the Prairies or as far east as Ontario. They were allowed to take a suitcase and a blanket each. In all the confusion of wartime their boats and houses and stores and farms somehow fell into the hands of white folks.

I was living in Greenwood, BC, at the time. Being six years old, I found it confusing when I saw the caricatures of evil Jap fighter plane pilots with their huge teeth and thick glasses, and then went to get my teeth fixed by a thin Japanese-Canadian dentist who shared my first name. Well, so did the king, and he knew what was what.

Community kitchen at Japanese-Canadian internment camp, c. 1943
(NATIONAL ARCHIVES OF CANADA/C-024452)

Remember those First Nations people who had been finding it a little difficult to live in the concentration camps called reserves? One way to get out was to join up and fight Europeans over there. The Native enlistment rate, at six thousand enlistees, was higher than the overall rate. Well, this would be a good deal, wouldn't it? After fighting for democracy in Europe they would come home to a country that would give them more freedom than they had in the past, wouldn't they?

D-Day and after

The six years of World War II (a little under four years if you are a USAmerican) made for a long and highly complex story that would take an entire book, if not several books, to tell even in outline. Fortunately, there are a lot of such books, and at any time a TV viewer with a channel changer will be able to find a program about the war, complete with historical film footage.

The long-awaited invasion of Europe started in Malta and Sicily in July 1943, and in Normandy on June 6, 1944. Notwithstanding the movies from Hollywood, there were a lot of British troops and Free French and fourteen thousand Canadians at D-Day. The Canadians are still being commemorated every year in Holland and Belgium because of their major role in killing and chasing young German men in those countries.

Lionel Shapiro, who also wrote my high school history book, wrote a novel called *The Sixth of June*, and it won the Governor General's Award for fiction for 1955. Thirteen years later Roch Carrier published his first novel, *La guerre, yes sir!*, which would later be adapted for the stage. In a wonky comedic fashion, Carrier tells the story of Quebec villagers irritated and confused by the WWII draft, and allegorizes the historic misunderstandings between rural Quebec and strange English Canada.

No one will ever get English-speaking Canadians and French-speaking Quebeckers to agree on the question of conscription. The English speakers say that the Quebeckers were cowards who would not fight for democracy. The Quebeckers say that they would not fight to protect anything that smacks of the British Crown, which has always oppressed them. Any outsider can see that both positions are ridiculous, but that has never stopped opponents from denouncing one another. In World War II Mackenzie King did not want to see conscription for overseas duty because that would persuade his Quebec members to jump ship.

Nevertheless the question would not just go away. In the middle year of the war, it became clear that the fighting could go on for a decade or two, and manpower was the country's most valuable resource. In late 1942 the government issued a strange but tactically shrewd referendum: would the people of Canada release the prime minister from his pledge that there would never be full conscription? Of course English Canada said you bet, and French Canada said forget it. King offered one of his enduring phrases when he declared that his aim was "not necessarily conscription but conscription if necessary." The reply from Quebec usually had the word *merde* in it.

After D-Day there were a lot of casualties on the Continent. Men got patched and thrown back into battle. On the home front there were women from the farms now making Bren guns. Boys and girls bought war savings stamps with pictures of tanks on them and wondered whether the war would still be on when they got out of school. In King's cabinet and the PM's Office there was a tussle between conscriptionists and antis. There were not enough recruits banging on the door. Mackenzie King finally decided to bite the bullet. He got help from his new Quebec lieutenant, Louis St. Laurent, and passed an Order-in-Council to turn sixteen thousand home-service draftees (called "Zombies") into overseas servicemen. St. Laurent went around *la belle province* describing the depth of King's unhappiness at the decision.

They held the usual riots in Quebec anyway. A lot of Zombies, there and elsewhere, headed for the hills. But thirteen thousand of them got onto ships and landed in England. About twenty-five hundred went into some degree of battle. A few got shot at and sixty-seven of them died. Of all the armies fighting against Fascism, Canada lost the smallest number of draftees. Still, King had taken a risk. He was relieved when he carried Quebec and won a majority in the election of spring 1945. FDR had died. Churchill had lost his election. Hitler and Mussolini had been killed. King and Stalin were still standing. He saw this as a sign from providence or history.

Switching empires

The war had brought full employment and boom manufacturing. At the beginning of peacetime things were good, and, following tradition, the Liberal Party of Canada took credit. Europe was devastated. England and France and Germany were broke. Now the USA had the richest economy in the world, and Canada's was second by an eagle's feather. It would not be long till the Canadian dollar was valued higher than the US one. Mackenzie King got his picture taken with the new US president, Harry Truman, and Dwight Eisenhower, who had commanded the USAmerican forces in Europe. As a young man King had worked for US billionaires, his grandfather had been harboured in the USA, and now he saw Canada's prosperity tied to the optimistic spirit of the US capitalist machine.

Oh, and he wanted to be the longest-serving prime minister in the history of the English-speaking world. The record holder was Robert Walpole, who pretty well invented the position in the eighteenth century. He had ruled for 7,619 days. All King had to do was stay in office till the end of April 1948. What a fortunate coincidence (except that King did not think anything a coincidence), in that 1948 would come to be known as the greatest year in civilization.

In the meantime, there were some interesting historical events to engineer. When the United Nations was formed in San Francisco just before the 1945 election, Canada was there as a founding member, advocating universal membership and participation in all UN agencies. When the Colombo Plan was instigated to promote economic growth in Asia, Canada was a founding member of that as well. But although he sent his two brightest stars, Louis St. Laurent and Lester B. (Mike) Pearson, to San Francisco, King did not think that the UN would work any better to preserve peace than the League of Nations had. For collective security he would throw in with the US, as he had shown when he signed that scrap of paper in FDR's rail car. John A. Macdonald's ghost was glad that his body had been buried with its back to the US.

King's man St. Laurent did more than anyone in the world to bring about the Cold War alliance called the North Atlantic Treaty Organization. When the Communists clambered to power in Czechoslovakia in 1948, North Americans did not need much urging to sign up with the Western European forces. It was a perfect union for King, because both the old mother country, Britain, and the adopted one, the US, were original signatories. King really did believe that the Communist menace was fearsome and that the US approach to Communism was right.

So when Ottawa got its own Cold War spy drama with the defection of the Russian file clerk Igor Gouzenko, King loved it and the Canadian people ate it up. The guy came on TV with a pillowcase over his head and told everyone that there were Commies in the Parliament Buildings.

People looked at the map and saw that Canada was right in the middle between the Soviet Union and the Capitalist one. We cozied up. We watched US television and US movies, and our magazines had Elizabeth Taylor instead of Elizabeth Windsor on the covers.

The monarchist organizations across the country had a lot to fume about in the late forties. On January 1, 1947, the new Canadian Citizenship Act came into effect, replacing British-subject status for Canadians. On the third, the seventy-two-year-old PM became the first person to receive a certificate. It was slow to catch on in some places. In 1963, when I was being entertained in the depths of the Vancouver Public Safety Building, the cop behind the desk asked my nationality. When I said Canadian, he said that the only Canadians were Indians. When I would not claim any other nationality the two cops on my side of the desk beat the living daylights out of me and threw me into a closet.

Nothing like that happened to Mackenzie King. His party told him that they could wait till he set his record, but then he had to go. It was wonderful having him. There were twice as many Canadians as there had been when first he was prime minister. But in 1948 it was not a good idea to look old. There would be an election in 1949, or 1950 at the latest. If the Liberal Party was going to reign forever, it had to get a new leader.

Mackenzie King went to his favourite fortune teller and checked it out. Then he told his party that if they got Newfoundland into Canada, they could have a new prime minister. Oh, and by the way, he said, I am leaning toward the Quebec guy, St. Laurent.

By the time World War II was over, Tom Longboat had retired to the Ohsweken reserve, where he had been a child named Cogwagee. When he needed a week's groceries he walked six miles and back to get them. He had once been the most famous human being on earth. He had met kings and potentates. Two hundred thousand Torontonians had turned out to welcome him back from Boston. He died in January 1949, and his spirit took off running.

NUCLEAR AND 17 UNCLEAR

Prime Minister Louis St. Laurent on swing with children,
probably during election campaign, 1949
(NATIONAL ARCHIVES OF CANADA/PA-123991)

We like to remember the fifties as being a lot like the "Archie" comic strip. There might be something to it—in most years the highest concentration of "Archie" readers has been in Edmonton, Alberta. But I don't remember anything about the atom bomb in "Archie." We were all afraid that we were going to be killed in an insane worldwide atomic storm set off by the fear and hatred between the Russians and the USAmericans. We didn't stop to consider that neither the Russians nor the USAmericans were likely to drop atom bombs on white people.

Our parents had been told that World War I was the war to end all wars. In the first years after World War II we were eager to try out this strange thing called peacetime, but we did not harbour any illusions about the end of war. We saw that the big manufacturing machine built to sustain the most recent war could be turned to making airliners and television sets and all the new gadgets that made us glad to be alive midway through the twentieth century. With the Canadian dollar ahead of the US dollar it even looked as if our first French-Canadian prime minister had been right.

Now our second French-Canadian prime minister smiled benignly with his old-fashioned and very Quebecky moustache as Canada grew and grew. While Louis St. Laurent was prime minister the vote was extended to the Inuit people, though it would not be given to other Native folks for another decade. The Supreme Court replaced the British Privy Council as the final court of appeal. Vincent Massey was appointed governor general, the first Canadian-born person to represent the English monarchy here. The Canada Council for the Arts would be inaugurated, and become the most important factor in the country's fight to stay out of Hollywood's sock drawer. The National Library would be invented, so that the story of Canada would not become a rumour known only to a few Cape Breton auto-repair workers. The Liberals under King might have snuggled us under Uncle Sam's arm, but his successor's government was looking for ways to keep our culture alive.

Counting on all fingers

By the end of the war there were US military men and machines all over Newfoundland and Labrador. Newfoundland was a handy place in mid-century. From Newfoundland, intercontinental planes, airliners or bombers, had their shortest jumps to Europe. For the US, Newfoundland would make a nice bookend to join Alaska, and Labrador would make another nice panhandle along what should be Canadian waters. Britain had been trying to get rid of Labrador for ages and had twice given Newfoundland responsible government, only to have the rock jump back into colonial status. But at the end of World

War II Britain was financially overextended overseas. It wanted Hong Kong and Gibraltar a heck of a lot more than it wanted Newfoundland and Labrador.

Canada had sent a lot of troops and civilians to Newfoundland during the war, too, and there were of course British officials and servicemen on the island. These were the best times Newfoundland had experienced in living memory. But the Brits pointed out that the 1934 recolonization was supposed to last only fifteen years. The voters among the population of 345,000 would have to make a decision. The possibilities were very much like those facing British Columbia before its entry into Canada: (1) independence, (2) join the USA, (3) join Canada. The first referendum seemed to favour independence, so those in favour of joining Canada caused a second referendum, and then said that the majority had chosen Canada.

With Newfoundland as a tenth province in 1949, the Liberal power structure went for an election. They figured that the grateful Newfies would vote Liberal and life would go on as it should. The Conservatives chose a boring man named George Drew as their leader and struck up an alliance with Duplessis and Camillien Houde, who was out of the concentration camp and back in the Montreal mayor's chair. This cabal portrayed the Liberals as part of the Communist threat, along with unions and the CCF. Sure, it was the morning of the Cold War, but this was not Washington. The Liberals, with Uncle Louis patting the heads of all the children he could reach, trounced the anti-Communist alliance and sat back for a while to let the prosperous country take care of itself.

The Cold War warms up

St. Laurent and his new secretary of state for foreign affairs, Lester B. Pearson, got interested in the Commonwealth of Nations and decided that Canada should take over as the Commonwealth's moral leader. Mackenzie King had never been much interested in international groups, unless they were led by the US military. Now Pearson and his prime minister joined with the Indian prime minister, Pandit Jawaharlal

Nehru, in encouraging the Commonwealth to promote economic advance in the newly independent states of Asia, and especially to recognize Mao's China. But the hysterical US reaction to "Red China" proved that Canada had switched empires. Even though progressive Northern European nations recognized China, Canada cuddled up to the USAmericans, who had persuaded themselves that they were taking a high moral position by backing Chiang Kai-shek's invasion of Taiwan.

In 1948 the Soviets had pulled their troops out of North Korea. In 1949 the US started leaving South Korea. In 1950 the anxiety about war got really high when the North Koreans marched into South Korea to explain their idea about reunification of the peninsula. This was only five years after the US atom bombs had obliterated two Asian cities. Most people assumed that the next world war would involve atom bombs, and the Soviets had figured out how to make atom bombs.

There was an emergency meeting of the Security Council of the United Nations. The Chinese Nationalist occupiers of Taiwan held the Chinese seat. The Soviets boycotted the meeting for that reason. The remaining members decided to send a multinational force to push the North Koreans back across the thirty-eighth parallel. A few days later the Canadian cabinet sat in a railway car of Mackenzie King's funeral train and decided to send naval and air support for the UN forces.

There were no riots in Quebec. A French-Canadian prime minister had made this decision, and the armed forces were not going to be sent to pull Britain's tail out of the fire. The majority of Quebeckers might have disapproved of the military call-up, but more than 30 percent of the army sent to Korea was made up of soldiers from the province.

There were a lot of WWII soldiers who had not been able to adjust to civilian life. And in 1949 the fist big post-war recession hit, making the army our principal employer in the early fifties. They would not get home for a few Christmases, though. The Chinese entered the war on the side of their North Korean allies, and back and forth went the freezing or sweltering armies, as jet fighters flew overhead.

Eventually 26,791 Canadians fought in Korea, and over five hundred were killed. It was a strange war. No one could figure out how it might end. In most wars you advanced until the bad guys were defeated and the disputed territory was back in the hands of the government you liked. Somehow everyone knew that this could not happen in Korea. Though there were seventeen UN countries fighting for the South, the US considered this their war, and they had atom bombs. When the US president told a press conference that the A-bomb was a possibility, the other sixteen countries wanted to know what was going on. The US said that since the UN had given the US responsibility for this war you could not expect the US to ask permission of its allies.

The Korean "Police Action" never did grab the imagination of Canadians. Who knew anything about Korea? Who had relatives there? Though the defence budget in 1953 was ten times what it had been in 1947, Canadians never did make as good anti-Communists as USAmericans did. When Gen. Douglas MacArthur was replaced by the relatively sane Matthew Ridgeway in 1951, and when the seemingly endless alternation between ceasefires and flare-ups finally resulted in an armistice on July 27, 1953, Canadians were just as happy to get that uninteresting war over and done with.

But that war confirmed a new fact for Canadians. We were now living on a globe that we had to keep track of, because the Communists were intent on taking over the whole works, and the Capitalists were intent on stopping them, and there were a lot of little countries up for grabs.

In Canada we saw a lot of US movies about the Cold War. We hardly ever saw any Soviet movies about the Cold War. This was hardly fair, was it? If you had a look at a map of the globe instead of the old Mercator projection, you saw that the Soviet Union was just about as close a neighbour as the US. But Canada was getting to be more and more like the US. In the US there were two main attitudes toward Canada: (a) where's that? or (b) what's the difference?

The US military, of course, had noticed what the globe looks like if you are looking down at the North Pole. As soon as the Soviets developed atomic weapons, the US decided that it needed to defend itself against delivery of these weapons, so they got interested in a series of defence perimeters in the space between the Soviet Union and the US. This would mean destroying Soviet bombers and missiles before they could reach, say, North Dakota or Vermont. If there were going to be atomic explosions, they should occur over Canadian snow. The Pinetree Line ran along the fiftieth parallel. I was a Royal Canadian Air Force photographer on the Pinetree Line. I was stationed in Manitoba but don't remember seeing a pine tree there. Our radar was supposed to check for anything that had got past the Mid-Canada Line. It ran across the country at the fifty-fifth parallel, which in Eastern Canada is way the hell and gone north, but which in Western Canada is halfway up the provinces. But the most dramatic and romantic line was the DEW Line (Distant Early Warning Line) along the seventieth parallel. These stations were entirely US outfits. If a Canadian and his dogsled got too close, he and his dogs could get shot. This was serious Cold War stuff. The situation did not seem strange to the US, which had missile bases along most the borders of the Soviet Union, and which would maintain that there was a natural US seaway between the islands of Canada's Arctic.

The US point of view was that we were enjoying a free ride. They were paying for the DEW Line, after all. And if there were any Canadians left after Armageddon they could help themselves to the radioactive scrap metal all over their country.

TV nation

During the fifties, the coaxial cables marched east and west from the Montreal/Toronto control room and across the country, bringing television pictures and the promise of more good times. Look at all these products, we were told. Tired farmers fell asleep while Giselle Mackenzie sang fifties songs with a smile on her face.

A lot of people like me remember Giselle Mackenzie and Shirley Harmer, and although we know that it was pretty bad stuff we were watching, at least it was Canadian pretty bad stuff. Most Canadians are fairly sure they want to keep Canada Canadian, but most Canadians are too dopey to notice the methods by which someone else is getting hold of it piece by piece. They would rather listen to USAmericans singing and pitching products than hear what is happening on CBC.

Yet it was a go-getter USAmerican who got some of Canada's megaprojects going in the fifties. C. D. Howe first came to Canada as a professor at Dalhousie University. Then he went west and built grain elevators from Toronto to Vancouver, becoming the richest grain elevator man in history. During the Depression he went into politics, and became Mackenzie King's most robust cabinet minister. During the war he was given special powers and the job of defence production. After the war he got the task of putting the economy back into private hands, and no one remembered to take away his special powers.

He had the biggest ego in Ottawa, and he got on people's nerves. When St. Laurent passed a bill in 1955 to ease back on Howe's power, Howe called the prime minister and his cabinet a bunch of wusses. He was the man who got Trans-Canada Airlines into the sky. Now as trade and commerce minister he was going to go underground. Since 1949 the oil companies in Alberta had been finding an oil gusher every time someone tried to dig a posthole. Howe wanted to get this oil across the country, and he didn't care where the money to do it came from, as long as the conveyance stayed in Canada. The dream of his first big pipeline would scare the bejabbers out of any ordinary politician. This line would run east across the prairies to Northern Ontario, into Quebec and down to New York. Impossible. Too big. Ridiculous, said the Tories and some of the Liberals. That's what they said about the CPR and the St. Lawrence Seaway, said Howe. I got the money for World War II, he reminded his government.

It took him a few votes and a few years and a few quasi-legal tricks in the House of Commons and a few strikes by US pipe makers, but the TransCanada Pipeline became the longest in the world, bringing oil to the eager furnaces of Southern Ontario. It was followed by the Trans-Mountain from Edmonton to Vancouver (imagine laying pipe over the Rockies!) and the Interprovincial line to Sarnia.

It was ironic that Howe would compare his pipeline to Van Horne's railway. The fifties saw the demise of steam locomotion and the birth of diesel. The oil boom gave noise to a trucking boom, and gradually shipping went more and more to road travel, which meant that the Trans-Canada Highway got a boost—the equivalent to a last spike was driven in 1963.

In 1958 the young Opera Festival association, which had grown out of the Royal Conservatory of Music in Toronto, became the Canadian Opera Company and began its annual tour with *La Bohème* and *The Tales of Hoffmann*. In 1957 Parliament had created the Canada Council. In 1959 *Canadian Literature*, a critical journal concerned with our serious literary writing, was founded at the University of British Columbia by its editor, George Woodcock. It was at the time a somewhat startling and most welcome idea. In 1957 the Festival Theatre opened in Stratford, Ontario, where the Stratford Shakespearean Festival had been running since Alec Guinness had played Richard III in a tent in the summer of 1953.

Tough cheese

When the French were still running the show in Quebec, they never once considered the notion that Native people might enjoy possession of land. But when in 1718 Louis XV granted seigneury to the Seminary of St-Sulpice at the joining of the Ottawa and St. Lawrence Rivers, it was with the understanding that its only purpose would be as a mission for the education and Christianization of the savages. In 1721 there were a thousand Natives living at the Lake of Two Mountains. The land was not ceded to the Natives themselves because they were not supposed to be smart enough to take care of it.

For some reason, the Mohawk living at what they called Kanesatake came to believe that this was their land. But when the English took over Quebec they honoured the Church's hegemony at the mission. In 1781 the Natives went to court to try to prove their proprietorship, but they lost. In 1841 there was a whole new generation of Mohawk who got it into their heads that they should run this place, but the government issued a special ordinance ensuring that the seminary was still in charge. This was the government's way of thanking the seminary for refusing to go along with the rebels in 1837.

But then with the presence of the British, the Mohawk started leaving the Catholic Church and becoming Protestants. For this reason the seminary began to import French-Canadian settlers, who, while they were not wealthy, had an economic advantage over the Natives. In the 1850s the government set aside land in other locations, and some of the Mohawk accepted that compromise, but most did not. Now they began to survey lots for themselves and to cut trees to sell as firewood. In response, the government threw some Natives into jail.

The government would continue to throw the leaders into jail for the rest of the century. Chief Joseph Onasakenarat, for example, was jailed eight times. In 1869 John A. Macdonald's cabinet brought down an Order-in-Council, reaffirming the seminary's control. Lake of Two Mountains became more and more white and more and more commercial. The village of Oka was established in 1875. In 1881 some Trappist monks from France arrived and built an abbey, creating one of the largest Trappist monasteries in the world. They became best known, perhaps, for their innocuous soft cheese.

Also in 1875 the Sulpician seminary got a court order and tore down the Methodist church that so many of the Mohawk had drifted toward. Then someone burned the Catholic church, and after several trials, the Native suspects were freed by an English-speaking jury. In 1878 yet another government inquiry found that the place belonged to the seminary. Then the seminary bought some land in Ontario and offered it to the Natives. Again a few went for it, but most wanted to stay where they had been born and brought up on land that their grandparents had lived on. In 1883 there was another government report that kept the land in seminary hands, but suggested that the Natives should get compensation because they had been led to believe that the seminary existed only to administer the land for the Native people.

More violence and more court cases led to 1912, when the Privy Council decided in favour of the seminary but said that the Native people should be recipients of a trust fund. A trust fund is not land, they rejoined. Then during the Depression the seminary sold most of the land, including the forest at Oka, to a Belgian real estate outfit. Anyone other than a Church official or a government agent could see that such a sale was not allowed by the original granting of the seigneury. A white folks' sawmill started turning the forest into lumber, and as soon as WWII was over, the Belgian company began selling plots of land for farming by white folks.

Alarmed, the Department of Indian and Northern Affairs bought up as much of the land as they could, and said, there, we have saved something for you lucky Indian folks. There weren't that many trees on this acreage, but it was something, eh? The Mohawk did not fawn all over themselves in gratitude. They hired lawyers and pressed their case. At least the violence of previous years had faded away, and by the end of the 1950s, the dispute was taking place quietly indoors while the scent of cheese wafted over Oka.

Dief and Mike

A lot of politicians were lawyers. Well, legislatures and parliaments make laws, so I suppose that makes sense. A lot of politicians were lawyers for rich people and rich corporations—Robber Baron Bennett and Brian Mulroney, for example. John Diefenbaker was a defence lawyer for poor farmers and Natives who had got into serious trouble with the law in Saskatchewan. Sometimes Dief travelled from courthouse to courthouse on a handcar along the CN tracks. He grew up in a shack on the bald-headed prairie, and he never forgot it when he was living on Sussex Drive in Ottawa.

He was a Progressive Conservative in a province that had been owned all through the century by the Liberals. He ran in every election that came along, and lost and lost until he got into the House by a fluke in 1940. Then he ran for his party's leadership over and over, and finally got that by a fluke in 1957. But he had known since childhood that he was Destiny's son. He would rise up out of the Prairies and demolish the tired old Liberal Party. Uncle Louis St. Laurent patted children's heads while a grassfire burned eastward. In 1957 the Liberals were chased back into Quebec. Dief did not have a majority, but he had a crowd of newspaper cartoonists and TV comedians pulling for him.

He was wonderful to watch. He leaned so far forward that he looked as if he would fall into the audience. He quivered and trembled in mock righteousness. His voice squeaked and thundered. He winked and grimaced and aped for the camera. Ottawa had not seen anything like this since John A. Macdonald. Dief the Chief never made a speech without quoting John A. He was a funny-looking guy with a peculiar way of talking, but people followed him as if he were another Elvis. In 1958 the Liberals threw Lester B. Pearson, the hero of Suez, at him, and the prairie fire burned them all down. The Conservatives got an amazing 208 seats. All the rest got 57.

Then he had to govern. The trouble was that he did not have a Quebec lieutenant, he did not have any alliances with big business, the USAmericans didn't like him and he could not shake his sympathy for the ordinary working joe. There was a high level of unemployment, and the Canadian dollar was living beyond its means. Did the Chief decide to ride it out the way Uncle Louis had done in the post-war era? No, he did what Robert Borden had done—he moved the Conservative Party to the left of the Liberals.

That sort of thing will get people mad at you. He got the US mad at him by going to a Commonwealth Conference and promising to shift 15 percent of Canada's trade with the US back to the mother country. He got the Brits mad at him by going to a Commonwealth Conference and joining the fight against South African apartheid. All the black prime ministers were in favour of discussing the problem and ousting the South African republic. (Those black prime ministers were in the commonwealth partly because Dief had argued so hard for the inclusion of newly independent black nations.) All the white prime ministers with one exception were in favour of forgetting the problem. Diefenbaker, the only white prime minister without a British name, was that exception.

John G. Diefenbaker
(NATIONAL ARCHIVES OF CANADA/C-6779)

Diefenbaker had the unfortunate habit of telling people what he thought about moral issues. He was probably the most reformist prime minister we have had, and the most patriotic. He tried to lean away from the Brits, and he tried to lean away from the US. When people asked him what he was leaning toward, he said independence. When asked how we would achieve this, he said look to the North. He had a marvellous vision of an opened North ensuring Canada's pre-eminence.

So maybe he was an Alice in Rideauland. He believed that black people should not be treated unfairly in South Africa or the USA, and that Native people should not be treated unfairly in Canada. He had represented Native people in scrabapple Saskatchewan courthouses. Now he gave them the vote. He made the first Native senator and the first female cabinet minister. He ended the immigration quotas for people of colour. He appointed a French-Canadian governor general (Georges Vanier). He made the government issue bilingual cheques, and he introduced instant translation into the House of Commons. He proclaimed the Canadian Bill of Rights, which forbade discrimination by race or religion or political beliefs. Unfortunately some less idealistic lawyers in provincial courts pointed out that they did not have to observe the bill because it was not entrenched in the constitution, the BNA Act. The constitution should be moved from London to Ottawa, said Diefenbaker. That is not going to happen, said the provincial lawyers.

Eventually all this idealism got under the skin of the US. How could they live next door to a loudmouth who stuck up for racial equality and Canadian independence? Dief had got along all right with sleepy old Dwight Eisenhower, that man who said that America should beware the military-industrial complex. But John Kennedy the rich crook's son was another matter.

First Diefenbaker made them mad by arranging big sales of Western Canadian wheat to China. The US was mad because everyone was supposed to buy into their Cold War. Kennedy and his testosteronic appointed cabinet were already pissed off at the man whose name they could never get right—after the US bullied Canada into allowing US-made missiles on Canadian soil, they were not able to force Diefenbaker to allow US atomic warheads with US technicians to tend them. When asked what should be in the warheads of these missiles, the Chief suggested sand. Kennedy and his hitmen started looking for a way to get rid of this Northern head of government.

Then when the Soviets noticed that there were US atomic missiles all along the Turkish-Soviet border, and figured the US would understand if there were Soviet missiles in Cuba, Kennedy and his crew went into High Noon mode to get the missiles out of Cuba, and people I knew in Vancouver headed for the mountains. Kennedy's bunch were mad at Canada anyway, for continuing trade with Cuba even after the Cuban government had taken the Cuban palaces away from US gangsters. Now during this macho showdown with the Russkies in October

1962, Kennedy figured that Canada ought to be his Bulgaria. To heck with NATO or NORAD or any defence agreement. This was a matter for the Monroe Doctrine.

Kennedy sent his warships into the Atlantic to intercept the Reds. The prime minister of Canada was supposed to send a telegram saying way to go, Jack! But Diefenbaker, according to his detractors, dithered. For instance, he mentioned the UN as a possible peacekeeper. When Kennedy phoned him and started yelling at him, Dief asked when Canada had been consulted on the matter. Kennedy cursed on the phone. The Canadian defence minister, Douglas Harkness, got the military ready for a crisis without notifying the Chief. Eventually the Chief said go ahead and issue an alert, and his entourage got ready to set up shop in the "Diefenbunker," the fancy bomb shelter the cabinet could converse in while the Parliament Buildings were being turned into radioactive dust.

Eventually the Cuban Missile Crisis was eased. Nikita Khrushchev kept his shoe on and said that he would take his missiles back home. Jack Kennedy promised in return that the US would never have anything to do with any invasion of Cuba. He had his fingers crossed behind his back.

Now it was time for Kennedy to figure out how to get rid of this old fart he called "Deefenbocker." If Canada were a Spanish-speaking country, he could just have the PM shot. Maybe he could send one of his girlfriends, maybe the one who was making it with Mafia bosses, up to Ottawa to compromise the old duffer or give him a heart attack. Instead he sent Gen. Lauris Norstad, the just-retired commander of NATO. Norstad actually looked like a hawk. When he came to Ottawa to make a speech, Diefenbaker sent his associate minister of defence, Pierre Sévigny, to represent the government. Sévigny would become famous for screwing a Soviet spy. Norstad was really browned off. He told reporters that Canadian fighter pilots had better carry atomic weapons or else.

Next day there were editorials that asked whether there was such a thing as an autonomous Canadian government. Mike Pearson, the famous Suez peacekeeper, said to himself, "Say, I could get a Liberal government elected if we—" Pearson the peaceable professor had always stated his aversion to atomic weapons. Now he said that we had a duty to show our friendship with our southern neighbours and to deploy US atomic missiles in Canada. There is a guy I could get along with, said Kennedy. Pretty soon *Time* magazine was running nice pieces about Pearson, and money was pouring into Liberal coffers, as they say, and Dief the Chief's days were numbered.

Back onside

The business-oriented Conservatives of Ontario wanted their party back. They didn't care a rap for human rights and national independence and all that expensive stuff. Still, in 1962 Dief got himself another minority, but the Libs forced an election in 1963, and now Pearson had his first minority government. Ah gee whiz, Pearson had always said, I don't know whether I am interested in politics. Jeepers, the Nobel Peace Prize, for me? Jiminy Cricket, I don't know whether I could be party leader. Gosh, become prime minister—me? In 1963 he had an expression on his face that said how did this happen? But Jack Kennedy saw him wink.

John Diefenbaker's government had done a lot for French Canada, but Maurice Duplessis died in 1959, and his Union Nationale was replaced in 1960 by the Quiet Revolution, also called Jean Lesage and the newly nationalist Quebec Liberals. Jean Marchand, the great union leader, had secularized the unions, pointing out that the Catholic Church had been on Duplessis's side when he quashed the great Asbestos uprising of 1949. Conservative rural Quebec was becoming less rural because a chain-smoking television journalist named René Lévesque was entering parlours and explaining the modern world. A wealthy young lawyer named Pierre Trudeau went so far as to suggest that education should take place outside the Church.

In a few years the hotshot young Liberals did create a lay school system, and inaugurated a network of CEGEPs, the Quebec version of community colleges. Lévesque, as a minister in the Lesage government, was involved in the nationalization of the huge electricity industry. In

1962 the Quebec voters again returned the Liberals, and when the Union Nationale was defeated, their allies in Ottawa began to look toward a few years in opposition.

For the US the sixties would mean a decade of war in Asia and political assassinations stateside. For Canada the sixties would mean Quebec. The Quiet Revolution had demonstrated to thinking Quebeckers that their province could pretty much go it alone as a country. They had the resources and the population and the intellectuals. They had the culture and a big wide river to the sea. These things were noticed by thinking English Canadians, too. The federal Liberal Party and the NDP, which was a party that had taken the CCF and added unions and moved rightward, soon adopted the two-nations concept—Canada should be seen not only as a group of ten provinces and some territories, but also as a country made up of two founding nations, using the word in the French sense, of course.

There were still some old-fashioned illiberal Quebeckers around. The Quiet Revolution people were glittery big-city folks with an intellectual leaning to the left. But in the 1962 election a stumpy guy in an old Quebec moustache, Réal Caouette, led a gang of Social Creditors into the House of Commons. These people proved that there was still a French-Canadian nationalism that was rural, Catholic and opposed to modern things such as public schools and homosexuality. A year later Caouette's group broke with the western Social Credit party and simply called themselves the Ralliement des Créditistes.

In 1963 the Royal Commission on Bilingualism and Biculturalism went to work, not so much to find out what people thought but to prepare Canadians to think differently, to introduce the idea that federal civil servants should speak both languages and that French Canadians in Saskatchewan should be able to relate to their federal government in French.

Yeah? Well, what about that flag? It has a Union Jack on it.

Lester Pearson decided that negotiations with Quebec City and Washington would go smoother if there was no Union Jack involved. This made John Diefenbaker, the trembling leader of the Opposition, see red. He wanted to go on seeing all the other colours in the Red Ensign, with all its colonial reminders. For six months in 1964 Members of Parliament debated the idea of a new flag. Fulminating old Legion types groused that this was somehow kowtowing to the French Canadians. Yet the Legion had adopted the Maple Leaf as its symbol years before. Canadians with maple leaves sewn on their clothing had fought in three foreign wars. Six months of argument showed that these grown men were not just bickering about a piece of cloth. Finally, Pearson invoked closure, and the Liberals stood and sang "O Canada!" with all its illiberal lyrics. Diefenbaker's crowd sang "God Save the Queen!"

The House of Commons has always been the place where guys in suits can get goofy.

On February 15, Canada's new flag with the red leaf was raised over the Peace Tower in Ottawa. Soon there would be red maple leaf flags fading to orange in the Canadian weather all across the land. In coming years the Canadian maple leaf would become so popular that young US tourists would sew it to their jackets and backpacks so that they would be treated more warmly in foreign countries.

18

CHANGE THE WORLD

Lester B. Pearson
(NATIONAL ARCHIVES OF CANADA)

Lester B. Pearson kept thinking about how nice it would be to have a majority government. He also noticed that in a few years Canada would be a hundred years old. Well, okay, it was a lot older than that already. But it would be easy to persuade Canadians that their country was going to be a hundred years old in 1967. Centenaries are always good for business, including the governing business.

So Pearson called another election for 1965. He had, he thought, got the French Canadians onside by flying the maple leaf. Big business would like the Auto Pact, a free trade deal with the US that dropped all duties on cars and car parts. He figured he'd attracted the softies by passing the Canada Pension Plan, a system whereby employees and employers had to contribute toward an investment plan that would supplement the old-age pension.

Unfortunately there was a series of spectacular scandals involving Liberals and the province of Quebec. Pearson slapped his hand over his eyes often in 1964 and 1965. Was some cheesy B-movie director running the country? A thug named Lucien Rivard seemed to have friends in both the Mafia and the Liberal caucus. No one ever told Mike until one day in the House, when Erik Nielsen, the puritanical Tory MP from the Northwest Territories, rose to ask questions that just baffled the PM. Politics in Quebec can be baffling. One night in the fall of 1964 Lucien Rivard asked permission to take a hose and make a skating rink in the yard at Bordeaux Penitentiary, where he resided. The temperature was 40 degrees above zero Fahrenheit. The rink was already full of water. Why not, said the warden, and Rivard used the hose to get over the wall.

Then there was Hal Banks. Banks was a USAmerican union thug who was brought to Montreal during the St. Laurent era to clean Communists off the waterfront. He and his guys were good with lead pipes and brass knucks. But they also formed monetary friendships with several Quebec members of the Liberal government. Eventually Banks was charged with assault and decided to head back to New York. Erik Nielsen asked the prime minister about this fellow, too.

It would be fun to tell all the stories about the scandals of the early sixties, but we would have to denude another Quebec forest to make the paper to print them on. Diefenbaker and his friends in the House just loved these stories. Dief would open his eyes wide in amazement and waggle his chops and lean waaaaay forward and describe another ethical horror. Lester B. Ballplayer longed for the days when he used to pitch for the Canadian contingent in the Washington embassy league.

Pearson washed his hands and then wrote a letter to Diefenbaker. I have just been looking at this dossier about your former cabinet minister and the East German prostitute, he said. Do you have any information I can add to it? Diefenbaker laid off the theatrics, and Pearson had himself his election. Did he get his majority on November 8, 1965? Read 'em and weep. Everyone gained seats except the Socreds and Créditistes, but Pearson had another minority government. He would have to pal up with the NDP again.

Smile on your brother

There are numerous points of view when it comes to Lester Pearson and national medicare. Some people, for example, say that there was a natural progression in the Liberal platform from Mackenzie King's old-age pension to Pearson's health plan. Others might point out that Pearson's dream of universal medicare was dreamed while Tommy Douglas's NDP was keeping the Liberals from falling to a non-confidence vote.

At the beginning of the twenty-first century Canada's first point of pride is its universal health plan. While global capitalists attack it in any way they can, hoping to make illness a capital resource, Canadians fear the loss of their greatest accomplishment. Many of them are old enough to remember the fight against the medical profiteers forty years earlier.

Tommy Douglas was a Christian who lived in Saskatchewan and watched what happened to farmers and workers during the Depression. How could he not be a socialist? He was there when the CCF was founded, and by 1935 he was a Member of Parliament. From 1944 to 1961 he was the premier of Saskatchewan, head of the first semi-socialist government since the white people took over the continent. His government would be innovative and it would work without waste. It would pioneer measures that other governments would adopt years later. Money poured into the province when US spy agencies sent their operatives to fight progress.

In 1957 Ottawa had passed a Hospital Insurance and Diagnostic Act that gave the federal government permission to make a deal with the provinces about acute care and laboratories. According to the BNA Act medicine was a provincial affair, so the feds had to tread carefully. In 1962, after a great struggle, the province of Saskatchewan passed a universal medical plan. On the anniversary of Confederation, 90 percent of the province's doctors went on strike for twenty-three days. I was in Berkeley, California, at the time, reading newspaper editorials about the Commie government up in some unknown Canadian place. US doctors were awfully afraid of the domino effect.

Diefenbaker had appointed a royal commission to look into a federal health plan, and in 1965 the Hall Report recommended medicare for all of Canada. Before the close of 1966 Pearson managed to pass the needed legislation. He wanted a health plan for his centenary celebrations. By 1972 all the provinces and territories had joined, and Canadian doctors, through their professional group, were in favour of it. It would do fine until some right-wing provincial governments at the turn of the century started their ideological attack upon it.

Try to love one another

By the mid-sixties there was a strange discrepancy between the Western world's younger people and its political leaders. Germany, France and Britain were led by old farts, and in North America we had Lyndon Johnson, a crude Texan wearing boots and a beer belly as US president. In Canada, while young people sashayed around in beads and huaraches and tie-dyed cotton, old Dief and old Mike stood up in their wrinkly suits and hurled ancient insults at each other's hearing aid. Canadian youth were marching against race hatred in Selma, Alabama, and strumming guitars at anti-war rallies in Toronto. In the early sixties the poets on both sides of the border had flipped a little revolution, and now the pop musicians were doing it for the post-literate generation. The US war machine, accustomed to blind support, now had to conduct a war in Asia against little non-white people without the usual jingoism, at least in the Northern states. Canadian companies made bombsights for US military jets and green berets for US commandos, but young Canadians marched in city streets, shouting insults at Lyndon Johnson.

The sixties were the most honourable years of the twentieth century, and the most hopeful, despite the usual mass killings in parts of the world. In the sixties a lot of young adults and adolescents actually acted as if civil rights were more important than financial investments, that a book of poems was more interesting than a skateboard.

As usual, the Liberals enacted legislation to benefit both sides of the economic-ideological wall. The Canadian Development Corporation would help new businesses, especially if they were launched in areas that had fallen on hard times. Old-age pensioners, who had never had a chance to contribute to the Canada Pension Plan, would get a minimum income according to the Canadian Assistance Act. The first social insurance cards were issued, and nervous Canadians were told that it would be illegal for anyone except the government's social programs to ask for a person's number. There were a lot of little acts that eased society as a whole a little closer to social democracy. Divorce and immigration and trades education, for example, were modernized.

There were a lot of people talking about "liberation" in the sixties. Yet when some women began to use the phrase "women's liberation," a lot of men in the liberation business remonstrated, cautioning that such a phrase was a mockery of real liberation, such as black liberation. Some revolutionary cells were generally democratic. Others expected their women to do the cleaning and Gestetnering. In 1966 in Quebec some women noticed that the movement toward decolonization in the province had not said enough about gender equality. They created a sisterhood called the Fédération des femmes du Québec and began to confront both sides of the political struggle with the need for attention to parity between the sexes. The women in the rest of the country spoke up, too. A gathering of groups called the Committee for the Equality of Women in Canada began trying to educate politicians and husbands across the country. In 1967 Pearson responded with another of his famous royal commissions, the Royal Commission on the Status of Women. It was chaired by Florence Bird, who from 1946 to 1966 was known in the CBC world as broadcaster Anne Francis.

The commission brought down its 167 recommendations in 1970, calling for affirmative action in employment and a full-out attack on discrimination. The committee broadened its membership and became the National Action Committee on the Status of Women, probably the most important movement to come out of the seventies. Smile on your sister.

1967

Still, when Canada hosted a world's fair on some islands in the St. Lawrence at Montreal to celebrate the hundredth birthday of Confederation, the official theme was *Man and His World*. In perfectly bilingual Montreal, of course, it was also called *Terre des hommes*. Women were allowed to come and have a look at the exhibits.

The approach to 1967 was characterized by what seemed a really un-Canadian orgy of patriotism. It never got to be as unselfconscious as the patriotism south of the border, but we were treated to an annoying patriotic song by someone named Bobby Jimby, and there were new flags everywhere. In the late sixties there was a big surge in Canadian culture. New publishers proliferated, fuelled by Canada Council grants. In Toronto the Coach House Press experimented with the new small computers and printed avant-garde poetry by people such as Joe Rosenblatt, bpNichol and Victor Coleman. A few blocks away an outfit called House of Anansi played the nationalist card with Dennis Lee and Margaret Atwood. Out in Vancouver Talonbooks combined far-out poetry and the rush of new Canadian drama. In Ottawa Oberon Books presented a lot of the best in Canadian short stories.

Small presses proliferated in all sizable cities, bringing the latest in leftish politics and the rock and dope culture. Little literary magazines sprang up everywhere, as the means of production got into the hands of the unwealthy young. Despite the US death grip on the distribution business, Canadian movies were making news, especially those created in Montreal and the Atlantic provinces.

Local communities across the country were encouraged to be useful and ironic in their government-supported Centennial projects. A town in Alberta built a landing pad for extraterrestrial spaceships. A town in Manitoba built a sewage system and had a ceremonial biffy bonfire. A Princeton, BC, Greyhound driver named Bomber Lacy painted portraits of ten Canadian prime ministers and the marathon swimmer Marilyn Bell on his bus.

My wife, Angela, and I moved to Montreal in the summer of 1967, and we got a 7.5-room apartment in the lower-middle-class corner of Westmount. It was a good thing the place was so big—we had people sleeping in most of those rooms until the end of Expo 67. It was an exciting place to be in those hopeful good times. The prettiest subway system in the country had opened the year before. People were already getting excited about the Summer Olympics that would be there in a few years.

But despite all the hoohaw there were lots of people in *la belle province* who thought that they were being oppressed by the tyrannical "English." In 1966 the Union Nationale had slipped back into power by gobbling up the rural vote, where there were not many voters per riding. The Liberals held on to the cities. A separatist party called the Rassemblement pour l'Indépendance Nationale won nearly 10 percent of the vote but no seats. There was a semi-underground outfit called the Front de libération du Québec that featured angry young writers by day and secret terrorists by night. Starting in 1964, these people had been setting off bombs in mailboxes in Westmount and expecting the people of Quebec to rise up spontaneously and take their land back from the English despots.

The most interesting bomber was a guy named Paul Joseph Chartier. On May 18, 1966, he brought a bomb with him to the visitors' gallery of the House of Commons. Those of you who were born since that time will have to try to imagine a House of Commons with no security screens and guards and all that modern stuff. The Liberals and Conservatives were throwing rude remarks back and forth at each other when Chartier got up to go to the bathroom. No one noticed anything odd, because the behaviour of the MPs often had this effect on spectators. But Chartier was going to arm his bomb. Unfortunately he must have misread the instructions. The bomb went off in the washroom, making a martyr of Chartier. A note written to the parliamentarians told them that he knew he was going to give his life to wake people up. Greg

Curnoe, the great nationalist painter from London, Ontario, made a group of four paintings centred by the words in Chartier's note.

The second most interesting bomber was a Frenchman named Charles de Gaulle. He was the president of France, darling of the aristocratic right wing and former leader of the Free French forces during World War II, most of which he spent in England. In July 1967, still wearing the military képi that was his trademark, de Gaulle made his state visit to honour Canada's centenary. Lester Pearson, the only Canadian PM ever to have been assigned to the front in a foreign war, met sixty foreign leaders during 1967. The normal protocol was that they would land at Ottawa first, and then perhaps visit Expo 67. De Gaulle came by ship and made his first stop at Quebec.

All over the world there were presidents and prime ministers that had got used to de Gaulle's high self-regard, and they tended to humour him. Even in Quebec he was not taken very seriously, but before his visit was over, the *nationalistes* would pretend that he was a great ally. When he landed, ironically at Wolfe's Cove, he shouted *"Vive le Canada! Vive le Québec! Vive la France!"* But his ship was not flying the Canadian flag, as it should have been. Then the president and the Quebec premier rode in a motorcade up the river to Montreal. Sometimes de Gaulle stood up in his képi and waved to the people he was liberating. When he stood on a balcony in Montreal, he started with his shouts again. *"Vive Montréal! Vive Québec!"* Then, reading from a placard in the crowd: *"Vive le Québec libre!"*

The *merde* hit the *fin*. Lester Pearson said that de Gaulle might as well forget about any big dinner in Ottawa. On television he reminded de Gaulle that Canadians were a free people, and that they had given their lives to liberate France. De Gaulle got onto his ship and followed the path of the WWII convoys home, and separatists in Montreal started making posters with his face on them.

The first Trudeau

When Expo 67 packed up and left, everyone expected the Canadian exuberance to continue, and that the world's shift toward peace and freedom would meet the country's preparedness to accept its bright destiny. And so on. But a lot of young Canadians would rather follow John Lennon or Bob Dylan or Robert Charlebois than the white-haired duffers who headed Canada's political parties. John Diefenbaker was born in 1895, Lester Pearson in 1897. Tommy Douglas was born in the twentieth century, but just barely.

The more that Canadians watched television, the more they thought that the US way of doing things was the normal way. Canadians were big fans of US political conventions, where presidential candidates would go through circus hoops while people in silly hats waved placards and balloons. In the sixties the TV fans got their wish, as the Conservatives and Liberals rented giant halls and brought in the clowns.

The Conservatives ran the first of these shows at Toronto in September 1967, while Expo was still roaring in Montreal. The defeats of 1963 and 1965 caught up to Diefenbaker, and Dalton Camp, a brainy party organizer from New Brunswick, engineered the rise of Robert Stanfield from Nova Scotia. Stanfield was a solid guy from an old political family; he had studied at Dalhousie and Harvard, and had been admitted to the bar in 1940. In 1948 he became leader of a provincial Conservative Party that did not have a single seat in the Nova Scotia legislature. In 1956 he became premier, and in the next few elections drove the Liberals into a six-seat enclave. He was a sure shot.

A few years earlier he might have made it all the way. But now national politics took place on television. Stanfield was honest and wise and calm and knowledgeable. But he was awkward, and gangly in an old way, and he had a head and face that could have been painted by an artist in the school of Maritimes Gothic. Still, if he had had to campaign against one of the old farts in the Liberal cabinet, he might have become Canada's good grey Uncle PM.

Mike Pearson remembered being recruited and groomed by Mackenzie King. The Conservative Party of Canada puts its seniors out on the ice floe, but the Liberals keep the generations talking to one another. Back in 1965, Pearson and his advisers were busy trying to recruit hotshot young thinkers in Quebec in order to fight off the looming separatist threat. A natural choice would have been René Lévesque, but he was fighting hard to move the provincial Liberals to the left. However, the "three wise men" did come over. Gérard Pelletier was a journalist and dignified troublemaker who edited the Montreal daily *La Presse*. Jean Marchand was a highly successful and intellectual labour organizer, and a member of the Bilingualism and Biculturalism Commission. And Pierre Trudeau—well, no one knew exactly what Trudeau was. He did have a law degree, and he had been an adviser to Marchand's unions. He was sort of a professor at the Université de Montréal. He was a writer, and founder along with Pelletier of the humanist intellectual and anti-Duplessis magazine *Cité libre*.

These three mages from the East came to Ottawa and became cabinet ministers. Trudeau was minister of justice by 1967, the year that Eric Kierans and others chased René Lévesque out of the Liberal Party. Trudeau took on the Criminal Code and gave it a good shake, reforming guidelines on divorce and abortion and homosexuality. Look at him in his fruity clothes, said sweaty old guys on tractors; he's obviously some kind of French-talkin' homo.

Trudeau was really good at getting on television, and he knew how to use it. You know those wooden things filled with holes that people used to keep woollen socks from shrinking on the clothesline? That's what Bob Stanfield looked like on television. Aw, what a shame, people said, that such a nice guy and accomplished fellow should have no chance at the polls because of what he looks like on TV.

Trudeau actually appeared in the House while wearing sandals. Some kind of homo beatnik hippie, said guys leaning on trucks in Weyburn. But Trudeau bought his clothes at the most expensive couturiers in Montreal and London and Paris. He was the first real dandy in the party since Wilfrid Laurier. His father had owned a string of gas stations. Pierre had a big powerful sports car. He could make quotations in Latin. For the next couple of decades US presidents would hate meetings with him because they looked and sounded so dumb in comparison.

Most important to the Liberal Party was his strong and intelligent federalism. He was an erotic figure who could beat back the chain-smoking hair-challenged René Lévesque, who had formed the Parti Québécois in 1968, and the other separatists in Quebec. Mike Pearson suggested that there was a Liberal policy of alternating leaderships between Francophones and Anglophones (a couple of words that entered the Canadian language about this time). In the spring parliamentary session of 1968 Pearson said hello and goodbye, adjourned the house and told his people to name a new prime minister. The justice minister was Mick Jagger with a brain. Women adored him. Men could put up with him. The Liberals made him their man, and figured Quebec was well in the fold. As soon as he had learned where the refrigerator was at 24 Sussex Drive, he called a general election.

You say you want a revolution

Nineteen sixty-eight was an amazing year. There were a lot of bodies in the street. The Vietnamese launched their Tet offensive and sent US men back home in record numbers of body bags. In the US itself military men and civilians were killing politicians, black activists, anti-war students and anti-poverty workers. In Paris students picked up paving stones and threw them at the regime. President Johnson said that he was going to quit, and de Gaulle should have. Revolutionary cells of young romantic leftists formed in Italy, Germany and Holland.

A lot of young Canadians went to the Democratic Party convention to get chased by police rioters, or to the US South to get attacked by sheriff's dogs. In Quebec there was a lot of riot envy. Pierre Vallières, a former editor of *Cité libre*, wrote a book called *Nègres blancs d'Amérique*, while sitting in jail in New York. Léandre Bergeron, a history professor, wrote a little neo-Marxist handbook for Patriotes titled *Petit manuel d'histoire du Québec*, which became a best-seller in 1971.

Some separatist agitators did not read and write so much as they threw Molotov cocktails and folding chairs. The streets in Montreal often looked like the wrestling rings that were so popular in the province. The day before the 1968 election happened to be St-Jean Baptiste Day, the yearly occasion when Quebeckers have a parade and try to feel what it's like to be a country. Trudeau, on this occasion, stayed in his seat while other dignitaries fled the reviewing stand that was being pelted with stones and bottles. He did not flinch or grab his hat. On television he looked like a well-dressed hero. The next day he won the parliamentary majority that Mike Pearson had always coveted.

Then he went to war with the separatists. In 1969 he brought in the Official Languages Act that had been called for by Pearson's Bi-and-Bi Commission. From then on Canadians would be able to turn the item over and read the English instructions. Fruit canned in the Philippines would have to have both French and English labels on the containers before they would be allowed into the country. Now the old gents around the gas station in Barrhead thought maybe they should keep their mouths shut or someone would be shoving French down their throats.

In 1970 René Lévesque led the constitutional separatists into the Quebec legislature. Seven Parti Québécois members now represented the intellectuals and the working class against both the Church and the Liberals. The criminal class and revolutionary thinkers were represented by the FLQ, which was five years older than the PQ. The FLQ did emit written statements, but their campaign would have seemed a little irregular outside of Quebec. Funds were often raised in robberies staged at credit unions, and mailbox bombings took the place of press conferences.

In October 1970 an FLQ cell kidnapped James Cross, the British trade commissioner. The FLQ wanted it to look as if they were acting against the colonial masters. They thought that English-speaking Canadians would be upset because it was an Englishman who had been nabbed. They had no idea that English-speaking Canadians too thought of Brits as foreigners. The kidnappers followed the procedure they had observed in political kidnappings elsewhere: they demanded the release from jail of some FLQ bombers, a public reading of their manifesto and safe conduct for the kidnappers. A few days later another cell kidnapped a famous French Canadian, Pierre Laporte, the minister of labour and immigration (yes, Quebec has a ministry of immigration) in the government of the Liberal premier, Robert Bourassa. The message was that anyone in the current government was a *vendu*, a traitor to the heroic people, etc.

Now the drama played out on television and the newspapers. The mysterious kidnappers' demands, the police movements, the rumours of Cuban spies in the cafes all made life entertaining and glamorous in Montreal. There was even real fear mixed with the theatre. One day as I was walking toward city hall, carrying my ratty old briefcase and wearing my usual Westminster police constable cape and yellow toque, a businessman went a long way out of his way not to be that close to me.

Trudeau took the flower out of his lapel and invoked the War Measures Act for the first time since World War II. In the House of Commons, only the sixteen NDP members voted against it. The act allowed emergency federal powers in case of an "apprehended insurrection," and that is what the prime minister said we had. Soon there were nineteen-year-old soldiers toting automatic weapons on Montreal streetcorners. Some French-Canadian poets and singers were thrown into jail and their books and records disappeared from store shelves. Across Canada angry voices called for all kinds of repressive action. In Vancouver a wild-eyed mayor in comic sideburns invoked the act in order to nab hippies and close down their newspaper.

There were two casualties. In Ottawa a teenage soldier shot himself while jumping out of an army truck. In a suburb of Montreal the body of Pierre Laporte was found in the trunk of a big car. He had been choked with the chain for his religious medal. His kidnappers were arrested. In December the government offered Cross's kidnappers a free ride to Cuba, and the Englishman was released.

The whole affair seemed entirely un-Canadian. Across the country and the political spectrum, people began to take the problem of Quebec-Ottawa affairs more seriously. Pierre Trudeau was a hero to the federalists and he was Pierre Elliott to the separatists.

Edging toward independence

Trudeau had predicted two things while preparing to become head man. He had said that the problem in Quebec was going to get worse before it got better. And he had said that Canada needed a new constitution, one that lived in the country. Now that he had been proven right about Quebec, it was time to fix Confederation.

First, he had a surprise wedding with Margaret Sinclair, a West Coast girl who liked headbands and crystals and tofu. He was fifty-one. She was about half that. They would start having babies every Christmas day. It was a storybook marriage for a man who usually read an entirely different sort of book. Now those guys leaning on their tractors in Edson would have to say, okay, maybe he isn't a homo, but he's still some kind of hippie Commie Frenchman. Still, in a lot of the country people liked him: he had appeared tough in Montreal more than once, and he produced head-of-government envy among foreigners whenever he travelled. His nickname for his regime, "the Just Society," caught on.

All kinds of interesting programs were developed across the country. A multiculturalism act declared that Canada was not a melting pot but a mosaic or patchwork quilt. When it was applied to immigration, multiculturalism put an end to the idea that Canada was a site for European relocation. By the early seventies the European newcomers were in the minority. Canada was making a new kind of country. With the Union Jack off the corner of the flag, the meaning of nation and of national unity was going to be incomprehensible to some old pukka folks. A lot of younger people in English-speaking Canada began sending their children to French-immersion schools.

Opportunities for Youth grants were given by the secretary of state to students who could come up with summer projects that sounded culturally valuable. Local Initiative Program grants were given by the department of manpower and immigration to fund community improvement projects and provide jobs. Democracy was being re-defined, and at the same time there was a huge wave of Canadian nationalism. New regulations forced Canadian radio stations to use a quota of Canadian material. Canadian singers became famous even without moving to the USA.

But Canada was still sleeping with Uncle Sam. When the US was finally driven from Indochina, it was faced with an unbelievable debt. It had been the most expensive war of all time. The US had dropped more bombs on villages every day than it had used in whole wars in earlier times, and these new bombs were *expensive*, man. President Richard Nixon let the price of gold fly through the roof and slapped an embargo on imports. Unfortunately, we depend on US imports.

President Richard M. Nixon and Prime Minister Pierre E. Trudeau in the hall of the Canadian Parliament, May 1972
(NATIONAL ARCHIVES OF CANADA/PA-175936)

For the rest of the seventies Canada tried to be socially progressive while its southern neighbour was squeezing the purse. A lot of the things that Canada might want to export to the US were the products of industries owned by USAmericans to start with. There were people in Canada who wanted a continental free trade system, otherwise called complete surrender to the US empire. A lot of these people were in Alberta, where oil is pulled from deep below the earth. A gaggle of foreign oil-producing nations called OPEC began to regulate their supply of fuel to the West, and the price of gasoline and heating oil went as high as the raw element had been deep. Ottawa sought means to explain to Alberta oil folks that the stuff under the ground was Canadian. In Alberta they were so used to working for head offices in Texas and Oklahoma that they even got most of their football players from those states. Albertans started to curse out Eastern Canadians, and do it with a drawl.

When Petro-Canada was created in 1975, to be a Canadian choice at the pump, as they say, Albertans reacted as if it were treason against Free Enterprise, a term used in the US to designate cowboy economics. Trudeau began to talk about a "National Energy Policy," a means by which Canadian ownership in the oil industry might be increased. The policy was being treated by Albertans as some kind of Commie plot. This is a province in which people would not use a $2 bill because they didn't have such a thing in the USA.

Remove those apostrophes

Albertans were not the only separatists to hassle Trudeau's new Canada in the seventies. In Quebec more and more people were getting more radical or less radical, and lining up behind the former television star René Lévesque. He was a really short guy with an overly obvious comb-over and cigarette ashes all over his rumpled clothes. They loved him. People did not love Robert Bourassa, the Liberal leader in the perfectly cut dark blue suit. Robert Bourassa was no Henri Bourassa, but he knew that he had better play the *nationaliste* card. In 1974 he passed Bill 22 and sent a shiver down the backs of English-speaking Canadians. The bill declared French the only official language of Quebec. English-language schools were not closed, but little children had to pass tough government tests to get into them. No one was going to sneak their kids into an English-speaking school! The Manitoba school question was history. No Liberal Party was going to take this problem to the Privy Council.

Bourassa's ploy did not work. Lévesque's Parti Québécois swept into power in 1976, the first time a group formed for the purpose of separation had made it that far. Newspaper cartoonists in Quebec and across the country were ecstatic. The mano-a-mano between Trudeau and Lévesque could begin. These two had known each other all their adult lives. Trudeau was patrician and tough. He had a face like a Japanese mask. Lévesque let emotions play on his face and figure at a rate of thirty a minute. Lévesque attacked his heart with all those cigarettes, but Quebeckers could hear it banging in his chest. Trudeau murmured like a patrician and was photographed diving from a thirty-metre board. You were never going to see René Lévesque in swim trunks.

In 1977 the Quebec government passed Bill 101, and now the shiver came *up* the backs of English-speaking Canadians. It was described as a bill to protect the French language, but its details suggested that it was a mechanism to attack the English language. People would not be jailed for speaking English in their own homes, but they had to use French at work. In public, French should be the only visible language. There would be no English billboards, and outside the big department store on Ste-Catherine, the big letters that had spelled EATON'S for a century would now say EATON. A lot of smiling PQ voters remembered their grandparents' stories about the way Eaton's would not let employees or shoppers buy or sell a hankie in French.

Bill 101 put an end to the government tests for little six-year-olds. From now on if you were a six-year-old you could get into an English-language school just through lucky DNA. The only kids who would make it in were the children of parents who could prove that they were in Quebec temporarily or children of parents who had been educated in English in the province.

There was a commission to watch over the compliance with Bill 101. It had an official and unilingual name, but in English it was usually called the "Language Police." The Montreal major league baseball team had a bilingual but stupid nickname, and seemed to get along all right in French, though it is unlikely that a US shortstop would think of himself as an *arrêt-court*.

In the first three years after the election of the PQ, 150 corporation head offices moved from Montreal to Ontario. The ones that remained ordered new letterheads.

In 1975 the Mohawk people at Oka made a comprehensive claim to what they thought was their acreage, including a forest that could be used for timber. They were rebuffed. In 1976 they tried again. The government reserved judgment for nine years.

19

INDEPENDENCE AND BACK

René Lévesque
(NATIONAL ARCHIVES OF CANADA)

After Pierre Elliott Trudeau died as a surprisingly old man early in the twenty-first century, there was a special big postage stamp, a made-for-television movie, a couple of new sculptures, all the cultural devices meant to canonize a former human being in the afterlife of history. But in the late seventies he was an enigma: he was the subject of the "Trudeaumania" that still lived, and virtual proprietor of the term "charisma," and yet his name was used as a cuss word by ordinary citizens, not only in the separatist regions of Alberta and Quebec.

It was from the separatist region of Alberta that his unlikely nemesis came walking—walking in a manner that suggested an imminent

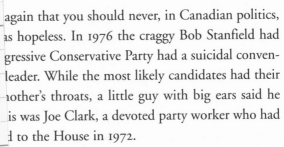

again that you should never, in Canadian politics,
as hopeless. In 1976 the craggy Bob Stanfield had
gressive Conservative Party had a suicidal conven-
leader. While the most likely candidates had their
mother's throats, a little guy with big ears said he
is was Joe Clark, a devoted party worker who had
d to the House in 1972.

of 1976 there were a couple of candidates from
there was Flora MacDonald, but though she had
hey were kind of worried about her first name.
really young fellows who went around talking in
ey would sound older. One had hardly any chin
much chin. Somehow the convention chose the
hin, and the next day the newspapers ran this
"

the federal election of 1979 Joe Clark started
setting records. He won a minority in Parliament, becoming the first
and last person ever to defeat Trudeau in an election, the first native
Westerner ever to become prime minister and the first man to become
prime minister while still in his thirties. He turned forty the next day.

But he was not finished setting records.

Joe Who was in a funny position. It was not so much that he had
been elected as it was that Trudeau had been diselected. Joe had never
been in a cabinet or even inside a lot of the rooms on Parliament Hill.
His party had been out of power for sixteen years. They had only two
members from Quebec. It was as if the drummer boy had been sent in to
command the big offensive. There was a recession, and it was Joe's job to
end it or ease it. What did he do? First he put off holding a session and
went for a few overseas visits, introducing himself to foreign leaders who
were seen to be whispering to one another behind their hands. He set a
record for the time—four and a half months—between winning an election and calling the House together. When he did call the House he
brought in a motion to raise the price of gasoline. The Liberals and New
Democrats saw their chance—they would become the consumer's heroes.

If Joe had been able to keep six Créditistes from Quebec onside, he might have squeaked through, but these gents stayed home when the big non-confidence vote was held. The Tories were defeated and Joe resigned. He had been prime minister for only 272 days, 49 of them in the House of Commons. He never got to govern with a majority, joining Mike Pearson with that distinction. He was the first PM to lose a motion on the budget, and he set the record for the shortest reign after winning an election.

Trudeau vs. Lévesque redux

Joe called the election for February 1980. And the Liberals were stuck without a leader, because Trudeau had quit and told them that it would take the queen on bended knee to get him back. If it had been summertime he might have been in buckskin in a canoe in some river far north. But it was January, and some of the less queenly Libs begged him to lead them into this election. Trudeau said okay, on the condition that he could win the election and then quit, thus making one of the oddest campaign promises of the late twentieth century. The reason he decided to come back was not the threat of Joe Clark, however—it was the threat of René Lévesque.

The Quebec premier was promising a provincial referendum on a peculiar semi-independence he called "sovereignty association." What that meant was that anything that Canada gives to Quebec would be allowed to keep coming, while any responsibility toward the federal state would be discontinued.

In the election campaign we got a new kind of Trudeau. His suits were expensive and more conservative in cut. He did not make quips that were lost on the semi-literate. He said that he was in favour of federalism, low gasoline prices and a National Energy Policy. People were scared of OPEC and Alberta. They felt that if living in Canada meant lots of winter and great road distances, fuel should not be ridiculously expensive. Voters gave Trudeau another majority. "Well, welcome to the eighties," he said, with that wonderful ironic drone he had to his voice.

Pressure from the separatists took various forms. In Alberta there was a lot of suspicion about Trudeau's National Energy Program, and there was a growing protest against his immigration policy. Where you find a Bible belt, unfortunately, you will find people who are not going to sit still for other people's ways. In the sixties in Calgary you could find newspaper cartoons with stereotyped Jews, and a sports column complaining that some hockey announcer had pronounced Hubert "Pit" Martin's name the French way. In the seventies, folks got restless when the damned CBC, that nest of Commie deviants, brought in French television. Then people from Asia and the Third World started appearing in Alberta cities and even in the schools. Rich guys from Hong Kong were buying big houses and shopping malls. When some good local businessmen wanted to clear Calgary's Chinatown and build something up to date, the Chinese managed to get them stopped.

At least the 100,000 USAmericans blended in nicely, unless they talked a little loud at a steakhouse. But here came some East Indians from Africa, and black people from the Caribbean, where there was never even any snow. There were boat people a long way from the ocean and, worst of all, Sikhs with beards and turbans and who knows what hidden under their clothes. A nicely symbolic struggle arose when it was rumoured that some Sikhs wanted to join the Mounties and still wear their turbans. Bumper stickers fought the good fight in defence of the RCMP, a great symbol of Albertan history. The fact that the Mounties had changed their headgear at least seven times in the past did not impress some guys. But then some of them claimed that there had been no Holocaust.

The separatists in Quebec got their watered-down referendum on May 20, 1980. It failed by just under two-thirds. Still, Lévesque and his PQ would be re-elected the following year. René Lévesque was the Tommy Douglas of French Canada. He was an honest man who genuinely wanted the greatest good for the most people. He hated avarice and corruption, and he tried his hardest to promote social justice. Quebec is a province not unfamiliar with crooked politics, and René Lévesque clearly saw some ways to improve the situation, never giving a thought to his own fortune. It is a tribute to the wisdom of the Quebec people that they supported him so emotionally and logically. His government made it illegal for corporations to donate campaign money to political parties. It introduced no-fault government car insurance and an agricultural land preservation act, providing an example for other provinces such as British Columbia. In a province in which battles between labour and management often led to fires and death, the PQ made it illegal for companies to hire scabs while its unionized workers were on job action.

The Alberta separatists were really people with their hearts and bank accounts in the USA. More and more one could read and hear remarks that painted "the Ottawa government," as Premier Peter Lougheed called it, as some kind of threatening foreign regime. In 1980 the Arab oil countries proved that they could cause long lineups at gas pumps in North America, and the US oil companies proved that they could raise Alberta's public opinion against those greedy guts in Ontario. "Let the Eastern bastards freeze in the dark," proclaimed bumper stickers on Alberta pickup trucks. Bumper stickers are very big in Alberta, just as they are in Texas. In Alberta there is a big sentiment for capital punishment and gun ownership.

Trudeau's National Energy Policy was aimed at having Canada own 50 percent of the oil business in Canada by 1990. This idea really browned off Lougheed and the Albertans. "I'd rather push this thing a mile than buy from Petro-Canada," proclaimed a popular bumper sticker. "This car doesn't brake for Liberals," announced another, with no apology or reluctance about the violent suggestion. The premier stood up and reminded citizens that "our forefathers fought hard to obtain these resources." People in Alberta did not think that that was a silly scene. They really hated Trudeau and the Liberals and back East and the idea of Canadian sovereignty.

When Pierre Trudeau said that he wanted Canada to be in charge of its own constitution, Peter Lougheed led the fight against any such possibility, and Albertans did not stop to consider the irony that their leader was now an ally of the premier of Quebec.

The Canadian North America Act

The term "Western alienation" entered the Canadian lexicon, and right wingers started referring to themselves as the Voice of Western Canada. They also started forming new separatist political parties. The Western Canada Concept demanded radical changes to the way Canada operates. A more bizarre group was the Edmonton-based West Fed. When it did not really catch fire, its inventor, Elmer Knudsen, renamed it the Confederation of Regions and moved it to New Brunswick. In provincial elections the various separatists got about 10 or 12 percent of the vote, a lot less than the nutbar movements of earlier decades. But there would always be a hefty supply of anti-Communist anti-Québécois voters in Alberta. It would not be long till the Bloc Albertois, called Reform, would rear its cowboy hat.

In August 1981 Premier Lougheed and the feds came to an agreement about oil pricing. The National Energy Policy would sort of remain, but the price of crude could go higher. Lougheed told his citizens that the usually perfidious Easterners were "sitting on the front porch and we're serving them coffee." Alberta voters like that kind of folksy figure of speech.

Now, we remember that Pierre Trudeau said that he was only prime minister until the party could find a successor. It should not, everyone thought, be too hard to find someone to tower over Joe Clark in the public imagination. A lot of people thought that the obvious choice would be John Turner, a handsome guy who knew how to yuk it up with the boys in those meeting rooms high up in those skyscrapers. But Trudeau knew that Turner would hack and cough and grab ass and fall on his bum. PET decided that he would hang around for a full term and go for history. He would bring the constitution to Canada.

In 1981 the constitution was still the BNA Act. The *B* stood for "British." That meant that despite all the efforts of Laurier and Borden and King, the Dominion of Canada was still not officially independent. Yes, we could and did make amendments: all we had to do was get Ottawa and the provinces to agree on an amendment and then submit it to London. Eventually London would grant the change to the Act. In

1965, for example, London said sure, go ahead with a government pension plan.

But still, there were a lot of Canadians who did not like all this submitting and granting. The population of the country was appearing less and less British, partly because people were coming from China, and partly because the grandchildren of British immigrants did not care all that much about the latest scandal in the royal family. In 1964 the Pearson government had got the provinces and Ottawa talking about patriation and amendment. The government came up with a plan called the Fulton-Favreau formula, named after Davie Fulton, Diefenbaker's minister of justice, and Guy Favreau, Pearson's minister of justice. It was complicated, but did work out a system of vetoes and majorities that protected the smaller provinces. All the parties agreed with it on principle, but then Jean Lesage lost his province to the Union Nationale, and the latter refused to sign the pact. So much for that.

In 1971 Pierre Trudeau's government tried again, this time at a first ministers meeting in Victoria. The resulting Victoria Charter went further than the 1964 agreement had, calling for democratizing welfare, reforming the Supreme Court and spelling out language rights. Quebec kept insisting that a province should be able to opt out of some social programs. Trudeau said we will talk about that later. Quebec said we want the wording right now. Trudeau said take it or leave it. Quebec said okay if that's how you feel about it, we will leave it. Some observers said that Trudeau's intransigence blew the agreement. Others say that the Quebec government did not dare accept the deal.

Trudeau wanted to go down in history as the man who brought the constitution home. Okay, if this is history, that's the least we can do.

There is no way, short of writing 250,000 words about it, that anyone could convey the exhaustiveness and exhaustion of the campaign for patriation. In the 1980 Quebec referendum campaign, Trudeau had promised that he would get the constitution out of the hands of the British. Over the next two years there was enough haggling to test the patience of a saint, but saints were in short supply in Ottawa and Quebec and Edmonton and Fredericton. Everyone wanted to get in on

the act—the provinces, the unions, the women, the French speakers, the
disabled. The Aboriginal community wanted recognition of Native rights,
and the Alberta premier wanted to make sure that the Native people
did not get any more than what they were getting now. On the floor of
the House of Commons there was a pile of hair, pulled out of the heads
of legislators who kept hollering and stomping around.

What was the main hassle? It was the amending formula, a phrase
that frightened the birds out of the trees in 1981. With the BNA Act it
was relatively simple: the provinces and Ottawa would agree on a petition, and the Brits would decide to make the legal move. Now, if
London were going to be out of the circuit, how would finality be
reached? In the USA, the least little argument about tee time at the
Wichita Golf and Country Club will wind up in the US Supreme
Court. But the USA is a federal state; Canada is a confederation. In
Canada we have what are called first ministers meetings, at which the
Conservative premiers do battle with the Liberal prime minister. That
was going to be the forum of the "amending formula."

The other delaying hassle was about Trudeau's proposed Charter of
Rights and Freedoms. As justice minister he had been a bold reformer.
He liked human rights and he was impatient to see them assured. But
the provinces were afraid that they might give up some powers to this
charter, and Joe Clark was now thoroughly convinced that he was the
defender of the little guy. He dreamed of a "community of communities," after all. René Lévesque wanted complete control of permission
when it came to using a language, and Trudeau wanted a country
entirely bilingual. Lévesque wanted to control television, his old bailiwick, but television was a federal matter.

There were a lot of ideas regarding an amending formula.

In September 1981 the Supreme Court came down with a nifty
pronouncement. People called it thoroughly Canadian. It said that it is
Canadian tradition that when it comes to matters that will affect provincial rights, the provinces must be consulted. But, it said, the federal
government could just go ahead and patriate the constitution if it
wanted to take that chance.

This contradiction led to the other phrase that would make all remaining birds lose their grip on the bough, the notorious "notwithstanding clause." This concept was brought in after all provinces except Quebec had agreed to a compromise procedure. The notwithstanding clause gives the province the power to override anything in the Charter of Rights and Freedoms that would run counter to the province's laws. That is, Quebec could pass a law making it illegal to curse the management of the Montreal Canadiens in English, and the lawbreaker could not appeal to the Charter's stand on bilingualism. In the unlikely event that an Ontario government minister should suggest that homeless people can be thrown in jail, all the provincial government would have to do is to pass a law making homelessness a crime.

Lévesque was still not satisfied. The separatist position was that Canada was not made up of ten provinces and a couple of territories—it was made up of two nations. And the French-speaking nation should have a veto on the constitution. They could opt out of federal programs, but they were not going to get financial compensation in doing so. They did not like the idea that people should be allowed to come to Quebec and look for work.

Prime Minister Trudeau with Queen Elizabeth as she
signs the Canadian Constitution, Apr. 17, 1982
(NATIONAL ARCHIVES OF CANADA/PA-141503)

Women's groups complained that their concerns were not specifically addressed. Native people appealed to Britain, reminding the Crown that their dealings had been with her. Conservatives and Péquistes and others dragged their feet as far as they could, but in March 1982 the Constitution Act cleared the House of Lords. On April 17, the Queen of England came to Ottawa and signed the Act. Some idiot set the whole procedure as an out-of-doors event, presumably so that some ordinary Canadians could exercise their right to look at Queen Elizabeth trying to keep her hat on as she sat and signed while the wind drove a persistent rain onto the fresh ink.

The Canadian Constitution was home. And it was as contradictory as the abjectly written national anthem. The Constitution starts with the Charter of Rights and Freedoms, which in turn starts with four fundamental rights. The first is "freedom of conscience and religion." But just before that the document says that everything depends on "principles that recognize the supremacy of God." This calls, I guess, for an individual notwithstanding clause.

From era to error

On a snowy Ottawa night in February 1984, Pierre Trudeau went for a walk, looking for a sign, as he wryly put it. All he saw was snow falling from darkness. He decided to quit.

Why not? Canada, along with the rest of the world, was going through the worst recession since the thirties. It was the first time a recession had smacked the country while the Liberals were in town. Time to quit.

Why not? He had been the boss for fifteen years, longer than anyone but Macdonald and King. He had fought the separatists and won. He had made Canada a bilingual and multicultural country. He had patriated the Constitution and got a real Charter of Rights and Freedoms going. He had helped the country join the sane world of metric measurements.

Yes, a lot of people used his name impolitely. But he had a way of winning elections, and when he was gone, of winning popularity polls.

Canadians perhaps felt themselves lucky to have him as head of government, especially when they looked around at other countries and noticed the contrast. He had been around longer than any other elected leader of his time, and he was a lot smarter. It was a privilege to have a prime minister who was intelligent, witty, rational, good-looking in his own way and compassionate. Although a child of great fortune, he had been a social democrat before entering politics, and among the bigwigs of the Liberal Party, he was the energy driving social reform. Financially, Canada was in poor shape in 1984, as were other capitalist countries, but morally better off than most.

A little voice was saying, "Thank your lucky stars." Another was saying, "You are not going to like what's coming."

While a lot of the country was wondering who could possibly replace Trudeau after all these years, the Mohawk people of Oka were still waiting for a decision on their land claim of 1977. They were not going to get much encouragement from Mr. Justice Donald Steele's judgment regarding the claim of the Bear Island people. If you go in the summer to the town of Temagami, just up Highway 11 from North Bay, you can take a tour of a big old lumber mill and a big old open-pit iron mine. For white people this is primary resource country. For the first white people the primary resource was beaver skins. Nearby Lake Temagami is shaped like a splatter, and has six hundred kilometres of shoreline, all Crown land, as they say, open to the public. Grey Owl, a famous white man, used to live near town. There are twelve hundred islands in Lake Temagami, and one of them is Bear Island.

The Native people of Bear Island have been there since the beginning of time, and the Hudson's Bay Company built a post on the island in 1870. The Temiskaming and Northern Ontario railway was built in 1903, and pretty soon the Native people were picturesque features of postcards to Toronto and Buffalo. The famous "Confederation" poet,

Archibald Lampman, suffered a cardiac relapse at the lake in 1896 and later wrote a pretty bad poem about a place that was

> Wild with the trampling of the giant moose,
> And the weird magic of old Indian tales.
> All day with steady paddles toward the west
> Our heavy-laden long canoe we pressed:
> All day we saw the thunder-travelled sky
> Purpled with storm in many a trailing tress,
> And saw at eve the broken sunset die
> In crimson on the silent wilderness.

You will notice that even the white poet urged upon university students of Canadian literature presents a landscape prepared for romantic colonial consumption. Archie Belaney was not the only colonialist white boy to dress up as a Red Indian and canoe around Bear Island.

A century after Archibald Lampman's heart attack, the people of Bear Island went to court to argue that they had been living on this lake since time began. The Teme-agama Anishnabay said that this fact should be seen as more important than the Ontario government's desire to develop the place commercially. The trial lasted 120 days. Many Teme-agama people spoke, and their ancestors spoke through them. At the end, Judge Donald Steele came back with a 284-page decision that ancestral ways were not relevant, and that the question of Aboriginal land was settled in the Proclamation of 1763. In 1763 the loquacious Ojibwa chief Minweweh had told the British, "Although you have conquered the French, you have not conquered us. We are not your slaves. These lakes, these woods and mountains were left us by our ancestors. They are our inheritance, and we will not part with them to anyone."

Steele made the Europeans' position very clear: "Aboriginal rights exist at the pleasure of the Crown, and they can be extinguished by treaty, legislation, or administrative acts." In other words, a minister of Indian affairs can cross out any Native rights with a stroke of his pen.

Besides, said Judge Steele, the way that the Indians had run the country was too primitive, that "the Indian occupation could not be considered true and legal, and that the Europeans were lawfully entitled to take possession of the land and settle it with colonies."

Pretty amazing language for a late-twentieth-century Ontario judge, would you say? In any case, the judgment by Judge Steele did not cheer up the Mohawk around Oka. Sure enough, two years later they would get the usual reply to the land claim they had mounted in 1977. Go live somewhere else, they were told.

After Trudeau's resignation, the Grits did not go automatically to their next English-Canadian candidate. A little competition between John Turner and Jean Chrétien made things on Parliament Hill a bit warmer in the spring of 1984. Not only was Chrétien a French Canadian but he was also an unquestioning Trudeau supporter. Turner, on the other hand, had dropped out of politics because of Trudeau and hung around in the financial district of Toronto, traditional Tory country. He was a collar-ad kid who had dated Princess Margaret, hacking and coughing in his characteristic way while she chain-smoked Dunhills. Turner won the leadership, and the Liberal Party belonged to big business.

The NDP was enjoying its greatest success under the leadership of Ed Broadbent. He got thirty-two Parliamentary seats in 1980, and in 1988 he would get forty-three. Broadbent was from big union country around Oshawa. The NDP was no longer a radical Christian Western agricultural human rights party but the voice of Ontario unions.

With the other two parties in the hands of big business and big labour, the Progressive Conservatives could not leave things in the hands of Joe Who. They needed Eastern big business too. Joe had defeated equally young Brian Mulroney in the 1976 leadership race. In 1983 Mulroney edged Joe 1584 to 1325 in the final ballot, and became leader of the opposition. Mulroney was born in Baie-Comeau, Quebec, a town owned by that Chicago-Irish newspaper tycoon, who shipped newsprint upriver on his own vessels. As a little kid Brian sat on this tycoon's lap and sang Irish songs for brand-new US $50 bills. He wanted to be a tycoon, too. He left Baie-Comeau, that town on the ironic forty-ninth parallel, and by 1977 he was president of the Iron Ore Company. The Iron Ore Company was mostly owned by USAmericans and owned the town of Schefferville over beside Labrador. In 1983 Schefferville was not turning in huge profits any more, so Mulroney shut it down, and a lot of aging miners wondered what to do.

Welcome to the post-Trudeau era. In 1984's general election, Mulroney's Conservatives won a majority. Trudeau's resistance to the US machine would be replaced by a smiling prime minister who held the door open and said everything is for sale. Trudeau's insistence on social justice as a key ingredient of democracy was replaced by the notion that money talks. In the Mulroney years money hollered, as the prime minister sang "When Irish Eyes Are Smiling" with President Ronald Reagan of the United States and compared Italian footwear with Prime Minister Margaret Thatcher of Great Britain.

Get a job

Brian Mulroney's party had been waiting for a chance to run the country, to steer it away from Liberal softness to good hard business sense. Mulroney was interested in keeping Quebec in the Canadian sphere and keeping Canada in the US sphere. His eager and vengeful cabinet ministers were fond of uttering words that came to strike terror into the hearts of social democrats—"privatization," "deregulation," "downsizing," "slashing." Civil servants asked what was in store for them, and the new prime minister in the very expensive Gucci loafers said, "A pink slip and running shoes." The CEOs of international corporations (which was the new name for US business) were glad that the Trudeau era was over. When he became the new PM, Mulroney gave his first big interview to *The Wall Street Journal*, where he promised that "super relations with the United States will be the cornerstone of our foreign policy."

Would this mean that the United Nations was less important? Canada has always kept up its payments of all UN dues. The US, on the other hand, is notorious for being far behind in its payments. In regard to a more regional group, the Organization of American States, Canada had always remained at most an observer, thus hoping to demonstrate its independence of the US. Brian Mulroney would slip Canada into the OAS.

For 120 years the Liberals had been promoting continental free trade and the Conservatives had been opposing it. During the campaign of 1984 the Liberals under businessman Turner had been promoting their traditional position, and Mulroney had been lining up with John A. Macdonald and John Diefenbaker. You will not hear anything more from me about free trade, he said over and over. Don't talk to me about free trade. It is bad for sovereignty.

But it is good for business, especially big business. By 1987 the Tories were negotiating with the US for an end to tariffs and import duties, and the installation of something called the Free Trade Agreement. Wow, thought the inexperienced, this would mean that I could buy a gadget in the US and I wouldn't have to pay duty on it when I came home. Unfortunately for Mulroney, there were a lot of experienced guys in the Senate, and because senators get appointed by the party in power, they were mainly old Liberals. You try to push the FTA through and we will delay the hell out of you, they threatened. So Mulroney went to the country in 1988, campaigning on free trade, of all things. He beat the collar-ad kid again.

For the next year or so, the voters looked around for the promised cheaper goods, and just could not find them. They could find a lot of For Sale signs on farms and businesses close to the US border, though. We can fix that, said Finance Minister Michael Wilson and his right-leaning friends, we just have to do a little more deregulating and privatizing. Gad, said unbelieving oldsters, what are they going to privatize next? The post office. Oh, don't exaggerate, Elmer. It's not as if they want their business friends to get their hands on Air Canada or the post office or the CBC.

Downsizing and all those other things caught on with provincial governments across the country. Mental health facilities closed and their workers looked for other jobs while their patients wandered the streets. Little old ladies wondered why they had to go to some drugstore across the city to retrieve a parcel mailed to them three weeks ago by their relatives up the valley.

No, the average citizen looked in vain for those cheaper goods promised by the FTA. What he did find in a couple of years was the GST. Oh, we had to remember a lot of initials. Mr. Wilson and Mr. Mulroney explained that the Liberals had got the country deep into debt by starting all kinds of social programs. The Tories could help get the country out of debt by either raising taxes or trimming programs and the jobs that went with them. Well, as you can see, the Tories do not favour taxes, so we have downsized and deregulated and all the rest. Well, then, said the citizen we have been talking about, isn't the GST a tax? It means that I have to pay 7 percent more for goods and services. Aw, well, that is really an illusion, he was told. We have removed a sales tax that the manufacturer had to pay, so the GST is really nothing additional. Oh, said the citizen, then if I were a businessman, I would like this GST. But how can I pay this tax that is really not a tax now that I have been downsized? Get a job, he was told.

WHOSE CENTURY IS THIS?

*Elijah Harper joins in a traditional drum song in
the Manitoba legislature, June 15, 1990*
(GERALD KWIATKOWSKI)

Brian Mulroney was proud of the fact that he had delivered Quebec
for the Conservative Party, the first man to do that in living memory.
But he was the custodian of a new Canadian Constitution that Quebec
didn't like. He had a terrific case of Trudeau envy. He had climbed to the
top of the business ladder and the political ladder, and he had a house
on top of the hill in Montreal, just like the Trudeaus. Now he wanted
to deliver Quebec, something that Trudeau had never managed.

In April 1987 he called the premiers of the ten provinces to a private
meeting in a little government enclave on the shore of Meech Lake, just
north of Mackenzie King's folly, Kingsmere. No one had ever heard of

Meech Lake, but in a few years there would be lobstermen and loggers using those two words as expletives. All the premiers knew that this was about Mulroney and Bourassa. The Quebec premier arrived at Meech Lake (Que.) with a potful of demands. Mulroney and the premiers got him to boil it down to five irreducible ones.

It was the old story. Quebec's picture of the country showed two founding nations trying to figure out how to live together or get divorced. The rest of the provinces saw the country as a confederation of ten provinces and a couple of northern territories.

It is easy enough for a lobsterman or a logger to say get tough with those losers. But a politician faced with the responsibility of keeping Quebec in the house knows that you have to give up a little on your assets and your principles. The premiers bit their top lips and went along with the five conditions for Quebec's agreement to the Constitution and remaining in the marriage. The term "distinct society" would be used to describe that province. There would be three Quebec judges on the nine-judge Supreme Court. The Constitution would recognize Quebec's department of immigration. All provinces would have a veto regarding parliamentary changes or the formation of new provinces. If there were going to be a new province, Quebec did not want it to be aligned with the other nation. Finally, if a province decided that it couldn't live with a new national social program, it could opt out and receive operating money instead.

Then the agreement had to go to the provincial legislatures. The deal was that once the proposal was passed by one province, the others had three years to sign up. Quebec, of course, passed its bill in June 1987. The House of Commons passed it by a wide majority. By July 1988 eight provinces had passed the legislation. Then the fit hit the land.

As soon as the agreement had been made public, Pierre Trudeau had stuck his OK Corral rose in his lapel and headed out to fight it. All his political life he had fought for a unified bilingual multicultural Canada. He had gunned down the separatists. Now this *arriviste* was giving half the country to the US and the other half to the separatists. Trudeau spoke everywhere, to the House, to the Senate, to the CBC, to the

Canada Club. Mulroney gathered with his chums and had a good
chuckle. Then he ran a federal election and got in again, with a smaller
majority. Meanwhile, Alberta was in court, trying to get rid of the old
law that provided for French-language education, and the Supreme
Court was striking down Quebec's ban on English signs. Quebec smiled
and invoked the notwithstanding clause, and it was again illegal to have
an English sign outdoors in the province. Northern Ontario towns
enacted legislation declaring themselves to be unilingual. Y'know, by
golly, said a guy leaning on his harvester in Saskatchewan, that Trudeau
might not be your regular fella, but at least he's sticking up for us against
them Kweebeckers.

Meech was in trouble in three provinces. In Newfoundland and
Labrador there was an election, and the new premier renounced the
outgoing government's approval of Meech. In New Brunswick, the only
officially bilingual province in Canada, the premier was anti-Meech. But
the main problem was Manitoba. Manitoba has a significant French-
Canadian component and had been the battlefield for French-language
rights. But Manitoba also has a highly significant multicultural population, lots of Eastern Europeans' descendants, for example. Manitoba also
has a highly significant Native population. In 1989 there was one Native
MLA in Manitoba—Elijah Harper.

Quebec politicians always tell the story of the way anti-French-
Canadian bigots killed the Meech Lake Accord. It is a convenient story
inside Quebec. But Elijah Harper was not after French Canadians. He
was after a gaggle of white men who had got together at a secret lake and
designed a future Canada that recognized a "distinct society" made up
of some white people. There is an irony staring you in the face, he told
Mulroney and his men. Nothing in this agreement you propose notices
that the Native peoples of Canada form several distinct societies—the
fact that you cannot tell us apart is bad enough, but the fact that you
don't notice us is worse. The fact that the two territories, where the
population is mainly Native, were not invited to the retreat speaks worse
of your plans.

Native land

There had been some progress for the indigenous peoples of Canada. By the end of the eighties there were five Native people in Parliament. The Native bands were administrating a majority of their federally funded projects. There were growing national associations such as the Native Council of Canada and the Assembly of First Nations and the Métis National Council. The Inuit formed an association to protect their languages and cultures.

The Native peoples would always make more progress with the federal government than with the provinces. The biggest provinces were the hardest nuts to crack: Quebec and Ontario and British Columbia had always led the fight against Indian rights. When the reserve system was begun in the nineteenth century, the federal government said that each Native family should have 80 acres. The BC authorities provided 10 acres. When BC entered Confederation it doubled that figure. Indians ought to be able to survive on 20 acres as long as they did not pursue a traditional Indian life but bent instead to raising crops. White families were granted 320 acres each.

Now Elijah Harper held a feather high and the cameras caught that image, and the Manitoba Legislature missed the deadline, and Native people across the country noticed. While the Quebec government pretended that Meech Lake had been drained by a bunch of anti-Quebeckers, First Nations people began demonstrations about land questions across the nation. When *les sauvages* got uppity in Quebec, the Quebec government sought revenge. The scene, yet again, was the forest at Oka.

One thing that really bugs the Quebec government is that the Native people in the province prefer English over French as the language of everyday life. So when the Mohawk and their allies dug in at Oka, the issue of Quebec language rights shared a social wreckage with Native land rights. This chapter of the Oka saga began in the summer of 1990 when some developers got permission from the town of Oka to hack down trees on some land near a Mohawk burial ground and double the size of the local golf course. What a wonderful symbol! The people of Kanesatake thought about Elijah Harper's feather, but they dressed themselves up like US commandos. Wearing combat fatigues and painting their faces, this Warrior Society, which comprised some men from Kanesatake and other Mohawk from Kahnawake and St. Regis/Akwesasne near Cornwall, set up a barricade, and welcomed the assistance of US Native veterans of the Indochina adventure.

Quebec sent in its police, the unloved Sûreté du Québec, there was a firefight and a cop was killed. Now reporters from all over the continent and elsewhere descended on this little cheese town by the St. Lawrence. The people of Kahnawake, across the river from Montreal, set up roadblocks on their reserve and blocked one of the bridges across the St. Lawrence. Angry white commuters threw concrete blocks through the windshields of Mohawk cars. Quebec blocked food and medical supplies, but Amerindians set up supply routes from the south, and the International Red Cross lent a hand.

Staredown: A Canadian soldier and Mohawk Warrior come face to face in a tense standoff at the Kanesatake Reserve in Oka, Quebec, Sept. 5, 1990
(CP/SHANEY KOMULAINEN)

Then Quebec asked for the help of the Canadian Forces, as it had during the 1970 crisis. The siege would last for seventy-eight days and cost $200 million. A lot of Native people would go to court again, and some of them would go to prison again. But the country seemed to have passed into a different phase of Native relations. There would be a lot more First Nations militants, some of them lawyers, some "warriors," and there would be more standoffs, usually on roads leading to places where white people like to ski or golf and make money off skiers and golfers. Some episodes would be really scary, such as the gunfire at Gustafson Lake in BC.

Free trade and globalization and Indian uprisings! What a contra-dictory world we lived in in the nineties. In the olden days Europeans came to the country and brought with them some exotic diseases that were extremely bad news for the home folks. In our own time world trade brings in insects and tree diseases to try to finish the job.

Mulroney tries again

Poor Brian Mulroney. Even my word processor's spell-check rejects him.

He took a bath in Meech Lake. Now the repercussions were not going to let him get dressed. There was the uprising of the Natives. There was the resentment of Quebec. Now nine MPs from Quebec waved goodbye and formed a strange new paradox, the Bloc Québécois, a federal party that was openly separatist. In a few years it would get even funnier as Her Majesty's Official Opposition was made up of anti-Canadians. Perhaps as comical was the Reform Party from the Prairies. Now that the traditionally protectionist Tories were free traders, maybe it made sense that this new party, which was to the right of most Latin American military coups, took the name of the Grits' progressive wing of a century and a half before. In a few years it would change its name to the Canadian Alliance, but it would be made up mainly of people who had called themselves Social Creditors in earlier days. It too would be the official Opposition for a while. This is what has happened in the country John A. Macdonald put together.

Okay, Mulroney had learned his lesson from Meech. This time he would have a more open and more inclusive constitutional meeting. Instead of forming a secret cabal at an unknown lake, the new parents of Confederation would meet in historic Charlottetown. Mulroney guessed that nearly half the Canadian citizenry would recognize the birthplace of Canada and applaud his symbolism. He gave Joe Clark the job of organizing and explaining.

First there was a television show that ran for a few weeks. It starred people, famous and less famous, who had innovative ideas about a new Canadian democracy. Pierre Trudeau told Canadians that with Mulroney and Bourassa running things, the country needed ideas from the people—and the people spoke up. Then the "first ministers" closed the big doors behind them and had a meeting. Eventually they came out, waving a long piece of paper, and the show was on the road again. This time there would be no grinding our way through the provincial legislatures—the vote would go directly to the Canadian people via referendum.

This one was even stupider than the first one. For one thing, the document was as vague as a Bolivian constitution. For another, its vagueness was spread out over too many topics. Taking to heart the complaints from people who had felt excluded from the Meech document, the composers now suggested satisfaction for everyone—Native people, women, Quebec, Senate reformers, racquet clubs, diet groups, Spanish dancers, action poets, second-string quarterbacks and so on. Pierre Trudeau stood up in a highfalutin Chinese restaurant in Montreal and denounced the deal as a dangerous erosion of his own Constitution. Preston Manning, the leader of the Reformists, denounced the deal as Mulroney's cave-in to the French Canadians. The Conservative Party tried to keep Mulroney out of the public eye, but every once in a while he would appear somewhere and say something a little too plainly.

The referendum was doomed. You weren't allowed to mix and meech. You had to take the whole menu or nothing. There were just too many things to vote against. If you hated Natives, or French Canadians, or women, or, say, Mulroney, you had to refuse the whole thing. On referendum day, October 26, 1992, 54.4 percent of Canadian voters voted against Charlottetown.

A lot of them were voting against the man in the expensive Italian shoes. One poll put Mulroney's approval rate at 14 percent of Canadians. The next one dipped below 10 percent. It was hard to imagine that this was the only Tory in the twentieth century to win back-to-back majorities. He did not have a chance in hell of winning in 1993. He was the first Tory PM in the twentieth century to hand over the job before an election. He looked around for someone to take the fall for him. Joe Clark would not meet his glance. He had to find someone who did not mind running and losing to Jean Chrétien, or someone who was dumb enough to think that a Conservative victory was possible.

Kim Campbell, a hotshot young cabinet minister from the West Coast, was willing to be the country's first female prime minister for a while. Jean Charest, a curly-haired Quebecker with impeccable English, ran against her. Campbell had been a local West Coast politician for a couple of other parties. Charest would go on to be a Quebec politician for another party. Campbell had the advantage of a really bad accent in French. She took the leadership.

After the election of October 1993, the Progressive Conservatives were the first party to have gender parity in the House of Commons. Charest was returned to represent French Canada, and Elsie Wayne would speak for Atlantic Canada. The West was left to the cowboys.

The Chrétien yawns, er, years

Jean Chrétien was always a political machine in the form of a man. He knew how to make himself useful to the Liberal Party, and he made sure that those Liberals who spoke English most of the time knew who he was and how helpful he always seemed to be. He was a federalist but he did not get in the face of the nearest separatist. He could not speak like an angel, but then Pierre Trudeau couldn't play golf. He always seemed to know the right thing to say, though he had an accent in both languages, and an hour later no one could remember what he had said. He was the perfect guy to run for prime minister.

In 1993 he ran against Brian Mulroney and defeated Kim Campbell in a mudslide. Remember Wilfrid Laurier's dread that Canada's voters would set up regional and sectarian redoubts? Now a hundred years after Laurier's ascendancy, the Liberals held Ontario and the Maritimes and some of Quebec. The Quebec separatists were the loyal Opposition. The West had returned the lowbrow right.

A year later the provincial voters in Quebec returned the Parti Québécois to power. The new premier was Jacques Parizeau. I don't know whether Parizeau was seen as a comic figure inside Quebec, but he seemed on the surface a most unlikely champion of independence. He had the credentials, all right—he was a veteran of the Quiet Revolution who became an adviser to René Lévesque. He had stood firm against Meech and Charlottetown, announcing that Quebec was not offered enough. He spoke very clearly and lost his temper easily.

But what was he doing with his outfits and English accent? He dressed like someone's satire of a British gentleman from the countryside come to London to do business. His little Mr. Peabody moustache was just the right touch. Why wasn't he wearing a monocle? He was a short fellow with a bay window covered by a weskit, and when he opened his mouth he spoke in a British accent from an Edwardian English comedy. I think I remember his saying things like "By Jove!"

In 1995 Parizeau presented another referendum on independence. Referenda are always worded a little oddly, because the government wants them to pass. This one asked whether voters agreed that Quebec should become sovereign after having made an offer to Canada for a new economic union. It sounded as if Canada were already another country. And what does "sovereign" mean, anyway? The campaign started slowly, and after a month, the polls showed sovereignty at 40 percent. But then Parizeau sent his man Lucien Bouchard, head of the federal Bloc Québécois and future premier of Quebec, out to rally the people. Where Parizeau was a sputtering straight-talker, Bouchard was a smooth operator, formerly Mulroney's Quebec lieutenant and a martyr because he had lost a leg and almost his life to flesh-eating disease. Bouchard would become the most charismatic leader in French Canada. Standing on an artificial leg that did not quite bend correctly, he told Quebeckers that after the breakup, Canada would come to Quebec on bended knee.

I was teaching Canadian studies in Denmark while this entertainment was capturing attention outside Canada. We knew that things were getting serious when Chrétien decided to get into the fight. He appeared with Charest and other Quebec federalists and promised Quebeckers that he would struggle manfully to get them the rights they seemed to have lost when Meech and Charlottetown failed. My students and the faculty at the University of Aarhus thought that I must be the resident expert on Quebec politics and kept asking me for inside dope and predictions. I thought back to the Quebec election, in which Liberals and Péquistes had finished in a virtual tie in the popular vote. The sovereignists might get 45 percent, I said.

There is a six-hour time difference between Denmark and Quebec, so I did not stay awake to see the results on television on October 30, 1995. But in the morning the first thing I did was to snap on the set, and a shiver went through my pre-coffee body. Ninety percent of the electorate had cast ballots, and the arithmetic was really close: 4.7 million people had voted, and 49.4 percent said yes, let's go.

You could hear voices from across the North Atlantic. They were whispering, "Next time." The drop in the no vote was a little like the emigration of Anglophones after the previous referendum. The explosive Jacques Parizeau pointed out that the vote would have succeeded if there just were not so many non-French people in the province. He spluttered, with TV cameras pointed at him, that the people had been deprived of their victory by "money" and the "ethnic vote." Antisemitism was still around, and not limited to Créditistes. Then he resigned as premier, saying something about vengeance next time. He would be replaced by Lucien Bouchard, who said just wait, we are going to have these referenda until we win. But in a few years this elegant man would also step down and hand the job to someone else. By the end of the century it was beginning to look as if Quebeckers had things other than independence to think about.

But just in case, the *fédérales* asked the Supreme Court to decide whether a province could just pass a referendum and jump out of the country. The Supreme Court came down with a typical ruling: no, a province could not do such a thing, but if such a referendum were to pass with a clear majority, Ottawa had to negotiate with the province in question. Whenever there is a major constitutional question to be settled, the Supreme Court of Canada says yes and no.

By the way, Jean Chrétien and the Liberals were re-elected in 1997.

Oh yeah, sure, I remember Canada

Traditionally, you will recall, the Conservative Party was in favour of tariffs and other controls that would protect Canadian enterprise from the encroachments of an expanding USA. The Liberals were traditionally continentalist. In the years after Mulroney, only the NDP gave a rap about the growing US control of Canadian resources and business. And the US is proof that the military goes where business wants to be. After the US military re-invaded Haiti in 1994, business concerns from Germany and France and Britain disappeared, while US corporations were all over the half island.

In that same year "Canada" signed an agreement called the North American Free Trade Agreement, or NAFTA. Now Mexico was included, and soon Chile, a country whose government had been turned rightward by the US, would be. Now US companies would be able to get their stuff made in Mexican factories where Mexican wages were paid. It would not be long until Canadians began referring to their dollar as a "peso." Outwardly respectable notables have suggested that Canada get rid of the Canadian dollar and "integrate" with US currency. Why not? Panama and the Dominican Republic already use the Yankee greenback as their money.

Perhaps the twentieth century really was Canada's. Or as close as we were going to get. Maybe it was Canada's last chance at a century, because there would be no such independent nation very far into the twenty-first century. Canadian children already call their female parents "Mom" instead of "Mum." Seemingly invulnerable Canadian financial institutions such as Eaton's stores first have to have US hamburger chains in their food fairs, then disappear entirely, to be replaced by big-box US stores, notably the strongly anti-union Wal-Mart. Soon after a couple of hundred Wal-Mart stores opened across Canada, it was officially named the richest corporation in the USA. In 2002 Target stores would begin to arrive, and gleeful suburban shoppers would load their bargains into the backs of their sport utility vehicles. Anyone my age who happens to find himself in a shopping centre (sorry—center) in Abbotsford or Kitchener feels as if his country has somehow disappeared. He does not feel as if he shares citizenship with all these people in Nike gear.

I suppose that we should consider ourselves fortunate that the US Air Force has not been the tool used to get these corporations here. Unless you count US nuclear warships running between our northern islands, and US guided missiles zooming across our West toward their practice targets, the US has not invaded us militarily since the Pig War. But other parts of the world are not so lucky. The US military is almost always active somewhere in the world, mainly demonstrating to foreigners that they should not experiment with forms of government or economy that are not approved of in Washington and New York.

It used to be that Canadians stood by and said tsk-tsk while the Yanks were doing this, preferring to employ our soldiers and sailors in peacekeeping roles. But as one century closed and another opened, with president Bushes, Canada sent fighters to shoot at people in the Islamic countries targeted by the US. A lot of people say that the forty-ninth parallel is disappearing, and this is happening while people in some unfavoured Islamic countries find new borders created within their own territory. These are called, in a kind of English that is becoming rather common, "no-fly zones."

It is a strange time to be living in what is left of this country. There are still five million people in Quebec who want independence. There are Native groups across the land who want a greater degree of independence. And the majority of Canadians are quite happy to watch as their own independence goes into the till at Blockbuster Video.

Long-Ago Person

In the year 2001 there were two interesting reburials of human remains. In one case the remains consisted of a skull and the bones of one leg. In the other case the head and one leg were missing.

The skull and leg bones belonged to Louis Joseph de Montcalm-Gozon, Marquis de Montcalm, the French general who lost New France on the Plains of Abraham on September 13, 1759. For 242 years his remains had remained inside a Quebec convent. But in October 2001 what was left of them was placed in a casket covered with a white-and-gold fleur-de-lys banner and borne on a carriage drawn by four horses through the streets of Quebec. Its destination was a little old cemetery in the Lower Town, where the casket was placed in a stone crypt. After 242 years the general was again with his soldiers. The pallbearers and escort were dressed in military outfits of the eighteenth century. The occasion was attended by Guy Bertrand, Marquis de Montcalm, who had flown from France.

The remains of General Wolfe are in England.

The other redisposition of mortal remains took place in the mountains of Northern British Columbia, close to the borders of Yukon and Alaska.

Remember that man who came out of the ice on a warm day in August 1999 on a glacier in far northern British Columbia? It turns out that he was discovered in Tatshenshini-Alsek Park, on land reserved for the Champagne and Aishihik First Nations, who speak a language called Southern Tutchone. Soon he was being called Kwaday Dan Sinchi, usually translated into English as Long-Ago Found Man.

Remembering the passionate conflict between scientists and Native groups that has occurred in recent grave discoveries, one might have expected a good tussle. But the story of Kwaday Dan Sinchi could stand as an example for all the squabbling factions in Canada. Scientists and government and Native associations listened to one another's counsel and reached a compromise that exemplified the Canada we have always told each other that we have. The biologists offered their work to the First Nations people, and several groups of First Nations people joined together in honouring the ice man.

Kwaday Dan Sinchi was the best-preserved Native "mummy" yet found in North America. He was discovered with some hunting tools, a woven hat, a cloak and a bag with chum salmon in it. He had been somewhere between eighteen and twenty-two years of age and healthy. He had apparently been caught in a sudden snowstorm and had died from exposure. Carbon-14 tests determined that his clothing dated from 1415 A.D. to 1445 A.D. Pollen grains were collected from his clothing, and samples were taken of his hair and the contents of his stomach.

Some Native people wanted to know as much as possible about the ice man's family tree, so officials agreed to take DNA samples from volunteers among the Champagne and Aishihik, as well as Tlingit groups. Native Americans in Alaska gave blood samples. White people and Natives were sent to the area in which Kwaday Dan Sinchi had been found, and they looked around for anything else that might have been stopped by the fifteenth-century snowstorm. Meanwhile, the body was being kept at the Royal British Columbia Museum in Victoria.

In the spring of 2001, eleven First Nations groups met in council and decided that their ancestor should be given a proper ceremony. The assembly decided that there would be a funeral and a potlatch. The body would be cremated and the ashes returned to the spot where the body had been found. Some people felt that the artifacts should be burned too, but the majority decided that they would be ceremonially blessed and kept for the knowledge that they might convey. The elders decided that the hunter's sacred medicine bag would remain unopened, and it was burned along with the body.

In July the funeral and potlatch were performed at Klukshu village in the southwest corner of Yukon. Native people came from all over the continent. Normally the host nation's customs would have been followed, but because no one yet knows what nation the Long-Ago Person belonged to, prayers were given by speakers for all the nearby groups represented. Chief Bob Charlie of the Champagne and Aishihik First Nations spoke of his happiness in seeing so many clans brought together and offered his hope that they would continue to meet.

The ashes were flown by helicopter to the place of discovery and consigned to the earth that had been bared by the warmer climate of recent years. Scientists and Native leaders shook hands and thanked each other for accommodating each other's beliefs.

Welcome to the nothings

No one really knew why, but Prime Minister Chrétien called an election for November 27, 2000.

Jean Chrétien and the Liberals were re-elected.

Bibliography

Abella, Irving, and David Miller, eds. *The Canadian Worker in the Twentieth Century*. Toronto: Oxford, 1978.

Allen, Ralph. *Ordeal by Fire: Canada 1910–1945*. New York: Doubleday, 1960.

Atwood, Margaret, ed. *The New Oxford Book of Canadian Verse in English*. Toronto: Oxford, 1982.

Bergeron, Léandre. *The History of Quebec: A Patriote's Handbook*. Toronto: NC Press, 1971.

Blakely, Phyllis Ruth. *Nova Scotia: A Brief History*. Toronto: Dent, 1972.

Bocking, D. H., ed. *Pages from the Past: Essays on Saskatchewan History*. Saskatoon: Western Producer Prairie Books, 1979.

Bothwell, Robert, and J. L. Granatstein. *Our Century*. Toronto: McArthur, 2000.

Bowering, George. *Bowering's B.C.: A Swashbuckling History*. Toronto: Viking, 1996.

———. *Egotists and Autocrats: The Prime Ministers of Canada*. Toronto: Viking, 1999.

Brown, Craig, ed. *The Illustrated History of Canada*. Toronto: Lester, 1996.

Bumsted, J. M., ed. *Documentary Problems in Canadian History*, vol. I, *Pre-Confederation*. Georgetown, Ont.: Irwin-Dorsey, 1969.

Careless, J. M. S. *Canada: A Story of Challenge*. Toronto: Macmillan, 1953.

Carstens, Peter. *The Queen's People*. Toronto: University of Toronto, 1991.

Cook, Ramsay, Craig Brown and Carl Berger, eds. *Confederation*. Toronto: University of Toronto, 1967.

Creighton, Donald. *Canada's First Century*. Toronto: Macmillan, 1970.

Davey, Frank. *Griffon*. Toronto: Massasauga Editions, 1972.

den Otter, A. A. *Civilizing the West*. Edmonton: University of Alberta, 1982.

Finlay, J. L., and D. N. Sprague. *The Structure of Canadian History*. Scarborough, Ont.: Prentice-Hall, 1989.

Francis, R. Douglas, Richard Jones and Donald B. Smith. *Origins: Canadian History to Confederation*. Toronto: Harcourt Brace Canada, 1996.

Fraser, John. *Eminent Canadians*. Toronto: McClelland & Stewart, 2000.

Graham, Ron. *The French Quarter*. Toronto: Macfarlane Walter & Ross, 1992.

Granatstein, J. L. *Yankee Go Home?* Toronto: HarperCollins, 1996.

Granatstein, J. L., et al. *Nation: Canada since Confederation*. Toronto: McGraw-Hill, 1990.

Greer, Thomas H. *A Brief History of the Western World*. New York: Harcourt Brace Jovanovich, 1987.

Harrison, Charles Yale. *Generals Die in Bed*. Waterdown, Ont.: Potlach, 1999.

Horwood, Harold, *Newfoundland*. Toronto: Macmillan, 1969.

Hutchison, Bruce. *The Unfinished Country*. Vancouver: Douglas & McIntyre, 1985.

———. *The Unknown Country*. Toronto: Longmans, 1948.

Keshen, Jeffrey, and Suzanne Morton, eds. *Material Memory: Documents in Post-Confederation History*. Don Mills, Ont.: Addison-Wesley, 1998.

Klinck, Carl F., and Reginald E. Watters, eds. *Canadian Anthology*. Toronto: Gage, 1974.

Lower, J. Arthur. *Canada: An Outline History*. Toronto: McGraw-Hill Ryerson, 1991.

MacFarlane, John. *Ernest Lapointe and Quebec's Influence on Canadian Foreign Policy*. Toronto: University of Toronto, 1999.

Mackenzie, William Lyon. *The Selected Writings, 1824–1837*, ed. Margaret Fairley. Toronto: Oxford, 1960.

McClymont, Ian. "Canadian Expansionism, 1903–1914," (thesis). Michigan State University, 1970.

McInnis, Edgar. *Canada: A Political and Social History*. Toronto: Rinehart, 1956.

McNaught, Kenneth. *The Pelican History of Canada*. London: Penguin Books, 1969.

Milne, David. *The Canadian Constitution*. Toronto: James Lorimer, 1991.

Morton, Desmond. *The Critical Years*. Toronto: McClelland & Stewart, 1964.

———. *A Military History of Canada*. Edmonton: Hurtig, 1985.

———. *A Short History of Canada*. Toronto: McClelland & Stewart, 1997.

Ormsby, Margaret A. *British Columbia: A History*. Toronto: Macmillan, 1958.

Palmer, Howard, and Tamara Palmer. *Alberta: A New History*. Edmonton: Hurtig, 1990.

Purdy, Al. *Beyond Remembering*. Madeira Park: Harbour, 2000.

Reid, J. H. Stewart, Kenneth McNaught and Harry S. Crowe. *A Source-Book of Canadian History*. Toronto: Longmans, 1964.

Richardson, Boyce. *People of Terra Nullius*. Vancouver: Douglas & McIntyre, 1993.

Sauer, Carl Ortwin. *Land and Life*. Berkeley: University of California, 1965.

Skeoch, Alan, and Tony Smith. *Canadians and Their Society*. Toronto: McClelland & Stewart, 1973.

Sluman, Norma. *Poundmaker*. Toronto: Ryerson, 1967.

Soucoup, Dan. *Historic New Brunswick*. Lawrencetown Beach, N.S.: Pottersfield Press, 1997.

Stanley, George F. G. *The Birth of Western Canada*. Toronto: University of Toronto, 1961.

———. *Canada Invaded, 1775–1776*. Toronto: Hakkert, 1973.

———. *The War of 1812: Land Operations*. Toronto: Macmillan, 1983.

Stewart, Walter. *True Blue: The Loyalist Legend*. Toronto: Collins, 1985.

Strange, William. *Canada, the Pacific and War*. Toronto: Thomas Nelson, 1937.

Tracy, Frank Basil. *The Tercentenary History of Canada*, vol. II, *From Champlain to Laurier, MDCVIII–MCMVIII*. Toronto: Collier, 1908.

Whitelaw, William Menzies. *The Maritimes and Canada before Confederation*. Toronto: Oxford, 1934.

Woodcock, George. *British Columbia: A History of the Province*. Vancouver: Douglas & McIntyre, 1990.

———. *100 Great Canadians*. Edmonton: Hurtig, 1980.

———. *A Social History of Canada*. Toronto: Viking, 1988.

Zaslow, Morris. *The Opening of the Canadian North, 1870–1914*. Toronto: McClelland & Stewart, 1971.

Index

Abbott, John, 151, 190, 191
Abercromby, James, 75
Aberhart, William ("Bible Bill"), 248
Aboriginals, 1–15, 18–19, 28, 41. *See also various First Nations and "cultures"*
burial customs, 9, 10, 131, 327; Christianity and, 40–42, 44–47, 249, 271–72; fur trading and (*see under* fur trading); land claims/grants and, 5, 9, 89, 128, 308, 309–10, 317–19; suffrage and, 265, 275
Acadia/Acadians, 48–49, 66–68
Act of Union, 149
Adams, Samuel, 92
agriculture
Aboriginals and, 12, 13–14, 182; in New France, 55–56, 64, 70, 71; Prairies and, 128, 168, 177, 182, 184, 199, 231; Red River Settlement and, 128, 168; wheat, 242, 246, 276
Alaska, 2, 5, 98; U.S. acquisition of, 154, 165, 166, 191, 206
Alberta
Confederation and, 207; oil and gas and, 231, 270, 295–96, 300–302; separatism and, 296, 302, 303; Social Credit Party and, 248–49
alcohol, 63, 133, 172, 234, 236
Algonquin, 15, 38, 51
American Fur Company, 116, 122–24
Amherst, Jeffery, 75, 80, 82, 84
Anglican Church, 108, 139
Annapolis Royal, 65–66
Arcand, Adrien, 257
Archaic culture, 9
Argenson, Pierre de Voyer d', 51, 52
armed forces. *See also various wars*
air force and, 254; Lloyd George and, 233; navy and, 209–12, 215–18; Oka and, 319

Arnold, Benedict, 94, 99–100
Asquith, Herbert Henry, 215
Assiniboia, 171
Astor, John Jacob, 116, 122, 123
Aulnay, Charles de Menou d', 48–49
Australia, 32, 90; rebel exile and, 142, 143, 145

Baille, Thomas, 133
Baldwin, Robert, 139, 144, 145
Baldwin, William, 144
Balfour Report, 239, 242
Bank of Canada, 246
Bank of Montreal, 137, 177
Banks, Joseph, 90
Banque du Peuple, 137
Batoche, 182–84, 186
Bear Island, 308–9
Belaney, Archie, 308, 309
Bennett, R. B., 241–46, 271
Beothuks, 4, 131
Bergeron, Léandre, 291
Bering, Vitus, 70, 71, 104
Bertrand, Guy, 326
Big Bear, 168, 180, 183, 185, 186, 188
bilingualism, 276, 279, 306, 307
Bill of Rights, 276
bison, 8, 11, 14, 126, 127, 128, 182
Black, William, 122, 123
Blackfoot, 185
blacks
gold rush and, 153; as refugees, 101–3; South Africa and, 274, 275; United Empire Loyalists and, 63, 99; U.S. Civil War and, 150; War of 1812–14 and, 119
Blake, Edward, 174, 175, 176
bleus, 156, 157, 158
Bloc Québécois, 319, 322
Bodega y Quadra, Juan Franciso de la, 105, 106

Boer War, 202–6
Bond Head, Francis, 141, 142
Borden, Robert, 95, 210, 215, 216, 229
    World War I and, 218, 221, 223–24
border, Canada-U.S., 96, 121–22, 149,
    206–7
Boston, 91, 92
Bouchard, Lucien, 322–23
Bougainville, Louis-Antoine, 79
Bourassa, Henri, 205–8, 233
    navy and, 210, 212, 215; World War I
    and, 218, 221, 223
Bourassa, Robert, 292, 296, 315
Bowell, Mackenzie, 181, 193
Braddock, Edward, 73
Brant, John, 119
Brébeuf, Jean de, 44, 46
Brendan, St., 22–23
British Columbia, 154, 159, 171–72, 175
    Aboriginals and, 10, 12, 15, 326–27;
    deportations and, 243; gold rush and,
    153, 154, 171, 200; Indian immigra-
    tion and, 216–18; internment camps
    and, 257–58; strikes in, 225–26, 227
British North America Act, 1867, 157,
    163, 164, 303
    amendments and, 242, 305; education
    and, 197; women and, 240
British North American Land Company,
    161
Broadbent, Ed, 310
Brock, Isaac, 118, 119
Brown, George, 157, 158, 161, 162, 165,
    174
Bulwer-Lytton, Edward, 154
Burgogyne, John, 95, 96
Burwell, Adam Hood, 124
Byng, Julian, 235, 236, 237

Cabot, John, 2, 19, 25–27
Camp, Dalton, 289
Campbell, Gordon, 226
Campbell, Kim, 321, 322
Canada Council for the Arts, 265, 271
Canada East, 149, 151, 156
Canada Pension Plan, 282, 285
Canada West, 149, 151, 156

Canadian Broadcasting Corporation, 270,
    301
Canadian Development Corporation, 285
Canadian Northern Railway, 199
Canadian Pacific Railway, 173, 176–79
Caouette, Réal, 279
Cape Breton Island, 66, 103, 114. See also
    Louisburg
Carignan-Salières regiment, 53
Carleton, Guy, 88, 93, 95, 102
Carlos V, 29, 31
Carrier, Roch, 260
Cartier, George-Étienne, 137, 157, 162,
    189
Cartier, Jacques, 28–31, 28–33, 40
Catholic Church
    Aboriginals and, 4, 25, 47, 249; civil
    rights and, 89; colonization and, 42,
    43; coureurs de bois and, 45; England
    and, 91; Facism and, 250, 251; faith
    vs. reason and, 68–69; family records
    and, 55; French Revolution and, 110;
    Henry IV and, 36; land ownership
    and, 69, 271; Louis Riel and, 184;
    Marice Duplessis and, 249; New
    France and, 52; Patriotes and, 141;
    Quebec, English rule and, 87, 92;
    Richelieu and, 42; slavery and, 63
Caughnawaga, 119
Chamberlain, Joseph, 202, 203
Chamberlain, Neville, 252
Champlain, Lake, 38
Champlain, Samuel de, 19, 36–46
Charest, Jean, 321
Charles I, 43, 44
Charles II, 56–57
Charlie, Bob, 328
Charlottetown, 158–59, 320
Charter of Rights and Freedoms, 305,
    306, 307
Chartier, Paul Joseph, 287–88
Château Clique, 135, 136, 177
Chinese Canadians, 178
Chrétien, Jean, 55, 310, 321–24, 328
Churchill, Winston, 215, 255, 261
Cité Libre, 290, 291
Civil War, 150, 155

Clark, Champ, 211
Clark, Joe, 299–300, 303, 305, 320
Clatsop, 123
Clovis people, 7–8
Colborne, John, 145
Cold War, 262–63, 267, 268–69
Coleman, Victor, 286
Colonial Office, 95, 108, 149
    Africa, India and, 202–3; Confederation
    and, 162, 163; Hudson's Bay Company
    land and, 167
colonists. *See also* immigration
    Aboriginals and, 54; American, 65, 73;
    French, 37, 42, 43; French Prostestants
    as, 33
Columbia River, 115, 116, 122, 123
Columbus, Christopher, 19, 25–26
Commonwealth Conferences, 242, 274
Communism, 241, 243, 248, 251, 282
    Cold War and, 262–63, 266, 267, 268,
    276
Company of New France, 42–43
Confederation, 129, 144, 150, 158–63,
    170–72, 182
conscription
    World War I and, 223, 225; World
    War II and, 253, 257, 260, 261
Conscription Act, 225
constitution, patriating the, 303–7. *See
    also* Meech Lake Accord
Constitution Act, 1867. *See* British North
    America Act, 1867
Constitution Act, 1982, 307, 314
Constitutional Act, 1791, 108–9, 113
Continental Congresses, 92, 93
Cook, James, 82–83, 90, 97–98, 105
Co-operative Commonwealth Federation,
    245, 248, 266
Cornwallis, Edward, 67, 94
coureurs de bois, 45, 52, 87
Craigellachie, 179
Crawford, Isabella Valancy, 196, 200
Cree, 57, 126, 182, 185
Crerar, Thomas, 229
Crimean War, 156
Cross, James, 292, 293
Crozier, L. N. F., 186

Curnoe, Greg, 287–88
currency
    Bank of Canada and, 246; Canadian *vs.*
    U.S., 261, 265, 274, 324; English *vs.*
    French, 87; Social Credit Party and,
    248

Dalton, Robert, 135
Darwin, Charles, 4, 165
Davey, Frank, 60
de Chastes, Aymer, 36
de Gaulle, Charles, 288
de la Roche, Marquis, 36
de la Tour, Charles and Marie, 48–49
de Monts, Pierre, 36, 37, 38
Debert, Nova Scotia, 7
"Declaration of Rights and Grievances," 92
defence
    C. D. Howe and, 270; with U.S., 255,
    262, 268–69, 276–78
Depression, the, 241, 245, 246, 251;
    Prairies and, 242, 244, 248
Detroit, War of 1812–14 and, 116, 118,
    119
Diefenbaker, John, 273–78, 279, 282, 289
"distinct society," 315, 316
Dollard des Ormeaux, Adam, 51, 231
Dominion Lands Act, 172
Donnaconna, 29
Dorion, Antoine-Aimé, 151, 162
Dorset people, 15–17
Douglas, C. H., 248
Douglas, James, 148–49, 153, 154, 172
Douglas, Tommy, 245, 283, 288
Doukhobors, 66
Drake, Francis, 32, 34
Drew, George, 266
Drumheller, Alberta, 6, 227
Drummond, Gordon, 136
Duck Lake, 186
Dufferin, Lord, 173, 176
Dumont, Gabriel, 180, 182, 186
Dunsmuir, James, 208
Duplessis, Maurice, 249, 253, 266, 278
Duquesne-Menneville, Michel Ange, 70
Durham, John George Lambton, 143–46
Durham Report, 143–46, 149

East India Company, 92
Edmonton, 57, 264
education
    Aboriginals and, 249; BNA Act, 1867,
    and, 197; churches and, 132; New
    Brunswick and, 198; Quebec and, 87,
    198, 232, 278, 296, 297; rights in
    Manitoba, 190–91, 192, 193–94; in
    Upper Canada, 132–34
Eirik the Red, 20
Eiriksson, Leif, 21, 24
Eiriksson, Thorvald, 21
Eisenhower, Dwight, 261
elections, federal
    1872, 173; 1874, 174; 1878, 176;
    1891, 189; 1896, 195; 1912, 212;
    World War I and, 221–22, 223–24;
    1917, 224; 1921, 229; 1925, 235;
    1926, 238; 1930, 241–42; 1935, 245,
    246, 248; 1940, 253, 273; 1945, 261;
    1949, 266; 1957, 274; 1958, 274;
    1963, 278; 1965, 282–83; 1980, 300;
    1979, 299; 1984, 311; 1988, 312,
    316; 1993, 321, 322; 1997, 324;
    2000, 328; rules, 236–37
Elizabeth I, 33–34
Emancipation Act, 150
Empress of India, 217
Evans, Slim, 243–44
Expo 67, 286, 287, 288

Family Compact, 133, 135, 139, 141, 146
Famous Five, 240–41
farming. *See* agriculture
Fascism, 241, 248, 250–51
Favreau, Guy, 304
Fenian Brotherhood, 143, 151
filles du roi, 54–55, 64
First Nations. *See* Aboriginals
fishing
    Basque whalers and, 22; cod, 25, 33,
    192; French and, 33, 35; rights, after
    War of Independence, 96; salmon, 15;
    Treaty of Tordesillas and, 27; U.S.
    "rights" and, 192, 233
flag, Canadian, 279–80, 286, 288
flu, 227

Ford, Henry, 211
forts
    Astoria, 116, 122, 123, 124; Battleford,
    185; Beauséjour, 73; Carillon, 73, 75;
    Chipewyan, 112; Detroit, 84; Douglas,
    128, 129; Duquesne, 70, 73, 74;
    Edward, 74; Frontenac, 75; Garry, 170;
    George, 115; Kamloops, 122; La Tour,
    48–49; Langley, 154; McLeod, 115;
    Niagara, 73; Okanogan, 122; Oswego,
    73; Pitt, 75, 84, 185; St-Frédéric, 73;
    Vancouver, 148; Victoria, 153; William
    Henry, 74
Francis, Anne, 285
Franciscans, 40–41
Franco, Francisco, 251
François I, 27, 29, 30
Francouer, J. N., 231
Franklin, Benjamin, 94, 96
Franklin expedition, 8
Fraser, Simon, 115–16
Fraser River, 111, 115–16, 153
Frederick the Great, 62
Free Trade Agreement, 312–13
French and Indian War, 62, 67, 92
French East India Company, 91
French Revolution, 109–10
Frobisher, Martin, 33
Frog Lake, 185
Front de libération du Québec, 287, 292
Frontenac, Louis de Baude, 52, 57, 62–63,
    64
Fulton, Davie, 304
fur trading. *See also* Hudson's Bay Company
    North West Company: Aboriginals
    and, 12, 37, 53–54, 84; alcohol and,
    63; beginnings of, 35; Champlain and,
    39, 40, 46; coureurs de bois and, 45;
    Dutch and, 46; Huguenots and, 42;
    La Vérendrye and, 64; Métis and,
    167–68; Mi'kmaq and, 131; monop-
    oly, 42; Montreal and, 47, 133;
    Napoleonic Wars and, 126; New
    France and, 57, 58–61, 62–64, 66;
    pemmican and, 126; Radisson,
    Grosseilliers, and, 51–52; Russians
    and, 70–71; Scottish merchants and,

87–89; Thirteen Colonies and, 89; after War of Independence, 96; on West coast, 70–71, 98, 105–7, 191

Galiano, Dionisio, 106
Galt, Alexander, 125, 151, 161, 162
Galt, John, 125
George, David Lloyd, 233
George II, 80
George III, 3, 80, 88, 90, 95, 96, 105
Godbout, Adélard, 253
gold
    California and, 153; Francis Drake and, 34; François I and, 27; Fraser River and, 153, 154; Jacques Cartier and, 28, 29, 30, 31; price of, 295; Yukon and, 199–200, 206
Golden Hind, 34
Goldsmith, Oliver, 134
Goodwin, Ginger, 225–26, 227
Gordon, Charles George ("Chinese"), 202
Gouzenko, Igor, 262
government, representative/responsible
    Canada West and, 156; Thomas Haliburton and, 139; Upper/Lower Canada and, 107–10, 136, 146
Government of Canada. See also various prime ministers
    cabinet and, 166, 231, 236–37; elections (see elections, federal); House of Commons, 163, 177, 280, 287; provincial powers and, 175, 197; Senate, 160–61, 190, 215, 240
governor general
    remedial legislation and, 198; Upper/Lower Canada and, 108
Grand Trunk Railway, 176, 199
Grant, Cuthbert, 128
Gray, Robert, 115
Grenouillère, La, 129
Grey, Albert Henry George, 207
Griffon, 59–60
Grosseilliers, Médard Chouart des, 51–52
Groulx, Lionel-Adolphe, 231–32, 233
La Guerre, yes sir!, 260

Haliburton, Thomas Chandler, 138–39
Halifax, 67, 94–95, 103, 118, 159, 224

Hancock, John, 91, 92, 95
Harkness, Douglas, 277
Harper, Elijah, 316, 317
Harrison, William, 118, 119
Hart, Julia Beckwith. See lumber trade
Harvey, William, 69
Hauptmann, Gerhart, 35
Hébert, Louis and Marie, 41, 45
Henry IV, 35–36, 39
Henry VII, 25, 27
Hepburn, Mitch, 253
Hill, James J., 177
Hitler, Adolf, 251–52, 261
Hochelaga, 28
Hospital Insurance and Diagnostic Act, 283
Houde, Camille, 250, 257, 266
Howe, C. D., 270
Howe, Joseph, 138, 139, 162, 165, 194
Howe, William, 95–96
Hubert, Jean-François, 110
Hudson, Henry, 39–40
Hudson's Bay Company, 56–58
    forts, posts and, 58, 308; gold rush and, 153, 154; land sale to Crown, 167, 170; Métis and, 167–68; monopoly, expiration of, 155; North West Company and, 88, 114, 128, 129, 133; Rupert's Land and, 114, 167; Selkirk and, 126, 128–29; settlers and, 86, 126; western Canada and, 131, 148, 167
Hughes, Sam, 204–5, 219, 220–21
Huguenots, 33, 39, 42
Hull, William, 116–17, 118
Hundred Years War, 23, 27
Huron, 15, 38, 44, 46, 47, 51, 63
Hutchison, Bruce, 252
Huygens, Christiaan, 69

Île d'Orléans, 55, 77
Île Royale, 66
Île St-Jean, 66
immigration, 165, 199
    from Britain, 125, 199, 232; from China, 301; from India, 216–17; multiculturalism and, 294, 301; Quebec and, 315; from Scotland, 126; Slavs and, 199; from U. S., 125; the West and, 176, 197, 198–98, 207

Imperial Conferences, 209, 239
Innu, 14, 36
Innuit, 265
insurance
    car, 302; health, 283–84; unemploy-
    ment, 242, 246
international boundary. See border,
    Canada-U.S.
internment camps, 256–58
Iroquois
    Adam Dollard des Ormeaux and, 51,
    232; agriculture and, 12, 13; as British
    subjects, 63; Champlain and, 36, 38;
    Dutch and, 46; Frontenac and, 57; fur
    traders and, 56; Huron and, 47, 63;
    Jacques Cartier and, 29, 30; Pierre-
    Esprit Radisson and, 51; treaty with
    France, 64
Iroquois Confederacy, 14, 39, 46

Jackson, Andrew, 247
Jackson, William Henry, 183, 188
James I, 37
James II, 62
Jamestown, 38
Japanese Canadians, 66–68, 257–58
Jefferson, Thomas, 114, 117
Jesuits, 46
    Aboriginals and, 12, 41, 44; coureurs de
    bois and, 45; education and, 132, 133;
    expulsion of, 87; Huguenots and, 39
Joe, Rita, 131
Johnson, Lyndon, 284, 291
Jolliet, Louis, 58
Jones, John Paul, 96

Kahnawake, 119, 318
Kamloops, 116, 122
Karlsefni, Thorfinn, 21
Kennedy, John, 276–77
Kennewick Man, 8–9
Kerouac, Jack, 45
Kierans, Eric, 290
King, William Lyon Mackenzie, 143, 229,
    241–42, 262–63
    Facism and, 250–52; Lord Byng and,
    235–37; social legislation and, 238,
    239, 283; sovereignty and, 233, 239,

253; World War II and, 252–53, 255,
    258, 260, 261
King George's War, 62
King William's War, 61–62
King-Byng affair, 235–37
Kirke brothers, 43–44
Klondike River, 199
Knudson, Elmer, 303
Komagata Maru, 216
Kootenay, 116
Korean War, 267–68
Kwaday Dan Sinchi, 326, 327

La Vérendrye, Pierre Gaultier de, 64
Labrador, 265–66. See also Newfoundland
Lachine Rapids, 29, 36
Lacy, Bomber, 286
Lafayette, General de, 109
Lakota, 126
Lampman, Archibald, 309
L'Anse au Foulon, 78
L'Anse aux Meadows, 22
Lapointe, Ernest, 235, 250, 253
Laporte, Pierre, 292, 293
LaSalle, Sieur de, 59–61
Laurentian culture, 9
Laurier, Wilfrid, 188, 189, 195, 197–98,
    229
    Boer War and, 202–4; confederation of
    colonies and, 203; Indian immigration
    and, 216; navy, sovereignty and,
    209–12, 215; Newfoundland and, 207;
    Red River Settlement and, 127; World
    War I and, 218, 220, 221, 223, 224
Laval, François de, 52, 62–63
le Jeune, Father, 45, 46
League of Nations, 249, 250, 262
Lee, Dennis, 286
Lemoyne, Pierre and Jean-Baptiste, 61
Lépine, Ambroise, 181
Lesage, Jean, 278, 304
Lévesque, René, 278, 290, 291, 292,
    296–97
    patriating the constitution and, 305,
    306; "sovereignty association" and,
    300, 301–2
Lévis, François-Gaston de, 79, 80
Lewis and Clark expedition, 114, 115

Liberal Party
    Alexander Mackenzie and, 151; 1874 election and, 174; Mackenzie King and, 235; Pacific scandal and, 173; Progressive Party and, 235, 236; Sandy Mackenzie and, 173–74; Wilfrid Laurier and, 188, 197
Liberal-Conservative Party, 156
Ligue des droits de Français, 231
Lincoln, Abraham, 155
Livesay, Dorothy, 247
Locke, John, 69
Longboat, Tom, 208–9, 226, 238, 244, 254, 263
longhouses, 12–13, 14
Lougheed, Peter, 302, 303
Louis XIII, 41, 42
Louis XIV, 47, 52–53, 54
Louis XVI, 109
Louisburg
    building of, 66; English-French battles for, 62, 73, 74, 75; French possessions and, 70, 71; Halifax as rival to, 67, 94; James Cook and, 82; James Wolfe and, 76
Louisiana, 60, 61, 67–68, 113
Lowell, James Russell, 166
Lower Canada
    British Parliament and, 136; Château Clique and, 135, 136; creation of, 108; education in, 133, 146; English establishment and, 110; English settlement in, 125; Executive Council, 136, 137; finances and, 136; legal system in, 114; Legislative Assembly, 108, 135, 136; Legislative Council, 108; Lord Durham and, 145; population in 1806, 115; population in 1838, 146; rebellion in, 137–38, 145; steamships and, 133; War of 1812–14 and, 119
Loyalists. See United Empire Loyalists
lumber trade, 130, 134, 214, 216
Lundy's Lane, 120

MacArthur, Douglas, 268
MacDonald, Flora, 299
Macdonald, John A., 156–63, 173

British Columbia and, 171–72; Louis Riel and, 168, 171, 180–81, 183, 187; National Policy and, 175–76; as prime minister, 165–66, 188–89, 197; Sandy Mackenzie and, 174–75, 176
Macdonnell, Miles, 127–28
MacGill, Helen Gregory, 239
Mackenzie, Alexander, 110–12, 114, 151
Mackenzie, Giselle, 269
Mackenzie, Sandy, 173–74, 176
Mackenzie, William Lyon, 133, 135, 139, 141–43
Mackenzie-Papineau Battalion, 251
MacNab, Allan, 116
Macphail, Agnes, 239, 240
Madison, James, 121
Maillet, Antonine, 67
Mainsonneuve, Paul de Chomedey de, 46, 47
Mance, Jeanne, 46
Manitoba
    Confederation and, 129, 171, 182; language rights in, 171; Meech Lake Accord and, 316, 317; population in 1871, 129; schools question, 190–91, 192, 193–94
Manitoba Act, 171, 190, 207
Manitoba Schools Act, 198
Manning, Preston, 320
Marchand, Jean, 278, 290
Maritimes. See also provinces of
    business and, 200, 231; Confederation and, 158–59, 161, 162, 163; education in, 132–33; 1806 population, 115; Lord Durham and, 144; Loyalists and, 99, 100, 103, 138–39; royal provinces and, 114; shipbuilding and, 200
Maroons, 103
Marquette, Father, 58
Marsh, Lou, 238
Martin, Abraham, 78
Massey, Vincent, 265
Mayflower, 40
McBride, Richard, 218
McClung, Nellie, 240
McDougall, William, 169–70
McGee, D'Arcy, 151

McGill, Peter, 137
McGill University, 133
Mckay, Alexander, 111
Meares, John, 105, 106
medicare. *See* insurance, health
Medici, Marie de', 39
Meech Lake Accord, 314–16
Meighen, Arthur, 215, 223, 229, 235, 236, 237
mercantile system, 55, 56, 87–89
Métis. *See also* North West Rebellion; Riel Rebellion
    Aboriginals and, 182; bison hunting and, 14; fur trading and, 167–68; North West Rebellion and, 182–88; Prairies and, 126–29, 148, 167–71, 182, 183; War of 1812–14 and, 119
Mexico, 2, 13, 61, 153
Middleton, Frederick, 186, 187
Mi'kmaq, 131
mining. *See also* gold; oil and gas
    Aboriginals and, 8; strikes and, 225–26
minutemen, 93, 99
Minweweh, 309
Mohawk, 271–73, 297, 308, 310, 317–19
Molson, John, 137
Monet, Marguerite, 182
Monongahela River, 73
Monroe, James, 148
Monroe Doctrine, 148, 207
Montagnais, 36, 38
Montcalm, Louis Joseph de, 73–76, 79, 326
Montesquieu, Baron de, 69
Montreal, 46
    Annexationists and, 151, 153; battles for, 47, 80, 93, 120; FLQ and, 293; French Revolution and, 110; fur trade and, 133; merchants and, 87–89, 107, 108, 144, 151; Patriotes and, 137; Radisson, Grosseilliers, and, 51
Moodie, Susanna, 135
Mulroney, Brian, 234, 271, 310–16, 319–21
Murphy, Emily, 239, 240

Murray, James, 79, 83, 87, 88
Mussolini, Benito, 249, 250, 251, 261

Napoleon I, 113, 117, 120
National Action Committee on the Status of Women, 285
National Energy Program, 295–96, 300–303
National Policy, 175–76, 186, 200, 211
National Resources Mobilization Act, 257
Naval Service Bill, 210, 215
Navy Island, 142
Nechako River, 115
Nègres blancs d'Amérique, 291
Neilson, John, 135
New Brunswick, 103, 114, 134
    Confederation and, 162, 163; Fenians and, 151; Meech Lake Accord and, 316
New Caledonia, 115, 153
New Democratic Party, 279, 310, 324
New England, 39, 54, 64, 65–66
New France. *See also* Quebec
    Aboriginals and, 51, 53–54, 56, 57, 63; agriculture in (*see under* agriculture); birth rates in, 54, 65; Catholic Church and (see Catholic Church); Company of, 42–43; company towns in, 55; expansion of, 58–61, 64; fall of, 75–80, 84, 91; filles du roi and, 54–55, 64; France and, 51, 52; Louis XIV and, 52–53; population in, 54, 61, 63, 64; as royal colony, 52–53, 54; trading posts/forts, 58, 64, 65, 66, 73; wars with Americans, 71, 73–74; wars with England, 61–62, 65–66, 74–80
New Orleans, 66, 70, 71
Newfoundland
    Aboriginals and, 4, 131; Confederation and, 159, 161, 162, 213, 263, 266; as Crown colony, 114; James Cook and, 82; Meech Lake Accord and, 316; Treaty of Versailles and, 227; U.S. and, 207, 265–66; World War II and, 255
Newport, Christopher, 38
Nichol, bp, 286
Nielsen, Erik, 282

Nixon, Richard, 295
Non-Intercourse Act, 117
Nootka, 13, 98, 105
Nootka Convention, 106–7
Norstad, Lauris, 277
North, Frederick, 96
North American Free Trade Agreement, 324
North Atlantic Treaty Organization, 262
North West Company, 88, 114, 115, 116
    Hudson's Bay Company and, 88, 114,
    128, 129, 133; Red River Settlement
    and, 127–29; War of 1812–14 and,
    122–24
North West Mounted Police, 172,
    185–86. See also Royal Canadian
    Mounted Police
North West Rebellion, 180–86
North West Territories, 167, 207
Northwest Passage, 25, 33, 90, 97–98, 105
Norton, John, 119
Nor'westers. See North West Company
Nova Scotia
    blacks and, 102, 103; business, National
    Policy and, 200; Confederation and,
    162, 163; Joseph Howe and, 138–39,
    162; land grants and, 37; as royal
    province, 114; separation debates, 165

Official Languages Act, 292
oil and gas
    OPEC, National Energy Policy and,
    295–96, 300–303; pipelines and,
    270–71; Turner Valley and, 231
Ojibway, 126
Oka, Quebec, 138, 272–73, 297, 308,
    310, 317–19
One Big Union, 227, 243
One Hundred Associates, 42, 43
Orangemen, 171, 181, 193, 194
Oregon, 149, 153
Organization of American States, 312
O'Sullivan, John L., 148

Pangman, Peter, 129
Papineau, Louis-Joseph, 135, 136, 137, 138
Parizeau, Jacques, 322, 323
parti populaire, 135

Parti Québécois, 291, 292, 296, 322
Parti Rouge, 151, 156, 158, 162, 205
Patriotes
    Catholic Church and, 141; La
    Vérendrye and, 64; Léandre Bergeron
    and, 291; Lord Durham and, 145;
    Papineau and, 137, 138; Upper
    Canada soldiers and, 141; World War
    I and, 225
Peace of Ryswick, 62
Pearson, Lester B., 262, 274, 277–78, 279,
    280, 288
    de Gaulle and, 288; health insurance
    and, 283–84; legislation, scandals and,
    281–84; Quebec separatism and,
    289–90, 291
Pelletier, Gérard, 290
Pemmican Wars, 126–29
pensions, 238, 282, 285
Petit manuel d'histoire du Québec, 291
Petro-Canada, 296
Petty, William, 69
Philip II, 33. 34
Piapot, 180
Pitt, William, the Elder, 74–75, 106
Plains of Abraham, 76, 78–79, 326
Plano people, 8
police. See also North West Mounted
    Police; Royal Canadian Mounted Police
    Quebec, Oka and, 318
Pontgravé, Sieur du Pont, 36
Pontiac, 83–84
Port Royal, 37, 62, 65–66
Poundmaker, 180, 182, 185, 186, 188
Prairies, 12, 166, 230–31. See also Red
    River Settlement; Rupert's Land
    agriculture and (see under agriculture);
    the Depression and (see Depression, the);
    immigration and (see immigration, the
    West); National Policy and, 186, 188
Prince Albert, Saskatchewan, 183
Prince Edward Island, 68, 103, 114
    Confederation and, 158–59, 162,
    173; Treaty of Utrecht and, 66
Privy Council (British), 191, 193, 203,
    265; Famous Five and, 240–41;
    Statute of Westminster and, 242

Progressive Party, 229, 230, 235
Protestants
Aboriginals and, 249; Acadians and, 67; Champlain and, 45; colonization and, 33; in New England, 65; New France and, 56 (*see also* Huguenots); North West Rebellion and, 186, 187; Red River Settlement and, 168, 170; Richelieu and, 39, 42
pulp and paper, 234
Purdy, Al, 16

Quadra Island, 107
Quebec. *See also* Lower Canada; New France
Aboriginals and, 271–73 (*see also* Oka, Quebec); Battle of the Plains of Abraham and, 76, 78–79, 326; Boer War and, 203–4, 205; Champlain and, 43, 44, 45; Confederation and, 159, 162, 163; constitution and, 304, 305, 306, 314–16; division of, 107–8; English rule of, 83, 86, 287; English settlers and, 86–89; English *vs.* French currency in, 87; Facism and, 250–51; Korean War and, 267; language laws and, 296–97, 316; legal system, after English conquest, 88, 89, 104, 107–8; Legislative Council of, 89; Louis Riel and, 180, 187, 188; Montcalm and, 74; nationalism, 231–32, 287–88, 290, 291 (*see also* Patriotes; separatism); Oka and (*see* Oka, Quebec); Quiet Revolution and, 278, 279; representative government and, 107–10; rights, treaties and, 5, 182, 316–18; scandals and, 282; Seven Years War and (see Seven Years War); size of, in 1774, 88–89, 91; Thirteen Colonies and, 92, 93; United Empire Loyalists and, 107–8; United States and, 117, 118, 119, 122, 147–48, 172; War of Independence and, 93–94, 95; women's rights and, 239, 285; World War I and, 220–21, 223, 225; World War II and, 253, 257, 259, 260, 261

Quebec Act, 83, 88, 91, 92
Quebec City, 94, 159
Queen Anne's War, 62, 63, 66
Queenston Heights, 118
Quiet Revolution, 278, 279, 322

Radisson, Pierre-Esprit, 51–52
railways. *See also* Canadian Northern Railway; Canadian Pacific Railway; Grand Trunk Railway
Alexander Galt and, 161; British Columbia and, 172–74, 175; freight rates and, 231, 238; R. B. Bennett and, 244; in 1850s, 155; the West and, 166, 172, 175, 176, 177, 188–89, 199
Raleigh, Walter, 34
Ralliement des Créditistes, 279
Ramsay, George, 136
Rassemblement pour l'Indépendence Nationale, 287
reciprocity, 155, 211, 212
Reciprocity Treaty, 155
Récollets, 12, 40
Red River Settlement, 148, 154, 166, 170–71
Louis Riel and (*see under* Riel, Louis); Métis and, 14, 167–68; Selkirk and, 126–29
referendums, 300, 301, 304, 320–24
Reform Party, 319, 320
Canada West and, 156, 157, 158; Upper Canada and, 139
Regina, 57, 186, 244, 245
Regina Manifesto, 245
Relations, 41, 46, 54
representation by population, 156, 157, 158, 160, 162
Richardson, John, 84
Richelieu, Armand du Plessis de, 39, 41–43, 44
Richler, Mordecai, 46
Riddell, Walter, 250
Ridgeway, Matthew, 268
Riel, Louis, 180–88
John A. Macdonald and, 168–71, 180–81, 183, 187; Red River Settlement and, 127, 168, 170

Riel Rebellion, 164, 170–71
    second (*see* North West Rebellion)
Rivard, Lucien, 282
Roanoake Island, 34
Roberval, Jean-François de La Rocque de,
    30, 31
Robespierre, Maximilien Marie Isidore, 110
Roosevelt, Franklin Delano, 255, 261, 262
Roosevelt, Theodore, 206–7
Rosenblatt, Joe, 286
Ross, Charles, 219
Roughing It in the Bush, 135
Rousseau, Jean-Jacques, 69
Royal Canadian Mounted Police, 243,
    244, 258, 301. *See also* North West
    Mounted Police
Royal Commission on Bilingualism and
    Bicuturalism, 279, 290, 292
Royal Commission on the Status of
    Women, 285
Royal Proclamation of 1763, 83, 86, 88,
    309
Royal Society, 83, 90
Rupert's Land, 114, 159, 169
Russell, John, 149
Ryerson, Egerton, 139

Saguenay River, 29, 35
Saskatchewan
    Confederation and, 207; North West
    Rebellion and, 182–86; provisional
    government, 184; Tommy Douglas,
    health insurance and, 283
Saskatchewan River, 182
Scott, F. R., 245
Scott, Thomas, 171, 181
scurvy, 29, 37, 79
Secord, Laura, 117
seigneurial system, 56
Selkirk, Thomas Douglas, 126, 128–29
Selkirk Settlement. *See* Red River
    Settlement
Semple, Robert, 128
separatism
    Alberta and, 296, 302, 303; Quebec
    and, 289–90, 291–93, 301, 322–23
    (*see also* Quebec, nationalism)

Service, Robert, 200
settlements
    Aboriginal, 12, 14, 15–16; Dominion
    Lands Act and, 172; Hudson's Bay
    Company and, 86, 126; on Red River
    (*see* Red River Settlement); Settlers'
    Union and, 183; in Upper Canada,
    124; in western Canada, 210
Settlers' Union, 183
Seven Oaks, 129, 170
Seven Years War, 62, 70, 74–75, 81, 82,
    96
Sévigny, Pierre, 277
Shapiro, Lionel, 260
Shelburne, Nova Scotia, 100
Sherman, William T., 159
Shield culture/people, 9, 10
Shippen, Peggy, 100
Siberian-Alaskan land bridge, 2, 5, 7
Sierra Leone Company, 103
Sifton, Clifford, 190–91, 198, 199, 212
    language rights and, 207–8
Simcoe, John Graves, 110
Sinclair, Margaret, 294
Sioux, 182
Sixth of June, The, 260
slavery, 63, 101–3, 150
Smith, Donald A., 170, 177, 179, 204
Smith, Mary Ellen, 239
smuggling, 91–92, 234
Social Credit Party, 248, 279
Société Notre-Dame de Montréal, 46
"sovereignty association," 300
Spain, 34, 35, 96, 104–7, 113
St. Laurent, Louis, 261, 262, 263, 265,
    266–67, 270, 274
St. Pierre and Miquelon, 62, 213
Stadacona, 28, 29
Stanfield, Robert, 289, 290, 299
Stanley, George, 122
Stansbury, Joseph, 100
Statute of Westminster, 242, 252
Steele, Donald, 308, 309–10
Ste-Foy, Quebec, 79
Stephen, George, 177
Stratford Shakespearian Festival, 271
strikes, 225–26, 227, 228

Supreme Court
    British Privy Council and, 265; consti-
    tution and, 304, 305, 315, 316;
    creation of, 174–75; Famous Five and,
    240–41; referendums and, 324

Tadoussac, 35, 36, 37, 42
Taft, William Howard, 211
Talbot, Thomas, 124–25, 133
Talon, Jean, 51, 52, 54
tariffs
    Eastern business and, 176, 211; U.S.
    trade, 156, 312, 324
taxes
    Canadian Pacific Railway and, 177;
    Confederation conference and, 161;
    French Revolution and, 109; gradu-
    ated income, 246; habitants and, 89;
    Mackenzie King and, 238; Mulroney
    and, 312; Thirteen Colonies and,
    91–92; World War I and, 223
Tecumseh, 118, 119
television, 269–70, 289
Temagami, Lake, 308
Teme-agama Anishnabay, 309
Tenochtitlan, 2
Tenskwatawa, 118
Thirteen Colonies, 89–93
    loyalists and (see United Empire
    Loyalists)
Thirty Years War, 42
Thompson, Annie, 191
Thompson, David, 116, 122
Thompson, John, 190, 192–93
Thule people, 16
Tilley, Leonard, 162, 163
Tippecanoe River, 118, 119
trade
    embargos/sanctions/tariffs, 116, 117,
    156; free, the West and, 211; with
    U.S., 274, 281, 295, 312–13
Traill, Catharine Parr, 135
Trans-Canada Airlines, 270
Treaty of Aix-la-Chapelle, 62, 70
Treaty of Ghent, 121, 123
Treaty of Paris, 62, 67, 81, 83, 102, 114
Treaty of Paris II, 96

Treaty of St-Germain-en-Laye, 44
Treaty of Tordesillas, 27
Treaty of Utrecht, 62, 66
Treaty of Versailles, 226–27, 233
Trelawney, Edward, 103
Trois-Rivières, 46
Trudeau, Pierre, 278, 290–91, 296–98,
    307–8
    constitution and (see constitution,
    patriating the); Joe Clark and, 299,
    300; "Just Society" and, 294; National
    Energy Policy and (see National
    Energy Policy); separatism and, 292,
    293–94, 296–97
Truman, Harry, 261
Tupper, Charles, 162, 165, 176, 190, 193,
    194–95, 212
Turner, John, 303, 310, 312

Underhill, Frank, 245
Union Nationale, 249, 278, 287
unions, 225, 227
    England's, 229; NDP and, 279;
    Quebec's, 278; scabs and, 302;
    Winnipeg General Strike and, 228
United Empire Loyalists
    slavery and, 63; War of 1812–14 and,
    119–20; War of Independence and,
    98–104, 107–8, 114
United Nations, 262, 267, 268, 312
United States. See also Thirteen Colonies.
    Aboriginals and (see under Aboriginals);
    Alaska and (see Alaska); Canadian
    defence and, 255, 262, 268–69, 276;
    Canadian resources and, 241, 311, 324;
    Canadian sovereignty and, 209–12,
    324–25; civil rights movement and,
    291; Civil War, 150; Declaration of
    Independence, 3, 95, 99; Diefenbaker
    and, 274, 276; emigrants from, 125;
    expansion of territory, 113–15, 118,
    121–22, 125, 148, 150–51, 154–55,
    206–7; Fenian Brotherhood and, 151;
    invasions of Upper Canada, 116–17,
    125, 142, 143; Korean War and, 267,
    268; Northeast secessionists and, 121;
    ocean rights and, 191–92; Prohibition

and, 234; rivalries with British North America, 114; trade embargos/sanctions and, 116, 117; Treaty of Versailles and, 227; Vietnam War and, 284, 291, 294–95; War of 1812–14, 117–24; War of Independence (*see* War of Independence); World War I and, 221, 224–25; World War II and, 255, 261
Upper Canada, 108, 139
  canals and, 133; education in, 132–34; 1836 election, 141; Family Compact and (*see* Family Compact); land grants in, 124; Legislative Assembly, 108, 139, 143; Legislative Council, 108; Lundy's Lane and, 120; population, 115, 146; reform/rebellion and, 139, 141–44; Toronto and, 134

Valdés, Cayetano, 106
Vallières, Pierre, 291
Van Horne, William Cornelius, 177
Vancouver, 57, 216, 243, 244, 258
Vancouver, George, 98, 105–7
Vancouver Island, 57, 107, 153
Vanier, Georges, 276
Vaudreil-Cavagnal, Pierre de Rigaud, Marquis de, 73–74, 80
venereal diseases, 90
Verrazano, Giovanni da, 25, 27
Victoria, Queen, 154, 202, 203
Victoria Charter, 304
Vietnam War, 284, 291, 294–95
Vikings, 20–22, 24
Ville-Marie, 46, 47
Vimy Ridge, 222
Voltaire, François Marie Arouet de, 69, 86
von Daniken, Erich, 20

Wacousta, 84
Walpole, Robert, 262

War Measures Act
  FLQ and, 293; Winnipeg General Strike and, 229; World War I and, 220
War of 1812–14, 117–24
War of Independence, 91–94, 95, 96
War of the Austrian Succession, 62
War of the League of Ausburg, 61
War of the Spanish Succession, 62
Wartime Elections Act, 223
Washington, British troops and, 121
Washington, George, 70, 73, 74, 92, 93, 96
  blacks and, 102; as king, 109, 163
Wayne, Elsie, 321
Welland Canal, 133
Wendat. *See* Huron
Whitman, Walt, 150, 166
Whitworth-Aylmer, Matthew, 137
William of Orange, 61
Wilson, Michael, 312, 313
Winnipeg, Hudson's Bay Company and, 57
Winnipeg General Strike, 228, 244, 245
Wolfe, James, 75, 76–79, 326
Wolfe's Cove, 78, 288
women's rights, 239–41, 285–86
Woodcock, George, 271
Woodland Period, 10–11
Woodsworth, J. S., 245
Word War I, 214–27
Workers' Economic Conference, 243
Workers' Unity League, 243
World War I, 218–21, 227
World War II, 252–61

York, 118, 133
Yorkton, Virginia, 96, 100
Ypres, 220
Yukon, 199–200, 206